IDOL ANXIETY

IDOL ANXIETY

Edited by

JOSH ELLENBOGEN

and

AARON TUGENDHAFT

STANFORD UNIVERSITY PRESS ∎ STANFORD, CALIFORNIA

Stanford University Press
Stanford, California

Printed in the United States of America on acid-free, archival-quality paper

Library of Congress Cataloging-in-Publication Data

Idol anxiety / edited by Josh Ellenbogen and Aaron Tugendhaft.
    pages cm
 Includes bibliographical references and index.
  ISBN 978-0-8047-6042-3 (cloth : alk. paper)—ISBN 978-0-8047-6043-0 (pbk. : alk. paper)
 1. Idols and images—Worship. 2. Idolatry. 3. Idols and images in art. 4. Idolatry in art.
 5. Idols and images in literature. 6. Idolatry in literature. 7. Art and religion. I. Ellenbogen,
Josh, editor of compilation. II. Tugendhaft, Aaron, editor of compilation.
  BL485.I35 2011
  202'.18—dc22   2011011025

Typeset by Bruce Lundquist in 10/14 Minion Pro

CONTENTS

CONTRIBUTORS

JAN ASSMANN is Professor of Egyptology (emeritus) at the University of Heidelberg and the 1998 winner of the prestigious Deutsche Historikpreis (German History Prize). He is the author of numerous books on ancient Egypt, Israel, and religion more generally, and has held visiting professorships at such institutions as the Collège de France in Paris, the Hebrew University of Jerusalem, and the University of Chicago.

RACHAEL ZIADY DELUE is Assistant Professor of American Art at Princeton University and is affiliated faculty in Princeton's Center for African American Studies. Her areas of research include landscape theory, race and visual culture, and visual theory. DeLue has served as a consultant to various museums and collections, including the Terra Foundation, and in June 2005 was a faculty member for a Terra-sponsored professional development program for public high school teachers in Chicago. She received her Ph.D. in art history from The Johns Hopkins University in 2001.

DANIEL DONESON is a Fellow in the Program on Constitutionalism and Democracy, the Department of Politics, at the University of Virginia. He has held fellowships at the Hebrew University of Jerusalem, the École des hautes études en sciences sociales in Paris, and the Frei Universität in Berlin. Doneson was educated at Swarthmore, Harvard, and the University of Chicago, where he received his Ph.D. from the Committee on Social Thought. His scholarly research and teaching focus on classical political philosophy, Jewish thought, German philosophy, and the theory and practice of modern liberal democracy, especially on the problematic relation between philosophy, religion, and politics.

JAMES ELKINS is E. C. Chadbourne Chair in the Department of Art History, Theory, and Criticism at the School of the Art Institute of Chicago. The author of numerous books, his work focuses on the description of visual experience in fine art, popular art, and nonart images of all sorts, including medicine, law, physics, and other fields; and in the conceptualization of visual experiences in general.

JOSH ELLENBOGEN is Assistant Professor of Art History at the University of Pittsburgh. He earned his Ph.D. in art history from the University of Chicago, and has also trained in intellectual history and history of science. His research focuses on history of photography, modernism, art historiography, and intersections between art and science.

MARC FUMAROLI is Professor of Rhetoric and Society in Europe (emeritus) at the Collège de France and a member of the Académie française. He is an historian of early modern European literature and culture, and the leading authority on seventeenth-century rhetoric. Fumaroli has been a regular visiting professor at the University of Chicago and Columbia University.

JEAN-LUC MARION is Professor of Philosophy at the University of Paris-Sorbonne (Paris IV) and the Andrew Thomas Greeley and Grace McNichols Greeley Professor of Catholic Studies and Professor of the Philosophy of Religions and Theology in the Divinity School and Professor in the Committee on Social Thought and the Department of Philosophy at the University of Chicago. Marion is the author of numerous books in the history of modern philosophy and in contemporary phenomenology. He is a member of the Académie française.

W. J. T. MITCHELL is Gaylord Donnelley Distinguished Service Professor in the Departments of English and Art History at the University of Chicago. He is the editor of the journal *Critical Inquiry* and author of numerous books and articles on the history and theories of media, visual art, and literature, from the eighteenth century to the present. Mitchell has been the recipient of numerous awards, including the Guggenheim Fellowship and the Morey Prize in art history given by the College Art Association of America.

MIKA NATIF received her Ph.D. from the Institute of Fine Arts, New York University, in 2006, and is currently a Mellon Postdoctoral Fellow at the College of the Holy Cross in Worcester, Massachusetts. Her expertise is in the art and architecture of the Muslim world, with a special interest in Central Asia, Iran, and India in the post-Mongol era. She is author of numerous articles and book chapters on Persian and Mughal painting and illustrated manuscripts, in such journals as the *Muqarnas, Studia Islamica,* and *Artibus Asiae.* Her current book manuscript explores the intercultural and artistic exchanges between India and Europe in the sixteenth and seventeenth centuries.

DANIEL SILVER is Assistant Professor in the Department of Sociology at the University of Toronto. He completed his Ph.D. in the Committee on Social Thought at the University of Chicago and his B.A. in philosophy and rhetoric at the University of California, Berkeley, studying in Germany and Greece in the interim.

ROSE ROSENGARD SUBOTNIK is Professor of Music (emerita) at Brown University. The author of influential studies on music and critical theory, she is the recipient of a Fulbright Scholarship to Vienna, a Guggenheim Fellowship, an ACLS Fellowship, and a Howard Fellowship. She has served on the Board of the American Musicological Society, where she was elected Honorary Member and winner of the H. Colin Slim Award for best scholarly article (2009).

DAVID SUMMERS is the William R. Kenan, Jr., Professor of the History of Art at the University of Virginia. Educated at Brown and Yale, he is the author of two major studies of Michelangelo, as well as of *Real Spaces: World Art History and the Rise of Western Modernism,* which appeared in 2003. He was elected to the American Academy of Arts and Sciences in 1996.

AARON TUGENDHAFT teaches philosophy and history of religion at New York University's Gallatin School of Individualized Study. He is a doctoral candidate in the Skirball Department of Judaic Studies at New York University and holds degrees in art history and in social thought from the University of Chicago. In 2008, he curated the exhibition "Idol Anxiety" for the David and Alfred Smart Museum of Art in Chicago.

EDITORS' STATEMENT

The idea for this anthology began on camelback. In January 2006, we were in Jordan doing research on the aniconic practices of Nabatean polytheism. At the time, Aaron Tugendhaft had already begun work curating "Idol Anxiety" for the University of Chicago's David and Alfred Smart Museum of Art. The exhibition, which would explore the diversity of practices associated with the notion of idolatry, was to run from April to November 2008. Tugendhaft had the idea of preparing an anthology of essays to complement the show and asked Josh Ellenbogen if he would act as coeditor. Ellenbogen agreed and work began on the present volume. It soon became apparent that the exhibition would come and go long before the anthology would be ready for publication. This allowed us to loosen the bonds between exhibition and book. Though they retain the same title, the two have become more cousins than siblings. Limitation of space restricted the exhibition to objects of a strictly religious character, preventing an exploration of idolatry's relevance beyond the realm of religion. Certain of the essays in this volume were accordingly chosen to broaden the themes of the show. Conversely, not all of the themes and cultures treated in the exhibition have found their way into the book; our beloved Nabateans, for example, had a cameo appearance in Chicago but find no mention here beyond this "Statement." Above all, while the show was an essay in a single voice, in putting together this volume we have embraced the multiplicity of voices natural to the anthology form.

We would like to extend a special thank you to Ike Harijanto for her help in copyediting and indexing this volume.

Josh Ellenbogen
Aaron Tugendhaft

IDOL ANXIETY

INTRODUCTION

JOSH ELLENBOGEN AND AARON TUGENDHAFT

When the inhabitants of ancient Mesopotamia made a new cult-statue for one of their temples, that object would first undergo an elaborate ceremony. This *mīs pî* or "mouth-washing" ritual consisted of numerous stages, over the course of which the object underwent a radical metamorphosis—it became the kind of thing one might appropriately treat as a god.[1] A crucial moment in the ritual occurred when the artisans flung into a river the tools that they had used to make the cult-object. Following this act, the artisans held out their hands so that a priest could symbolically chop them off with a wooden sword. As the artisans, each of whom had just completed fashioning the object, extended their hands they would ritually chant: "I did not make it; I swear I did not make it; I did not make it; I swear I did not make it."

This claim has its counterpoint in the polemic of the anonymous Hebrew prophet whom we know as "Second Isaiah," an Israelite exile living in Babylonia.[2] As a witness to Mesopotamian cultic practice and as one familiar with the thinking to which it corresponded, the prophet gleefully insisted, in order to discredit the Mesopotamian cult-object, on the fact of its human manufacture: "The makers of idols all work to no purpose. . . . They are craftsmen, they are merely human" (Isa. 44:9, 11). What appeared to his Mesopotamian neighbors as a god was, to the Israelite prophet, simply a work of human hands. This indictment of the cult-object has provided a basis for discourse on "idolatry" ever since.[3]

The phrase *idol anxiety* likely brings to mind a figure like Second Isaiah and his abhorrence of Mesopotamian cultic practice. In this introduction, however, we want to suggest that anxiety over idols may in fact reside beyond the confines of the biblical tradition. As we believe the *mīs pî* ceremony reveals, the very cultures that biblical polemic often casts as "idolatrous" themselves had a notion of "idol"—in the sense of an object that could not achieve its cultic task—and therefore devised an elaborate system of rituals to prevent such a failure.

This situation calls into question the classic dichotomy of cultures, on the one hand, that recognize the problem of idolatry but refrain from engaging in the practice and, on the other, of ones that engage in it without recognizing it as problematic. We want to suggest that the anxiety that objects can become idols is far more ubiquitous, even if certain cultures do not possess the terminology to frame the issue as such. An object's collapse into the category of "idol" marks a form of breakdown that can be understood on a culture's own terms. Recognizing a particular culture's expression of anxiety can function as a guide to how that culture defines success and failure with regard to religious objects. From such a perspective, it is not only Second Isaiah who has a notion of idol, while his Mesopotamian hosts are oblivious to such a "failed object." As the care taken in the *mīs pî* to ensure success exemplifies, the Mesopotamians well knew how an object could fail. As they themselves put it, without undergoing the ritual process "the image does not smell incense, eat food and drink water."[4] It remains a dumb thing, rather than achieving the purpose of being a god. By contrast, and crucially, when it does succeed as a god it is not, at least by the definition we propose in this introduction, an idol.

Moshe Halbertal and Avishai Margalit, in their book *Idolatry*, define their project as "principally a conceptual analysis of idolatry as it is seen by its opponents. . . . It is an attempt to understand a phenomenon through the way it defines the 'enemy.'"[5] They recognize that traditional discourse on idolatry has been "polemical and hostile," aimed at "the other."[6] Since their work focuses on Jewish sources, "the other" at issue here is the polytheist or pagan (they use the terms interchangeably) "other" of monotheism. These two scholars focus on how the monotheistic portrayal of paganism as idolatry constitutes an act of "self-definition through its idea of what is excluded."[7] To this interpretation, idolatry marks an anxiety, but always one that is aimed outward—against a group that is other.[8] In contrast to Halbertal and Margalit, we want to turn attention to how anxiety over idolatry can arise within groups themselves. Moving beyond "idolatry" as a polemical accusation, such an approach allows us to reorient our inquiry to the forms of anxiety that shadow the human interaction with things and the divine, and the various strategies that given groups have developed for overcoming these anxieties.

This situation points to one of the broadest goals of the present introduction. The category of the idol turns on the selection of certain interactions with objects as dangerous and others as desirable. Which interactions appear threatening and which appear suitable correlate to a larger set of issues: the understandings of representation, likeness, being, and making that given cultures develop.[9] Rather than aiming artificially to fix the character of idols as a specific class of thing, we want to highlight some of the variables that can play a role in any culture's specific negotiation of success and failure in its religious use of objects.[10] In order to do so, we propose tracking the basic conceptual categories and forms of interaction that emerge as significant in the Mesopotamian *mīs pî* ritual, comparing them to other historical manifestations of idol anxiety. The result will be a kind of "grammar of the idol," a guide to the variables that must be considered when attempting to interpret a culture's approach to the use of objects in religious contexts.[11] Furthermore, because the idol engages with the categories of representation, likeness, being, and making that govern all human interactions with objects, a broader heuristic purpose for such a grammar presents itself. Attention to the anxieties surrounding idolatry can provide insight into the ways, in particular times and places, human beings have negotiated their relationship with objects more generally.[12]

Before proceeding with our grammar, it may be useful to say something more about the term *idolatry* itself, with its long and complicated history. Given the polysemous nature of the term, we need to clarify what we primarily do and do not have in mind when we talk about idols in this introductory discussion. That the word *idolatry* fuses a Hebrew concern with Greek terminology provides an immediate indicator of the problems involved here. As might be expected, the fit between the Hebrew and the Greek is not precise. The term idolatry itself derives from two Greek words: *eidōlon* ("image") and *latria* ("worship"). Biblical Hebrew lacks any term meaning "worship of images," and no single term that clearly corresponds to the Greek *eidōlon*. The Jews who produced the ancient Greek translation of the Old Testament, the Septuagint, used the word *eidōlon* to translate various Hebrew terms. Some of these Hebrew words (e.g., *pesel, tzelem*) approximate the root meaning of the Greek *eidōlon* fairly closely, and do not possess any negative connotation when taken on their own—they simply mean "image" or "likeness." Other terms rendered in the Greek by *eidōlon*, however, make matters more complex. For example, the Hebrew word *elohim*, translated by *eidōlois* at 1 Kings 11:8, literally means "gods." Similarly, the *eidōlois* of the Septuagint version of Deuteronomy 32:21 corresponds to the Hebrew term *hevel*, whose literal meaning is "vapor" or "breath," and figuratively can mean "insubstantiality," "worthlessness" or "vanity" (as in the famous opening of Ecclesiastes). By translating such varying Hebrew terms with this one Greek word, the Septuagint collapses distinctions between images, divinity, and lack of truth or substantiality. When the compound word *eidōlolatria* appears in the Pauline letters—that is, after the composition of the Hebrew biblical books and their translation into Greek—it is glossed as "fornication, uncleanness, inordinate affection, evil concupiscence, and covetousness" (Col. 3:5). Clearly, then, the term has already taken on vastly broader connotations than its etymological basis would suggest.[13]

A univocal meaning for the terms *idol* and *idolatry* is impossible on the basis of such divergent data. Accordingly, one will find a variety of approaches to these concepts in the pages of the present anthology. As editors, we have not tried to impose a consistent definition of idolatry on our contributors. In this introduction, however, we focus on the idol as a material thing and on the concerns that surround human interaction with it.[14] The grammar of the idol that we propose, therefore, proceeds as follows. Using primarily the *mīs pî* ritual and related Mesopotamian practices, we will consider the following five determinants of the idol: the question of making, the concept of likeness, the representational or presentational status of objects, understandings of human power, and the immanent or transcendent character of the divine.

Today, we know the Mesopotamian *mīs pî* or "mouth-washing" ritual from a series of cuneiform tablets dating to the first millennium B.C.E., though the ceremony itself probably first appeared in older epochs. The most extensive manuscripts come from Nineveh and Babylon. These texts allow for a reconstruction of the *mīs pî* as a ceremony consisting of ten or eleven phases, over the course of which the new cult-statue leaves the workshop and is inducted into the temple. The first day of the ritual begins with preparations in the city, countryside, and temple, followed by purification rites and an incantation in the workshop. The procession then moves to the river, into which the artificers of the object throw their tools. Then follows another incantation, and an appeal for the image's brothers, the other gods, to count it among them. The first day comes to an end when the celebrants take the image from the riverbank to the orchard, where they place it facing the sunrise. On the second day, the ritual resumes with further offerings and incantations in the orchard. At this point, the moment comes with which our discussion started: the artisans declare that they did not make the object and the priests symbolically chop off their hands. Following more incantations, the procession marches to the temple gate and then, after yet another series of incantations, to the sanctuary niche. The priest then leads the object to take its seat, the celebrants recite two more incantations and prepare a last offering. The *mîs pî* then concludes.

Through this ceremony the inhabitants of Mesopotamia convey their need to confront the question of making as a central concern in using a statue to attain contact with the divine. If making a thing is tantamount to possessing power over it, then forgetfulness regarding a thing's genesis can prove transformative of its nature. By the logic of this rite, casting the tools into the river upon completing the image returned them to the gods of craftsmanship, and so established those gods as the actual makers of the cult-statue. The act of ritually severing the artisans' hands with a wooden sword graphically reiterates this idea. Such a deed buttresses the claim that the cult-statue was not humanly made, but rather, as a god, was born to the gods in heaven. By this displacement of genesis and agency, the thing was divested of the human manufacture that would have rendered its worship unacceptable.

A similar denial of human manufacture operates in many cultural traditions, although the particular form that it takes varies widely.[15] The Mesopotamian ritual, for example, does have certain parallels with the later Christian idea of the *acheiropoiēton*—a work "not made by human hands." Veronica's veil comprises the most famous example of this latter tradition. Folk etymology derives the female saint's name from the Latin word *vera*, meaning "true," and the Greek *eikon*, another word for "image." The tradition tells of how Veronica supplied Christ with her veil to wipe his brow as he was carrying his cross to Golgotha, and how the image of his face became miraculously impressed upon it. The resulting "true image" of Christ achieved its accuracy because it came into being without the mediation of a human hand. As Gilbert Dagron has summarized: "In order for the icon to live the painter and the painter's art must disappear—or at least they cannot serve as active intermediaries, but only passive instruments in the elaboration of the image."[16]

This elimination of mediation centers on the idea that direct contact between signifier and signified ensures an image's accuracy. Human artistry is evacuated from the image in order to guarantee that that image is a perfect likeness. In this respect, the Christian denial of manufacture differs markedly from the Mesopotamian one. The tradition of the "true image" introduces a concern with accurate likeness to the divine—a concern that this tradition links to the problem of making—that plays no part in the *mīs pî* ritual. Whatever else we might say of the object as it issues from the *mīs pî*, we cannot call the object a likeness of the divine. It is the divine.

Nonetheless, even if we cannot say that a Christian species of likeness makes up a valid concern in the Mesopotamian context, the concept likeness has other applications to the Mesopotamian cult-object. This point becomes more apparent in a text related to those that describe the *mīs pî* ceremony, although the text treats a separate matter.[17] In the thirty-first year of the reign of the ninth-century B.C.E. Babylonian king Nabû-apla-iddina, the monarch made a decision to restore the image of the god Shamash. The Suteans had destroyed the original image some two centuries before. Between the period of the cult-object's destruction and its restoration, worshippers had used a sundisk as a replacement for the missing image. Strikingly, the stone tablet that describes these events indicates that restoration of the cult-object required access to the destroyed original so that it could serve as a model. The text begins by relating how "a relief of (Shamash's) image, an impression of baked clay—his figure and insignia—was discovered on the opposite side of the Euphrates, on the West Bank." On the basis of this model, the king ordered the priest Nabû-nadin-shumi to fashion a new image, a task the priest accomplished "through the craft of Ea" and other gods. The king then had the *mīs pî* ritual performed upon the restored image.[18] That deciding to refashion the image of the god required, as a warrant, the discovery of a previous model indicates that the question of likeness does have application in a Mesopotamian context. In order for it to become an object of worship, the cult-image had to look a certain way, and even to resemble a particular original. Yet the god Shamash does not himself provide the original, at least if we understand that word in terms of a freestanding antecedent on which artificers must model their copy. Rather, a previously existing image plays this role.[19]

Putting matters this way has the advantage of making a related group of questions pressing. Above all, it demands we consider carefully the issue of antecedence, which one might also view in terms of the presentational or representational status of the cult-object. This matter has the broadest importance, since it directly impinges on two of the other primary variables in our grammar of the idol: the nature of human power and the immanence or transcendence of the divine. In the case of the Mesopotamian tradition, we cannot really speak of the cult-object that issues from the *mîs pî* ritual as merely a way to refer to or represent a divine antecedent. The cult-object makes the deity present. At a functional level, the object itself serves as the divine original for worshippers, and so the whole question of representation is problematic in relationship to it. This becomes clear, for example, when we turn to a case documented in the Amarna letters. In the fourteenth century B.C.E., Egypt ruled the city of Qatna, a part of the same Akkadian culture to which the later Babylonian king Nabû-appla-iddina belonged. The Hittites raided the city of Qatna, stealing the cult-object for the god Shimigi (the Hurrian equivalent of Shamash) from its temple. When Akizzi, the mayor of Qatna, wrote to Akhenaten in Egypt to explain the situation, he spoke of the theft of Shimigi, not of a statue of Shimigi: "The Hittite king has taken Shimigi, the god of my father."[20] Since the cult-object does not simply represent Shimigi but has an "equality of essence" with the god, or "manifests" the god, or constitutes "the real presence" of the god, to steal the cult-object Shimigi, on one level, is to steal Shimigi.[21]

Of course, even if the Mesopotamians mean the cult-object itself to establish the presence of the divine, we cannot say that the cult-object ever became fully coterminous with the divine. The king Nabû-apla-iddina, in the previous story of remaking a destroyed image of Shamash, could undertake such a refashioning precisely because the destruction of the Shamash image had not actually entailed the destruction of Shamash. The text in fact states that the king has the ritual performed on the cult-object Shamash "before Shamash."[22] Since Shamash comprises the audience of the *mîs pî*, we cannot say that the cult-object Shamash simply is Shamash. At one and the same time, Shamash is the cult-object of the *mîs pî* and a separately existing entity that stands at a distance from the *mîs pî*, one that that can watch over the rite and the object it consecrates.

Such distance between the cult-object and divine presence only grows accentuated in other, quite different traditions. Here, the suitability of a mediating thing's relation to the divine turns on establishing and stabilizing its referentiality, its capacity to represent a divine that must always remain external to it. The defense of images that St. John of Damascus (d. 749) undertook centered, in part, on the claim that the mediating thing could be confined to the referential.[23] It would not itself become the recipient of veneration but would abet the veneration of a deity that stood fully apart from it. The continued power that the Christian tradition wields in this regard enforces ways of thinking that often make it difficult to grasp alien practices, such as the *mīs pî* ceremony. Nonetheless, what makes for a proper or improper use of a cult-object depends on the presentational or representational duty with which the users of an object task it. Just as securing the proper status of the cult-object in relation to making becomes a vital matter, so does establishing the suitable status of the object in regard to its representational or presentational duties.

This issue actually correlates to the matter of human power. In general, where a given cultural tradition asks the object to make the divine present, the fear that haunts the use of cult-objects does not concern the weakness or inadequacy of humanity's productive power. Rather, the anxiety turns on the fear that humanity's powers are in reality too great. Therefore, actualizing these productive powers in the absence of divine authorization appears as a dangerous pretension in mortals, an unseemly competition with the gods. To avoid this peril, it becomes necessary to establish some check on the potentially dangerous overflow of human power. Rebuilding the image of Shamash required a divine warrant; the *mīs pî* ritual denied that humanity's dangerous power had played any part in making the cult-object. If traditions that aim for presence are anxious about the unseemly overflow of human power, however, those that prioritize representation most often worry about the limitations of human ability.

Where representation becomes the object's primary purpose, and where limitations on humanity's ability successfully to represent become a paramount concern, anxieties often cluster around the referent of the made object. For example, in such a system, the divine that one means to signify can simply be beyond visual depiction, and so the object that seeks visually to refer to it itself becomes perilous. Such cases would correspond to the ineffable deity of negative theology. If the thing one seeks to represent does not have such a nature that its visual depiction is simply absurd, however, then the question of accuracy in depiction can arise. The Incarnation in Christianity, for instance, had a decisive effect on establishing accuracy as a central category for evaluating images, as expressed poignantly by John of Damascus: "Of old, God the incorporeal and formless was never depicted, but now that God has been seen in the flesh and has associated with humankind, I depict what I have seen of God."[24] When God became flesh and matter, the status of the fleshly and material underwent a general transformation, with the broadest ramifications for questions of image making.[25] God now became a referent capable of being represented. Such cases make clear how issues of presentation and representation must be considered in relation to how they correspond to concerns over the adequacy or inadequacy of humanity's productive capacities.

At the same time, it is easy to see how the questions of divine immanence and transcendence comprise powerful variables within the above schema. Whether the divine stands in the role of a transcendent creator, in the sense that it manufactured a material world of which it is not a part, or whether it exists in the same universe as men and material things, holds implications for what forms of human manufacture will appear as particularly threatening. This statement holds true not only for objects that might seek to represent the divine but also for those objects that represent the mundane. In those cases where a transcendent creator is posited, for example, questions can arise regarding any attempt at making a likeness of the material objects that that creator had first brought into being. Such an act can cast human maker and divine maker into parallel—and possibly competitive—roles with each other. This idea comes to the fore in the biblical Decalogue in Exodus, especially if we consider the prohibition of images in light of the commandment to observe the Sabbath. By specifying that "graven images" depict those things "in the heavens, on earth, and in the sea" (Exod. 20:4), the image prohibition concerns itself precisely with those things that are not God, that is, with likenesses of the works of Creation. The later commandment that establishes the Sabbath reiterates this idea, which reads: "For in six days the Lord made heaven and earth and sea, and all that is in them" (Exod. 20:11). The repetition of language makes the issue clear: humanity cannot make likenesses of the things that God created during the six days of creation. God as Creator is distinct from the things He has created. Though not yet articulated as "transcendence," the problem that this philosophical notion comes to address is already present *in nuce*. The issue at play in the biblical prohibition of images, therefore, is distinct from the question of producing a likeness *of* the creator, although the form any such likeness might take would also be decisively shaped by the immanent or transcendent status of the divine.

All attempts to articulate the relationships between the human, the divine, and the things that mediate between them will have to take into account the kinds of variables that we have sketched out in this introduction. Such an approach allows for idolatry to be treated as a locus of concern rather than a polemical accusation. Attunement to cultural anxieties over idolatry provides an opening through which one can better appreciate the forms of negotiation and set of solutions brought to bear in any particular case. We have touched on only very few examples in this introduction. Many more are taken up by the contributors to this volume, to whom we would now like to turn our attention.

···

This introductory discussion has privileged the question of how human beings understand the things of the world, and how they comport themselves in relation to them. In taking this approach, it finds inspiration in Jean-Luc Marion's insight that "the idol does not indicate . . . a particular being or even class of beings. [The] idol indicate[s] a manner of being for beings, or at least for some of them."[26] Marion's position, one of the most important treatments of the idol that exists in the literature, is itself famously rooted in a particular and original treatment of Heidegger. Out of a desire fully to exploit the vantage that Heidegger's work opens, we have chosen to bring together a large number of works that specifically attempt to develop Heideggerian accounts of the idol. Over a third of the essays contained in this volume, in fact, proceed from Heidegger's work in one way or another. The notion of failure, for example, that we ourselves employ in the above originates in Heidegger.[27] Further, aside from Marion's essay in this collection, the contributions of David Summers, Daniel Doneson, and Daniel Silver all provide accounts that respond to and expand upon Heidegger's thought. This is not to say that all these contributions develop Heidegger's thought toward the same endpoint; by connecting our definition of the idol to Heidegger's notion of breakdown, for example, the argument of our introduction moves in a different direction than Marion's notion of the idol as a "first visible."[28]

Furthermore, since the themes we have identified as central to understanding the idol—how human beings construe making, representation versus presentation, the nature of human power, and so on—clearly can be approached from various perspectives, we have decided to bring together voices from several disciplines. This allows the anthology to explore how the question of the idol plays out in distinct realms. History of religion, philosophy, literary criticism, art history, and musicology make up some of the main fields from which we draw our contributors. Additionally, because many of the objects historically associated with idols now go by the name of art, and because more and more scholarly voices seek to bring discussions of the idol to their treatments of art objects, we have looked in particular for essays that treat art objects in light of the idol. Many of these essays, such as those of W. J. T. Mitchell, Rachael DeLue, and Rose Subotnik, do so by developing studies of particular artworks. Other essays, such as that of Jim Elkins, engage in a more purely theoretical discussion of the stakes at play in taking an originally religious concern and applying it to modern artworks.

The essays in this anthology fall into three sections, beginning with what might best be called its historical section. The essays of Jan Assmann, Marc Fumaroli, and Mika Natif comprise this part of the book, since they bear upon the main religious traditions that have historically discussed idolatry: Judaism, Christianity, and Islam. While these three essays address the conceptual questions we have already raised, they also develop different aspects of the question of idolatry. Assmann's essay on the Old Testament, for example, centrally concerns itself with what it could mean to have a visible support for the worship of a nonvisible God. It significantly expands on this question, however, by raising an issue of paramount significance to discussions of idolatry, that of medium. Although Assmann integrates the question of medium into other contexts, such as the transition from monolatry to monotheism and the politics implicit in the development, his account puts particular weight on the image/text distinction and its theological import. To Assmann, the Old Testament's concern over establishing proper media for relating to the divine sees to it that "where Images are, Torah shall be," so that "images must disappear in order to make room for the word."

Assmann argues that "images idolize the world and blind the eyes from being able to look beyond the world and focus on the creator," so that, "instead of establishing contact, images block communication with God." Such a position treats idolatry as largely a problem of seeing, so that the attention of worshippers is arrested on the material thing that should only serve as a vehicle for attaining contact with the divine. While this treatment has broad parallels with many of the essays that appear in this anthology, above all W. J. T. Mitchell's piece, it also establishes links with other essays in the historical section, particularly Marc Fumaroli's essay on Christianity. Fumaroli's account, like Assmann's, argues that the error of idolatry in the Old Testament is one of gazing, in which worshippers do not look through the material thing meant to provide contact with God, but instead "stop . . . on the object itself."

Here, "the crime is in the orientation of the gaze that abusively transforms a work of art into an idol." For Fumaroli, Christianity develops Judaism's privileging of the gaze, ultimately "subjectiviz[ing] the notion of the idol" in a full and comprehensive way. For this reason, because images lose any intrinsically idolatrous dimension, "holy images will be able to enter into Christian worship in broad daylight," a situation that has the capacity to "make unheard of images flourish, animated by two sorts of life, the life of bodies and that of souls." By this formulation, Fumaroli means to encapsulate the trajectory of artistic development that finally culminates in the Renaissance, and so his essay aims to carve out a way of understanding the tradition of Christian religious art most broadly.

A very different, but equally significant, approach to the same group of questions appears in Mika Natif's essay on Islam. Natif's essay, which attempts a fundamental reconceptualizaton of Islam's attitude toward images, first provides an overview of actual imagistic practices in Islam through time. She demonstrates that Islam's attitudes toward image making were a good deal more ambivalent than they are often claimed to have been. While an overview of this kind has its own conceptual import, the true analytic thrust of Natif's piece emerges in her question: "Was resentment of images ever due to strictly religious problems?" For Natif, the emergence in the ninth century of a religious discourse that aimed at the rigorous prohibition of figural representation was the fruit of "a sociopolitical power struggle, and not a religious or spiritual one." While Assmann's piece indicates the importance of political questions in anxiety over idolatry, Natif gives greater weight to this issue, in particular considering tensions between the caliphs and the ulema (religious scholars) in the emergence of Islam's famous ban on images. By this means, she does nothing less than provide a new way of considering the question of idolatry as it functioned in one of the three main religious discourses on the subject.

Natif's essay also carefully considers how the sociopolitical tensions it examines, along with the influence of Aristotelian philosophy, established particular techniques by which Muslim artists chose to render bodies, depicting them as "flat, almost transparent, without the forms of muscles, while *dīv*s are shown with heavy bodies, with muscles, hair, and genitalia." For this reason, Natif's essay serves as a transition to the anthology's next section, which focuses on the production and analysis of actual art objects, and includes essays by W. J. T. Mitchell, Rachael Ziady DeLue, David Summers, Rose Rosengard Subotnik, James Elkins, and Jean-Luc Marion. By highlighting how, in Natif's argument, certain strategies of representation became religiously safe, we do not mean to suggest that particular visual, technical, or aesthetic forms are automatically immune to anxiety over idolatry, any more than that particular forms must engender the fear of it. W. J. T. Mitchell, whose essay initiates the section in this volume that focuses on actual artistic practice, has underscored this point in other published work. By emphasizing that *idol* is fundamentally a name for a particular mode of relating to things, Mitchell has shown that "it is therefore important to stress that one and the same object (a golden calf for instance) could function as a totem, fetish, or idol, depending on the social practices and narratives that surround it."[29]

In Mitchell's present essay, he develops these ideas into a case study of a single object. He picks up the specific matter of the Golden Calf, as depicted by the great painter Poussin, in order to articulate an alternative model for discussing Poussin's painting of it, one that Mitchell roots in an unusual reading of Blake and Nietzsche. The particular model to which Mitchell's approach tries to be an alternative is that of conventional art history, a method that emerges as oddly iconoclastic in Mitchell's account. By iconoclastic, Mitchell means primarily ways of approaching images that strive to get past or behind their visual character in order to render them what Mitchell calls "a sign or symptom" of some proper antecedent. Such an approach dovetails with the theological imperative, discerned by Fumaroli, that one's gazing not "stop . . . on the [sacred] object itself," and it constitutes, according to Mitchell, a central drive of art history. Art-historical explanation has recently held that Poussin's work is conventionally pious, in that it consists in "signs and citations that point toward an invisible and unrepresentable foundation." The religious duty of the spectator thus consists in "revers[ing] the significance of 'visual prominence,' and see[ing] that the primary subject of the painting is 'the hiddenness of the divine.'"[30] Insofar as this account requires "relating to the picture as a sign or symptom of Poussin's [own pious] intentions," art history stands in the same relation to Poussin's work as it imagines Poussin did to "visual prominence," striving to yoke it to an extravisual foundation.

In opposition to this reading, Mitchell suggests we see the work through the eyes of Blake and Nietzsche. Mitchell argues that Nietzsche, in *Twilight of the Idols*, turns the tables on the iconoclastic gesture by renouncing the drive to image destruction. As Mitchell notes, Nietzsche holds that "the eternal idols are not to be smashed but to be 'touched with a hammer as with a tuning fork.'" Nietzsche, here, seeks not to smash idols, but instead to "sound" them "with a delicate, precise touch that reveals their hollowness . . . and perhaps even retunes or plays a tune upon them." In terms of what this perspective means for the Poussin painting, Mitchell suggests we consider the possibility that the work has a more ambiguous relationship to idolatry's founding moment than one of simple iconoclasm, so that Poussin emerges as being of the devil's party without his knowing it: "Could Poussin's painting, without his quite knowing it, be *sounding* the idol with a hammer, tuning fork, or (more precisely) a paintbrush?"

Mitchell's work has set an important part of the program for how scholars think idolatry in relation to art objects. Rachael DeLue takes Mitchell's work in a new direction, using it to analyze contemporary art that confronts racist imagery. She approaches the work of the artists Kara Walker and Michael Ray Charles via Mitchell's suggestion that we ask of pictures, understood as a material array of formal and symbolic elements, less what they mean or do, but instead "what they *want*—what claim they make upon us, and how we are to respond."[31] Such a grant of agency to pictures, aside from the general methodological provocation it offers, appears as especially apt in DeLue's treatment, since she seeks to understand how "Walker and Charles make their imagery behave as would things not altogether lifeless and inert." DeLue argues that these artists, who interrogate and appropriate historical racist imagery, make the objects they produce seem animate and alive "by way of an excess of representation that fashions brute matter into a set of qualities associated with life and volition." Via such a representational excess, which DeLue takes to turn on the formal aspects of the works as well as how audiences understand the question of human making, the images of Walker and Charles acquire a dimension that "pushes them toward a category of object relations already vexed and fraught: that of idolatry." Obviously, Walker and Charles do not mean to bring off a worship of vile, racist imagery. But by compelling a viewing of such imagery that approaches veneration, they collapse "the adoration of the idolater and the revulsion of the iconoclast into a single experience." For DeLue, the double bind these works initiate—a painterly iconoclasm that incites viewers to veneration and destruction—encompasses their main purpose, the creation of a space for "deliberative thought, what the extremes of idolatry and iconoclasm refuse to allow."

The next four essays that appear in this anthology's discussion of art objects, although they maintain continuity with the questions this introduction treats, also insert these questions into novel contexts. For some time, David

Summers has been engaged in an independent methodological project meant to establish new ways of addressing art objects, ones that move away from the binary of form and content, and the notion of style as it is typically deployed. Rejecting a notion of "visual arts" to develop one of "spatial arts," a concept that refers to humanity's physical being-in-the-world and the production of social space, Summers's thinking has much in common with that of other contributors to this volume. In particular, his effort to analyze the artifactual shaping of social space owes much to Heidegger's writings on art, and it is vitally concerned with the issue of substitution.[32] What Summers attempts in his contribution to this volume is to situate idolatry relative to his larger project. In an essay that provides its own programmatic treatment of idolatry and iconoclasm, Summers ranges from the Golden Calf to the contemporary art of Nam June Paik, but of particular note is his emphasis on the role of place in how users of objects form relations with them. While contributors to this volume are unanimous about the importance of substitution making the divine present, Summers explores how such substitution is intrinsically related to questions of location. That is, while "presence entails some form of *substitution*," Summers demonstrates that "icons are usually meant to make a presence accessible in a designated place and in response to specified behavior." By taking this position, Summers not only identifies a determinant of how relations with icons are imagined, but helps explain a dimension of idol anxiety that other commentators, from Mitchell to Halbertal and Margalit, have noted.[33] The charge of idolatry often unfolds in relation to territory, carrying the imperative not only to smash icons but to cleanse space. Of the power that images come to exert, we need to ask not just how images may seem to act as agents but what is the place in which they do so.

Rose Subotnik's essay advances the goals of the anthology simply by the nature of its subject-matter. Aware that "it is difficult at first glance to see how a musical performance could become an object of worship," Subotnik formulates an answer by navigating between Adorno and Benjamin. These two figures have a special significance for Subotnik's work in music theory, since their approaches represent the most fully developed models we have for considering popular music, the cultural form she examines from the vantage of idolatry. Adorno himself argues that false values emerge from popular music "like an idol," and his attempt to describe the dynamics of how such music culturally functions makes noticeable use of a religious vocabulary. While Subotnik argues that Benjamin's thoughts on aura also provide a means to think music via idolatry, she claims that "what neither [Benjamin nor Adorno] offers is an alternative to Marxism as a framework in which to think about the relation of music to idolatry." Subotnik's essay tries to develop such an alternative, above all by privileging the question of collective memory. By providing a common object in relation to which members of a collective can form memories, popular music comes to play a vital role in community-formation, creating a species of bulwark that can stabilize individual life. As Subotnik argues, "In an age that no longer provides religious guarantees of permanence in the cosmos, bulwarks of this kind have a genuine existential value."

James Elkins, for his part, engages with issues of a foundational status for this volume's intellectual presuppositions, as well as larger strands of the contemporary discussion of idols. Elkins begins by noting, rightly we feel, that many of the secular discourses that scholars currently construct around art objects have a provenance in religion. He concerns himself both with the discussion of the sublime and, of special significance to *Idol Anxiety*, iconoclasm. Elkins is at pains to point out that his endeavor is not one of "investigative journalism," an effort to show that contemporary accounts of art objects are really "covert theology." Instead, his piece seeks to establish a conceptual framework in which to consider the stakes of employing originally religious concerns and anxieties, such as those expressed in iconoclasm, as a means to discuss artworks without any apparent concern for religion.[34] Elkins indicates that "the themes around iconoclasm are not limited to religious images, but it is not yet clear when it makes sense to invoke them." In an effort to bring clarity to this matter, Elkins wonders what would happen if texts on artworks, ones that "have no open allegiances to religion or belief, were temporarily reassigned to their original sources in religious and theological writing."

Elkins concludes his essay in this volume by asking why it is that we, at the end of the first decade of the twenty-first century, find concepts such as iconoclasm and its related terms so compelling as a means to discuss art objects. Rooted as it is in his understanding of the idol, Jean-Luc Marion's aesthetics provides one possible response to Elkins's query. Beginning already with his early theological writings, the idol has played a crucial role in Marion's thinking.[35] For Marion, the significance of the idol is rooted in its etymology—*eidōlon*, from the Greek root *eidō*, "to see." As he writes in *God Without Being*, "the fabricated thing becomes an idol, that of a god, only from the moment when the gaze has decided to fall upon it, has made it the privileged fixed point of is own consideration."[36] In his later phenomenological work, Marion has developed the importance of this category, particularly for aesthetics. "The privileged occurrence of the idol," he writes in *Being Given*, "is obviously the painting."[37] In his contribution for this volume, Marion provides a phenomenological account of the difference between seeing and appearing that expands upon this insight. In effect, Marion develops an aesthetics that brings to bear for the work of art—or what he calls the "aesthetic visible" in its relation to the "common visible"—distinctions that originate in and underlie his earlier work on the idol. Accordingly, Marion's essay provides a valuable example of how the concept of the idol can provide a basis for broader investigations with wide philosophical import.

The last two contributions to this volume continue to develop philosophical approaches to our theme, broadening the discussion that Marion initiates. While Marion builds on arguments from Heidegger's early work, Daniel Doneson takes as his starting point Heidegger's later essay "The Origin of the Work of Art." Doneson situates the problem of the idol within the broader trajectory of Western metaphysics, as Heidegger understood that trajectory. In Doneson's account, designating something an "idol" is itself based in the aesthetic tradition initiated by Plato, a tradition Heidegger claims is unable properly to account for the work of art. Instead, Heidegger says the artwork sets the truth to work. Doneson aims to elucidate this bold and complex claim by fleshing out how the artwork "opens up a world" and "sets forth the earth." After explicating Heidegger's account of such an artwork—not beholden to the idolatry of aesthetics, so to speak—Doneson comes to ask whether today, after "the death of God," artworks can function in an analogous way to such premodern works as the Mesopotamian cult-statue, the Greek temple, or the Christian cathedral. He suggests that the artwork may still be at work, but not as the site at which the beholder can "plug in" to the beyond or "the holy." Rather, the artwork can become a kind of "anti-idol," a site at which we "unplug" from our absorption in the rest of life, so as to expose or reveal "its ex nihilo character to itself from out of itself."

Like Marion and Doneson, Daniel Silver also takes inspiration from Heidegger—this time from the 1929–30 lecture course published as *The Fundamental Concepts of Metaphysics*. Building an analogy with our opening discussion of the *mīs pî* ritual, Silver reads the lecture course as Heidegger's response to the felt collapse of a cultural practice (philosophy) that occurred in the early twentieth century. Silver dubs Heidegger's pedagogical attempt to awaken a philosophical mood in his students "a kind of latter-day *mīs pî,* one designed not to infuse cult-objects with divine presence but to infuse philosophical practice and settings with 'the mystery' and 'inner terror' necessary to live up to their promise." Heidegger's mood awakening provides a unique form of response to the anxiety of cultural collapse, because its aim is not to manage or minimize the anxiety but rather to find spiritual resources in describing and tuning into it as a mode of engaged, living experience. Silver develops this argument through an explication of Heidegger's treatment of boredom as a "fundamental philosophizing mood." His essay provides an example of how "idol anxiety" may be at play in a place where one might least expect to find it, but also—by the essay's conclusion—it proposes a new way to understand the *mīs pî* itself. Contrasting Heidegger's attunement to moods in human action with standard utilitarian and voluntaristic understandings, Silver argues that whereas to these standard approaches the activity of the *mīs pî* would look like nothing more than conspiracy or reassurance, from the perspective of mood attunement "the ceremony would be designed to tune priests and artisans into the power of a certain mood to open up a way of engaging with their situation." Silver's focus on mood awakening thus provides a rich model for rethinking those forms of human action that have traditionally been labeled as "idolatry."

1

WHAT'S WRONG WITH IMAGES?

JAN ASSMANN

The prohibition of images is perhaps the strangest commandment in the Decalogue. It is understandable enough that God does not want other gods to be worshipped along with him; that his name not be abused; that he wants us to keep the Sabbath and to honor our father and mother; and that he forbids murder, adultery, theft, wrong testimony, and the covetous desire for the wife, house, and possessions of others. All this is quite normal and can be found in other cultures. But why forbid images? What does God find wrong with them? And what do we learn about the concept of "image" from the fact that God forbids the making and the worshipping of them?

Let us recall the text of the commandment:

> You shall not make for yourself a carved image, or any likeness of anything that is in heaven above, or that is in the earth beneath, or that is in the water under the earth. You shall not bow down to them or serve them, for I the LORD your God am a jealous God, visiting the iniquity of the fathers on the children to the third and the fourth generation of those who hate me, but showing steadfast love to thousands of those who love me and keep my commandments. (Exod. 20:4–6; cf. Deut. 5:8–10)

The Decalogue occurs twice in the Bible, in Exodus and in Deuteronomy. Depending on how one breaks up the commandments, the prohibition of images either belongs to the first commandment, the prohibition of worshipping other gods ("You shall not have other gods besides me") and forms its commentary (i.e., "You shall not make for yourself any carved image"), or the prohibition of images forms a commandment of its own.[1] What is the difference between these two ways of reading? If the prohibition of images forms the commentary of the commandment "No other gods!" it means: do not make images, because every image tends to turn into another god. We are here in a world, to quote Hans Belting, "before the age of art"; images are not made for aesthetic pleasure, for decoration and embellishment, but for worship. Worship is the only raison d'être for the production of images. To prohibit the production of images, therefore, means to prohibit the adoration of the visible world. The visible world in its shapes and forms must not be adored and in order to avoid this mistake, it must not be represented in images.

In another passage, Deuteronomy gives a reason for this prohibition—the only passage in the Bible where such a reason is given:

> Therefore watch yourselves very carefully. Since you saw no form on the day that the LORD spoke to you at Horeb out of the midst of the fire, beware lest you act corruptly by making a carved image for yourselves, in the form of any figure, the likeness of male or female, the likeness of any animal that is on the earth, the likeness of any winged bird that flies in the air, the likeness of anything that creeps on the ground, the likeness of any fish that is in the water under the earth. And beware lest you raise your eyes to heaven, and when you see the sun and the moon and the stars, all the host of heaven, you be drawn away and bow down to them and serve them, things that the LORD your God has allotted to all the peoples under the whole heaven. But the LORD has taken you and brought you out of the iron furnace, out of Egypt, to be a people of his own inheritance, as you are this day. (Deut. 4:15–20)

God is invisible. Therefore, he cannot be worshipped in anything visible—be it an image or a heavenly body. It is interesting to note that images are here given the same status as sun and moon and stars. This shows that images have a cosmic status; adoring them means adoring the visible world. This restriction amounts to a radical disenchantment of the world. To worship images means to worship the world, that is, "cosmotheism." The visible forms, especially the heavenly bodies, are given to the other peoples as objects of worship. They are the gods of the others and must not be worshipped by Israel, which has acquired a special status where anything visible is banished from communication with God.

The composer Arnold Schönberg gives just such an interpretation of the prohibition of images in his notebooks, written while working on his opera *Moses und Aron*. Images, he writes, are false gods: "There is a false god in everything that surrounds us; he can look like everything, he originates in everything, everything originates in him; he is like the entire surrounding nature and nature is in him as in everything. This god expresses the worship of nature and identifies every living creature with God." The prohibition of images establishes a new relationship between man and the world. Man is emancipated from his symbiotic embeddedness in and dependence on the world. Instead, he confronts the world as a subject confronts an object. This is the relation between man and the world that underlies the *dominium terrae*, the commandment to rule the world: "And God said to them, 'Be fruitful and multiply and fill the earth and subdue it and have dominion over the fish of the sea and over the birds of the heavens and over every living thing that moves on the earth'" (Gen. 1:28; cf. Gen. 9:2). The order of images, by contrast, presupposes divine immanence, that is, an "enchanted world." Images are prohibited because they are all too powerful: they enchant or divinize the world.

If, however, the prohibition of images constitutes a commandment of its own instead of being an explication on the prohibition regarding "other gods," the implication is not so much that every image becomes another god, but rather that no images should be made—including an image of God himself. This is not so much a matter of loyalty, of not worshipping other gods, but of not worshipping God in the wrong way. Yahweh, the god of Israel, must not be represented in an image. Let us keep these two meanings apart by calling the commentary meaning "political," because it is a matter of loyalty and binding, and the other, the independent commandment meaning, "theological," because it concerns the unrepresentability of God. We must not forget, however, that on both readings the prohibition of images is given a political commentary that explains it by reference to God's jealousy and his distinction between friend and foe: "You shall not bow down to them or serve them, for I the LORD your God am a jealous God, visiting the iniquity of the fathers on the children to the third and the fourth generation of those who hate me, but showing steadfast love to thousands of those who love me and keep my commandments" (Exod. 20:5–6; Deut. 5:9–10). God resents the making of images for it is an act of defection and apostasy. This shows that the political meaning was, at least originally, the dominant interpretation. The prohibition of images divides the world into two parties: the idolaters and the iconoclasts, the first being the enemies and the second being the friends of God. So what's wrong with images? They prove that you are an enemy of God.

Before proceeding, let us summarize our results. Images are forbidden for two reasons:

1. Because every image represents a (false) god. This is a question of loyalty. Images are other gods and provoke god's jealousy.

2. Because no image is able to represent the invisible God. This is a question of God's nature. Given the invisibility of God, images constitute the wrong medium to establish contact with the divine.

The concept of medium, as introduced in the second reason, leads us to our next step. If images are the wrong medium, is there an alternative? Is there a right medium of establishing a contact with God, or does the prohibition of images throw us into an abyss of negative theology?

Arnold Schönberg, for one, opted for the second possibility; in his opera *Moses und Aron*, he interprets the prohibition of images in an extremely radical way. Moses condemns not only the Golden Calf, but the whole Bible as an image: "wrong as only an image can be." Schönberg's Moses despairs of the communicability of any idea of God, not only through images but also through words. At the end of the opera, he collapses with the cry: "O Wort, Du Wort, das mir fehlt! [O word, thou word that I lack]." Such a radical position of negative theology, however, by no means corresponds to what the Bible intends by imposing the prohibition of images. The Bible luxuriates in verbal images of God and these are obviously fully admissible. There is nothing wrong with language. Schönberg calls God not only invisible but also unimaginable. This does not correspond to the biblical view. On the contrary, imagination is everything. The biblical texts constantly invite us to imagine God, to form mental images of God in order to love him, to fear him, to obey him. The visible images must disappear in order to make room for the word and the mental images it evokes. Where images are, Torah shall be. Where Torah is, images must be no longer.

Between these two meanings of the prohibition of images—the political one and the theological one—lies a shift in religious orientation which may be described as a shift from monolatry to monotheism. Monolatry means the exclusive worship of only one god while acknowledging, in principle, the existence of other gods. Monotheism means the denial of the existence of other gods. Jealousy is only possible where other objects of love and worship exist.

Jealousy belongs to monolatry, not to monotheism. Therefore, the Bible, to a large extent, presupposes the existence of other gods, but forbids worshipping them and explains this interdiction with the idea of God's jealousy. Only in its later stages, with Deutero-Isaiah, is the existence of other gods denied, and with this step the motif of jealousy disappears. There are no other gods. With this denial Israel achieves the shift from monolatry to monotheism.

Let us have a look at what may be considered the "primal scene" of idolatry, the forbidden worship of images: the story of the Golden Calf. The scene occurs while Moses is atop Mount Sinai, receiving the law from God.

> When the people saw that Moses delayed to come down from the mountain, the people gathered themselves together to Aaron and said to him, "Up, make us gods who shall go before us. As for this Moses, the man who brought us up out of the land of Egypt, we do not know what has become of him." So Aaron said to them, "Take off the rings of gold that are in the ears of your wives, your sons, and your daughters, and bring them to me." So all the people took off the rings of gold that were in their ears and brought them to Aaron. And he received the gold from their hand and fashioned it with a graving tool and made a golden calf. And they said, "These are your gods, O Israel, who brought you up out of the land of Egypt!" (Exod. 32:1–4)

Meanwhile, God informs Moses that the people are committing a great crime. God wants to destroy the people and to found a new one for Moses, but Moses prevails on Him to forgive and to give the people a second chance.

> Then Moses turned and went down from the mountain with the two tablets of the testimony in his hand, tablets that were written on both sides; on the front and on the back they were written. The tablets were the work of God, and the writing was the writing of God, engraved on the tablets. . . . And as soon as he came near the camp and saw the calf and the dancing, Moses' anger burned hot, and he threw the tablets out of his hands and broke them at the foot of the mountain. He took the calf that they had made and burned it with fire and ground it to powder and scattered it on the water and made the people of Israel drink it. (Exod. 32:15–16, 19–20)

Moses destroys both the tablets and the calf, the one out of anger and the other to humiliate and punish. What could be the meaning of grounding and diluting the Golden Calf and of making the people swallow it? The eating of sacred animals is—in the Egyptian imagination—the worst possible religious crime. Drinking the diluted calf seems to be the equivalent of eating a sacred animal. Again, we meet with the strange power that is attributed to images. The image is treated like a sacred animal in the Egyptian sense—not as a representation, but as an incarnation of the divine, not as a copy of a divine body, but as a divine body itself. But Moses does not rest here. This is not enough. He also orders a massacre.

> Then Moses stood in the gate of the camp and said, "Who is on the LORD's side? Come to me." And all the sons of Levi gathered around him. And he said to them, "Thus says the LORD God of Israel, 'Put your sword on your side each of you, and go to and fro from gate to gate throughout the camp, and each of you kill his brother and his companion and his neighbor.'" And the sons of Levi did according to the word of Moses. And that day about three thousand men of the people fell. (Exod. 32:26–28)

The execution of this punishment is presented as a model of "zeal": human zeal and divine jealousy are cognate words in Hebrew. *El qanna'* means "jealous god"; *qana'im* is the denomination of the zealots. Moses and the Levites act as *qana'im* in making themselves tools of God's jealousy. This is what it means to be a zealot. The story teaches that God's distinction between friend and foe prevails over human bonds of kinship and friendship. What's wrong with the Golden Calf? It represents another god, a false, a forbidden one—and representing and adoring another god is the greatest sin that an Israelite can commit.

Why this desire for representation? Why is it necessary to create an image in order to establish contact with the divine? Let us return to the question of medium. Contact with the divine—what does this mean? We must place ourselves back into a world, several millennia distant, where any contact with the divine is culturally institutionalized. There is no way of entering a temple and praying to God the way we are accustomed to do in our churches or mosques or synagogues. Any contact with the divine is institutionally framed in the form of a cultic scene. The cultic scene is cut out from the continuum of space and time as a frame of intervision, interaction, and interlocution. There is something to be seen, to be performed, and to be said. In the Greek mysteries, this triad of intervision, interaction, and interlocution or interaudition is called *deiknymenon* (what is shown), *dromenon* (what is performed), and *legomenon* (what is spoken). In this conception of the cultic scene, everything is symbolic. The image represents the deity, the priest represents the people, and the words to be spoken bestow the sacramental significance to the performance. In the scene of the Golden Calf, the calf represents the deity, the action consists in a sacrifice or sacrificial meal and in what the Bible calls "playing," a euphemism for erotic pleasure. The spoken element occurs in the declaration: "These are your gods, Israel, that brought you up from Egypt!" (Exod. 32:4).

The new religion that God and Moses are negotiating on Mount Sinai deprives the cultic scene of the element of intervision. There are rites to be performed and words to be spoken, but there is no image to be seen. God must not be represented. This is a revolutionary innovation. Moreover, the cultic scene is no longer the only medium and frame by which to establish a contact with the divine. Now, instead of the cultic image, there are the tablets with the word of God that Moses shall explicate as the commandments and prohibitions of the Torah. Every Israelite is expected to learn this Torah, or instruction, by heart, to study it day and night and to transform its prescriptions into lived reality. Instead of the priest before the image, the new religion sets the human being before God. We are now in a position to better understand the principle, "Where images are, Torah shall be." The images must disappear to make room for the word. And the word will not be confined to the sacred space and time of the cult; rather, it determines the whole of life. The monopoly of the word amounts to a complete restructuring of sacred space. The whole world becomes sacred, all of life becomes a service to God, and the whole people become priests—"a kingdom of priests" (Exod. 19:6).

Let us again pause and summarize. What's wrong with images?

1. They are too powerful. Every image represents a god and requests worship. Images are *other* gods. This aspect of the prohibition of images presupposes a world full of gods, an enchanted world, and cosmotheism as the general religious orientation, which the Bible seeks to overturn.

2. They are unable to represent the invisible true God. Images are *false* gods. This aspect denies the existence of other gods, presupposes a disenchanted or disanimated world, where images are nothing else but powerless dead matter.

As we have seen, between these two aspects lies the turn from monolatry to monotheism.

Within the horizon of monotheism, the error of idolatry lies not so much in disloyalty and defection, but in benighted madness, in the incapacity to understand the senselessness of one's actions. The other religions that are built around the cultic scene with image, ritual, and recitation are debunked as sheer nonsense. For this demonstration or denunciation, biblical literature avails itself of an ancient genre, the satire of trades.[2] This is a well-known literary genre, which is especially well attested in ancient Egypt, a society distinguished by its high level of division of labor and professional specialization. Its method is to depict the specific activity of a member of a given profession or trade in isolation and complete abstraction from all sense-making frames and contexts of the social division of labor. A specialized profession is shown as an absurd hustling and bustling without any meaningful purpose and result, in a perspective much like that of Samuel Beckett or Franz Kafka.[3] It is with a similar kind of willfully uncomprehending gaze that the caricatures of this genre regard the rites of foreign religions.

In reading some of these texts in the Bible we immediately become aware of their interdependence. It seems obvious that we are dealing with examples of a rather tightly defined genre or with texts following a common model. In the first two examples, we encounter the usual confrontations between the God of Israel and the gods of the "nations," who are demoted here from the rank of *elohim* ("gods") to mere "idols":

Why should the nations say,
"Where is their God, now?"
But our God is in the heavens.
He does whatever he pleases.
Their idols are silver and gold,
The work of men's hands.
They have mouths, but they don't speak.
They have eyes, but they don't see.
They have ears, but they don't hear.
They have noses, but they don't smell.
They have hands, but they don't feel.
They have feet, but they don't walk,
Neither do they speak through their throat.
Those who make them will be like them;
Yes, everyone who trusts in them.
Israel, trust in Yahweh!
He is their help and their shield. (Ps. 115:2–9)

Similar satire appears in Jeremiah 10:1–16 and Isaiah 44:9–20. These texts give a new answer to our question. What's wrong with images? They are just helpless matter, pieces of wood or stone without the power to help themselves let alone others. This view of cult images is extremely unfair and reductive, because no Egyptian or Babylonian would mistake a statue for a god. An image becomes a medium for establishing a contact with the divine only after complex rites of consecration and investiture, only temporarily, and only within the special, temporal and social frames of the cultic scene. All this was, of course, well known to Jeremiah, Deutero-Isaiah and other biblical writers, but they abstracted from this knowledge for the sake of satire.

What cults of images are about is most explicitly stated in a much later Egyptian text, written in the third century c.e., in view of arising Christianity: the hermetic treatise *Asclepius*. This texts devotes several chapters to the statues "animated and conscious, filled with spirit and doing great deeds, statues that foreknow the future and predict it by lots, by prophecy, by dreams and by many other means; statues, that make people ill and cure them, bringing them pain and pleasure as each deserves."[4] Images are not dead matter but are vessels of divine presence. They provide an interface between the divine and the human worlds, between heaven and earth. "Do you not know," the text continues, "that Egypt is an image of heaven or, to be more precise, that everything governed and moved in heaven came down to Egypt and was transferred there? If truth be told, our land is the temple of the whole world." Images are the means of bringing the divine down and making it dwell in Egypt. Images, in the eyes of those who believe in them (let us call them "iconists"), achieve precisely what their opponents (the "aniconists") say they prevent: making god dwell among the people and ensuring sacred communication. Images and sacred animals are media of divine immanence. Iconoclasm would deprive the world of this divine animation and would turn it into mere inanimate matter, doomed to pollution and decomposition. The hermetic treatise continues by giving a vivid description of what it calls "the old age of the world" (*senectus mundi*):

> Divinity will return from earth to heaven and Egypt will be abandoned. The land that was the seat of reverence will be widowed by the powers and left destitute of their presence. . . .
>
> Then this most holy land, seat of shrines and temples, will be filled completely with tombs and corpses . . . a torrent of blood will fill the Nile to the banks and pollute the divine waters.
>
> Whoever survives will be recognized as an Egyptian only by his language; in his actions he will seem a foreigner.

In their weariness the people of that time will find the world nothing to wonder at or to worship. This universe—a good thing that never had nor has nor will have its better—will be endangered. People will find it oppressive and scorn it. They will not cherish this entire world . . . a glorious construction, a bounty composed of images in multiform variety, a multiform accumulation taken as a single thing.

No one will look up to heaven. The reverent will be thought mad, the irreverent wise. Whoever dedicates himself to reverence of mind will find himself facing a capital penalty. They will establish new laws, new justice. Nothing holy, nothing reverent nor worthy of heaven or heavenly beings will be heard of or believed in the mind.

How mournful when the gods withdraw from mankind! Then neither will the earth stand firm nor the sea be sailable; stars will not cross heaven nor will the course of the stars stand firm in heaven. Every divine voice will grow mute in enforced silence. The fruits of the earth will rot; the soil will no more be fertile; and the very air will droop in gloomy lethargy.

Such will be the old age of the world: irreverence, disorder and disregard for everything good.[5]

The worship of images is a worship of the cosmos or—to use a word coined in the eighteenth century—a "cosmotheism." Images are not mimetic reduplications of visible reality but vessels of the invisible, intramundane powers that animate the world from within.

According to the aniconists, images idolize the world and blind the eyes from being able to look beyond the world and focus on the creator. Instead of establishing contact, images block communication with God, whose presence can only be felt, to quote Stefan George, like "air from another planet" blowing.[6] For the iconists, the divine is not like air blowing from other planets, but rather the very air that is blown in this world and that makes it an abode habitable for both men and gods. To the aniconists, this happiness with and within the world as it is seems like blind entanglement. Idolatry, they declare, is *Weltverstrickung*—entanglement within the world, addiction to the visible and the material.

In the final part of this essay I want to look at what became of the prohibition of images in occidental Christianity. As is well known, Christianity readmitted images, images of the visible and even images of the invisible. With its incarnation in Jesus Christ, the word became visible and even left an imprint on the handkerchief of Veronica—whose name means "true image" (*verum icon*). In the history of monotheism, Christianity meant a huge iconic turn. However, the Ten Commandments remained valid, among them the prohibition of images and the incrimination of idolatry. The writings of the Church Fathers are full of violent invectives against the idolaters. Idolatry is treated as madness, an illness, a kind of addiction and a satanic performance. The traces of Christian iconoclasm are to be seen everywhere in Egypt. Occidental Christian history is thus informed by a deep conflict between iconism and iconoclasm, between a culture of the word and a culture of the image. After the first iconic turn in late antiquity there was a recoiling in the form of Byzantine iconoclasm, which lasted for a century until the conflict was finally resolved in favor of images.

A similar wave of iconoclasm occurred with the Reformation. Sculptures, paintings, and even organs were removed from Protestant churches and destroyed. On the other hand, the Reformation led to an enormous boom in "word culture": in writing, printing, and reading, in teaching and preaching, in philology and hermeneutics. With the Counter-Reformation of the sixteenth and seventeenth centuries, however, the pendulum swung in the opposite direction and another iconic turn triumphantly sets in, especially in the Catholic countries of the south. The Enlightenment of the eighteenth century and the beginnings of modern bourgeois culture, by contrast, once again show many traits of an anti-iconic word culture. The historian Carl Schorske, without referring to the long religious conflict between iconism and aniconism, identified a constant swaying between what he calls a culture of grace and a culture of the word in the history of Vienna between 1760 and 1930.[7] Rococo Vienna under Maria Theresa represents the culture of grace, which remained present among the Viennese aristocracy well through the nineteenth century. The severe classicism and rationalism under Joseph II, on the other hand, represents the culture of the word, prevailing in bureaucratic and bourgeois culture right up to the present time. What Schorske described for Vienna in the eighteenth through twentieth centuries may, I think, be easily generalized for the whole of occidental history. Heinrich Heine gave vivid expression to this double-facedness in European culture: "Humans are either Jews or Hellenes, beings with ascetic, iconophobic drives, addicted to spiritualization, or beings of a serene and realistic disposition, proud of unfolding their potentials."[8] (Note the irony: Jewish asceticism is presented as a matter of "drive" and "addiction", Greek pride and serenity a matter of "nature".)

Sigmund Freud held similar views about Judaism and its proneness to spiritualization. In his last book, *Moses and Monotheism*, he outlines his ideas about monotheism as an advance in spirituality or intellectuality—that is, in "word culture"—and sees the Jewish people as the paragon of this movement. The Jews owed this advantage in intellectuality to the prohibition of images, which forced them to turn away from the sensual and to concentrate on the intellectual:

> Among the precepts of the Mosaic religion is one that has more significance than is at first obvious. It is the prohibition against making an image of God, which means the compulsion to worship an invisible God. I surmise that in this point Moses surpassed the Aton religion in strictness. Perhaps he meant to be consistent; his God was to have neither a name nor a countenance. The prohibition was perhaps a fresh precaution against magical malpractices. If this prohibition was accepted, however, it was bound to exercise a profound influence. For it signified subordinating sense perception to an abstract idea; it was a triumph of spirituality over the senses; more precisely, an instinctual renunciation accompanied by its psychologically necessary consequences.[9]

In his *Critique of Judgment*, Immanuel Kant—writing 150 years before Freud—interprets the prohibition of images in a similar way: "Perhaps the most sublime passage in the Jewish Law is the commandment: Thou shalt not make unto thee any graven image, or any likeness of any thing that is in heaven or on earth, or under the earth, etc. This commandment alone can explain the enthusiasm that the Jewish people in its civilized era felt for its religion when it compared itself with other peoples, or can explain the pride that Islam inspires."[10] In the last decade of the eighteenth century, when Kant wrote his Third Critique, the "sublime" was the central category of aesthetics. The sublime is the opposite of the beautiful. Whereas the beautiful appeals to the senses and attracts humans to the visible and the sensual world, the sublime transcends our sensual and conceptual capabilities of comprehension; it repels the senses and tears humans away from their everyday entanglements, exposing them to the horrors of the unknown and leading to a transformation and "sublimation" of their nature. This reminds us of Freud's concept of "sublimation," which leads to a totally different conception of the power or impotence of images. What is wrong with images? They lure the mind into sensual attractions and lead to cultural regression.

In his later days, Goethe seems to have fostered similar opinions about images and image culture. In one of his *Zahme Xenien* (Tame Invectives) he wrote:

Dummes Zeug kann man viel reden,
kann es auch schreiben.
Wird weder Leib noch Seele töten,
es wird alles beim Alten bleiben.
Dummes aber, vors Auge gestellt,
hat ein magisches Recht.
Weil es die Sinne gefesselt hält,
bleibt der Geist ein Knecht.[11]

[Silly stuff may be said enough,
and may also be written—
this will kill neither body nor soul,
nothing will be changed.
Silly stuff, however, put before the eyes,
raises a magic claim.
Since it keeps the senses enthralled,
the mind is made a slave.]

This sounds as if Goethe were writing in and against the age of television and advertisement. What's wrong with images? Their magic claim. What Goethe calls their "magic claim" is the kind of constraint they exert on our imagination as long as they operate outside language and verbal reflection. A verbal statement may be answered by means of rejection, elaboration, modification, or counterstatement. But how does one answer images? This is precisely what we must learn in order to escape their magic claim and withstand their power to enslave the mind. The solution seems to lie not in the prohibition of images but rather in the acquisition of iconic literacy.

THE CHRISTIAN CRITIQUE OF IDOLATRY

MARC FUMAROLI

Christian theology's revival of Neoplatonism and Stoicism, two philosophical perspectives critical of images, only partially explains early Christianity's repugnance (or, at the very least, extreme distrust) toward artistic images.[1] The New Testament does not annul the Old Testament, it completes it; the Decalogue remains an article of faith, for the new Law as for the old. Now the second commandment of the Decalogue, unceasingly reaffirmed in the Bible, forbids the human fabrication of images modeled on the creatures of God, as such images are always susceptible to being adored like the gods and of being treated as idols, diverting to themselves the adoration due to the one God, and to him alone.[2] Sacred history justifies the absolute terms of the law and announces its expectations. While God manifests himself to Moses on Sinai and dictates his law to him, the impatient people have Aaron mold them a golden calf to which they offer sacrifices. This betrayal unleashes the anger of the Lord that Moses has great difficulty in calming, and which he feels himself. A little later, "irritated by the journey and their suffering," the people, still on route to the Promised Land and reduced to subsisting on manna alone, curse Moses and blaspheme his God. Punishment is not long in coming: it arrives in the form of serpents that bite "like fire," echoes of the serpent that seduced Eve and introduced evil and the appetite for evil into humanity. Once more, Moses intercedes, and the divine clemency orders him to have a serpent of bronze molded and to hoist it up a mast so as "to serve as a sign that whoever was wounded and looked upon it would be healed."[3] Certain Jewish traditions, received into Christian literature

beginning in the fourth century have it that this brazen serpent had been transported thereafter to the temple of Jerusalem, where, over time, it became the
object of idol worship. The reformer-king Hezekiah, purifying the worship in
the temple, is said to have had it destroyed as Moses had done with the Golden
Calf molded by his brother Aaron.[4]

In the text of Numbers, the Brazen Serpent, coiled around and raised upon
a mast, is given as a simple sign. By this means, Moses invites the eyes and
the hearts of the Israelites to direct themselves beyond it toward the heavens
that will heal them, but without stopping on the object itself. In the time of
Hezekiah, it seems that this pious manner of employing the serpent had been
forgotten, and that the sign had become an idol. Ignoring this development,
John the Evangelist interprets the serpent of Moses hoisted on its mast as the
prefiguration, the prototype of the cross on which Jesus had been lifted "so
that whoever believes in him would not perish, but would have eternal life"
(John 3:14–15). Before him, Philo of Alexandria had seen in the Brazen Serpent
a symbol of the Divine Logos. After him, a sect of Gnostic Christianity, the
Ophites, went so far as to see in Christ himself the true and perfect Serpent,
saving intermediary between the Father and matter, of which the serpent in
the Garden of Eden was the impure emanation.[5] When Christians sought out
justifications in Scripture for their "holy images," the Brazen Serpent served
as proof (along with the cherubim that framed, by the express command of
God, the Arc of the Covenant) that the God of the Old Testament himself did
not condemn artistic images, as long as they referred to God, instead of being
pretexts for idolatry.

For their part, Western painters have frequently represented this biblical
episode, in the light of John, as a legitimating allegory of their art. At the
height of the Age of the Enlightenment, in 1733, Tiepolo gave his version of
it in a prodigious narrative fresco, now preserved at the Academy of Venice.
One sees Moses in it in the distance, an old man showing the Hebrews, with
a grand sweep of his arm, the Brazen Serpent that he has had placed on the
trunk of a tree: in the foreground, certain Hebrews turn their regard toward
the divine sign, and are saved; others, their backs turned and exposed to the
burning bite of the serpents, or already bitten and cadaverous, have not been
able or are not able to benefit from the saving glance. Heroic male nudes,
worthy of the *ignudi* of the Sistine Ceiling, twist themselves in vain to escape the serpents' bites; desperate young mothers seek in vain to protect the
infants at their breasts, while a splendid young woman, languid, her head

turned toward the Brazen Serpent, eyes lifted to the sky as in ecstasy, is preserved from the assault of the serpents. A tragic sense of the mystery of grace
presides over this drama of the gaze. The carnal gaze, which sees nothing but
the serpents looking for someone to devour, is neighbor to the spiritual gaze,
which finds support in the Brazen Serpent so as to elevate itself to the invisible mercy of the divine. Tiepolo could not have been ignorant of either John's
typology of the Brazen Serpent, nor of the argument that it furnished to the
Christian art of images. The importance he gives to the direction of gazes
and attitudes in this dramatic fresco well and truly makes the biblical legend
into an allegory of the art of painting. But this artist, who has been taken too
frequently for a kind of immoderate Watteau, was, as Roberto Calasso has
recently shown, a great interpreter of myths, symbols, and mysteries, and
remained faithful to the biblical letter of Numbers.[6] Neither more nor less
than Poussin in his *Manna* (Louvre), Tiepolo has hidden nothing of the piti-
less character of the divine mercy accorded by the God of the Old Testament
to his unfaithful people. There are two levels of seeing: one that attaches itself
to accidents, the other that goes to the essence, one that destroys and another that saves; the painter, like Moses and God, does justice to these two
vocations without attacking human liberty. Displayed during the eighteenth
century in the choir of a church in Venice, this fresco was rolled up after the
disaffection of the church in 1810, and remained so until 1893, when it was put
on display at the Academy in the state of a superb ruin, which, luckily, no one
had ever sought to restore. Its wounds render it that much more gripping.[7]

The version of the biblical story that would have it that the Brazen Serpent,
having become an object of idolatry, was destroyed by Hezekiah, attests that
even the signs chosen by God to call the faith of his people back to him can
change their sense entirely according to the gaze that the spectator brings to
them and become pretexts for idolatry. In the Bible, in effect, the art of imitating visible beings or things, in sculpture or drawing, is inseparable from
the irresistible inclination of the people of God to betray his alliance and return to the ways of their idol-worshipping and polytheistic neighbors, from
the moment an image resembling any of his creatures should interpose itself
between them and him. Thus the rigor of the divine interdiction: it guards
against every temptation to idolatry for a people prone to give themselves over
to it, as all of their neighbors did.[8]

The biblical critique of polytheistic idolatry, supreme blasphemy toward
the true God, was adopted in its entirety by Christianity. Even the most icono-

phile strains of Christianity never doubted the invisibility of the divine essence, and Christian negative theology always provided a counterweight to the tendency of positive theology to weaken divine transcendence. An iconoclastic ferment, in the Byzantine East as well as in the Latin West, in more or less radical forms, repeatedly combated a cult of images that threatened to backslide into idolatry.

However, from its first centuries, Christianity also avoided reifying the interdiction on the fabrication of images—which the Old Testament takes for the inevitable occasion of idolatry—with the same rigor found in Judaism (and later Islam).

The Bible mentions above all sculpted images, *simulacra*. Statuary in *ronde bosse* and three dimensions, the preferred art of Greco-Roman polytheism, would thus be sacrificed by Christians, from their earliest times, to the second commandment. It has again disappeared from among us. But "flat paintings," mosaics and bas-reliefs, less explicitly targeted by Scripture and more apt to represent the Christian mysteries symbolically and sacred history narratively, would be spared, although not without violent iconoclastic flare-ups aimed at these Christian arts. Today, painting, drawing, and bas-relief are again confined to catacombs, after having valiantly combated for a century and a half to preserve their spiritual preeminence as an art, against the collective and sensory fascination exercised by technological images—our new idols.

The virulence of the treatise *On Idolatry*, written by the Christian Tertullian of Carthage in the second century, rises to the level of the wrath of God and Moses against the Hebrew people returning to their infamous adoration of idols. It anticipates the vehemence of Calvin against Catholic "holy images," of Kierkegaard against the religious scholasticism of the nineteenth century, of Baudelaire against photography and naturalism, and perhaps even Susan Sontag's irritation, in her *Regarding the Pain of Others*, against the perverse modern attraction for photographic images of war, massacres, torture, and physical suffering that pretend to "denounce" what they depict.[9] "Idolatry," Tertullian writes,

is the chief crime of mankind, the supreme guilt of the world, the entire case put before judgment. For even if every sin retains its own identity and even if each is destined for judgment under its own name, each is still committed within idolatry. Do not observe rubrics, just examine the deeds. The idolater is at the same time a murderer. Do you ask whom he has killed? Not a stranger nor an enemy, but himself—if this contributes anything to the extent of the indictment. By what schemes? By those of his error. With what weapon? Affront to God. With how many strokes? As many as his idolatries.[10]

For the Cato of Latin Christianity, idolatry is another word for demonolatry. The idolater is a murderer of his own soul because he makes himself the accomplice of demons, murderer of that which man receives from God, a soul created "in his image." Now the fact that man receives his soul from God is the only thing that makes him capable of being a witness to that which, in him, has betrayed God. Demons furnish the alibi that makes the human soul forget its divine origin, and thus the consciousness of what separates it from the divine, depriving it of the salutary desire to rise from its fall and make amends for it. Complicity with demons, idolatry engenders spiritual suicide. The juridical language that Tertullian, in good Latin, affects, gives the black intensity of a Dostoyevskian denouement to his description of sacrilegious crime, its accomplices, and the criminal who is his own principal victim. The artistic image, which ancient *otium* associated with a delectable contemplation, here figures as the mask of a disguised murderer in a life-or-death intrigue.

Nonetheless, the idol, for Tertullian, is only the *occasion* of the crime. It is not the cause of it. The crime is in the orientation of the gaze that abusively transforms a work of art into an idol, in obedience to the injunction of a demon. One is thus far from the biblical necessity that linked idol, idolatry, and polytheism to the point of identifying them, supposing that only the destruction or absence of idols could suppress idolatry and polytheism by eliminating their cause. For Tertullian, idolatry has no need of the material support of the idol to render its victims willing slaves of the enemies of God and to take from the Creator that which creatures formed "in his image" owe to him. Idols of stone or wood are merely one of the channels used by the cult of demons, fallen angels who seek to insinuate themselves into the imagination of carnal man, where they find psychological idols ready and waiting to welcome them. It is not the idols themselves—inert and neutral material—that make the pagans who adore them criminal and Christian artists who fabricate them culpable, but the evil subjection to the will of demons. *In themselves, idols are nothing.*

This sentence is capital. It subjectivizes the notion of the idol. It has lost nothing of its exactitude for indicating the emptiness of the greater part of art called "contemporary," deprived even of that commerce with the surreal that

André Breton and his friends, painters and poets, wanted to substitute for the Christian supernatural. So much the more does it apply to fraudulent attempts to associate these productions with an idea of the "sacred" of Christian ancestry. For Tertullian, it is the human appetite for evil, not idols, that demonizes artistic images. Such images are and do what we are and do with them.

Nonetheless, for the Christian theologian of the second century, the adoration of demons in an abusively divinized material form adds, to the offense against God supplanted by his creature, blasphemy toward the incarnation of the Son in the body of a man and toward the Eucharist, body and blood of Christ hidden under the species of bread and wine. Inhabited by demons that their adorers cause to enter into their souls through the eyes, idols constitute so many monstrous inversions of the double nature of the Savior and of the sacramental species under which he hides himself and continues to sacrifice himself for us. Anthropomorphic statues of demon-gods are an anti-Eucharist of sight and imagination. One senses already, in reading Tertullian, that the days of Greco-Roman statuary will be numbered if Christianity becomes dominant. The Christ-image will reabsorb and surpass all the graven idol-gods.

As neutral as it might be, the notion of the idol in Tertullian, because it is subjective, nonetheless prepares the moment when—the origin, the intention, and the sense of artistic images having been reversed so that they become signifiers of the divine signified, rather than the demonic—holy images will be able to enter into Christian worship in broad daylight, and participate in the eviction of the pagan demon-idols that, until then, were the sole occupants of the public space. To purify, sanctify, and liberate public spaces from demons and idols, where they ruled for so long without rivals: such is the primary task of the Church of Christ from the moment it emerged from the catacombs and its clandestine existence. Certainly, the relics of Christ and his martyrs, charged with their real presence like the Eucharist, are the most effective exorcisms. But the irradiation of their holiness needs relays: just as Christian demonology gives itself, as a counterpart, an angelology, itself renewed from the Old Testament, the critique of pagan idolatry seeks a counterpart in a Christian iconology. How can such an iconology be reconciled with the second commandment? Who inhabits, invisibly, the images of art? Whom does one see, so as to venerate or adore him, behind images made by human hands? From where does the magnetic field, of which the artistic image is the foyer, come—the occasion of death for some, victims of the serpents whose bite burns, and the occasion of salvation for others, protected and healed by the sight of the Brazen Serpent? Will the artistic image be the exclusive privilege of demons, those fallen angels seeking to drag souls down with them in their fall, as the Old Testament would have it? Or can it, as with faithful angels, become one of the channels of the grace that Christ brought into this world so as to steal souls away from demons? All these questions were implicit in Tertullian's diatribe against idolatry. They were inconceivable under the reign of the second commandment understood in a literal sense. In the long term, these questions opened a bitter and recurring theological and philosophical debate, but in the short term they were sacrificed to urgent practical concerns. Would the vandalism of Moses and Hezekiah recommended by the Old Testament have been sufficient to counteract images harboring deceptive powers and facilitating their mortal possession of sinful man's senses, his passions, and his imagination? Was it not right to oppose them with more effective Christian images—more effective precisely because they owed their efficacy not to men or demons but to Christ, Mary, the martyrs, and the Christian's faith in their liberating and saving presence that the era of Grace had begun? The relic, a metonym for the whole of Christ, of his mother and of his martyrs, and the images that lend a face and mute narration to relics, will be the first Christian antidote to the idols of pagan demonolatry.

Poor beginnings, seeds as inadequate to the masterpieces of classical Greco-Roman art as the cross of the Savior had been to the luxurious abodes of *otium*, peopled with images, beloved of the Greek and Roman aristocracy. But these were seeds that in growing, and in absorbing in their slow and haphazard germination the spoils of pagan Egypt, would enable unheard-of images to flourish, animated by two sorts of life, that of bodies and that of souls: the Ghent altarpiece of the Van Eyck brothers and the *Sacred Conversations* of Giovanni Bellini and of Fra Bartolomeo.

Christianity, an emblematically philosophic and learned religion, did not therefore reject artistic images as radically as the Mosaic law had done; it inherited from that law a vigilant suspicion of the visual arts' penchant toward idolatry, but it nourished or modulated this suspicion with the psychological and artistic reflections on images pursued by the different ancient schools of philosophy, rhetoric, and pedagogy. Above all, not content simply to amplify the allusive formula of Genesis that makes man a creature "in the image" of his Creator, it introduced the concept of the Image into the very breast of God, whereas the Old Testament applied it only to man and to idolatrous arts. The

God of the Bible is known only through hearing. The Christian God knows himself in his Image, and this image, in becoming incarnate, made itself visible to the eyes of men so as to remind them that, "created in his image and likeness," they vandalized this filiation, and to announce to them that they might restore it to a state more perfect than it was for the first couple. In becoming incarnate, Christ suffused grace into the visible world, where he was vandalized on the cross and where he was resurrected, ransoming bodies as well as souls and reopening the visible world to the presence of the invisible. If it is true that the life of Christ and its Old Testament prefiguration gave rise, very early, to a narrative topic and typology proper to Christian art and objects of modern iconology, Christian art, in the very fact of sight ransomed and reoriented by the evangelical gaze, has an inexhaustible and unprecedented principle of optical research and formal invention, as painters discovered little by little.

The theology of both the Latin and the Greek Church Fathers, as well as the dogmatic decisions of the successive ecumenical councils, turn around the concept of the Image: the Christ as image of the Father and Person of the triune God. The progress in the definition of the perfect image at the heart of the mystery of the Trinity has not been without consequence for the problem of the psychological image and for that of the artistic image in the era of grace that was inaugurated, for a humanity fallen away from its imperfect resemblance with God, by the incarnation of the perfect Image-Son of God.

Two centuries after Tertullian, in the fifth century—when the Roman Empire, though still in existence, had already been profoundly Christianized—St. Augustine neither calls back into question the existence of traditional artisanal activity nor condemns the images, paintings, mosaics, and bas-reliefs that artisans fabricate—now for a Christian clientele. But he never ceases calling attention, as a theologian and philosopher, to the risks of idolatry that come along with these images. Like Tertullian, Augustine holds that the idol "is nothing": the pretension of pagans to adoring the powers of nature in terms of anthropomorphic traits molded in gold or silver is only an alibi for giving themselves over to the cult of bad angels. An image made by the hand of man cannot be the object of adoration, and if it is adored, it is only as the pretext of a perverse worship. The only image that is adorable is the perfect Image, equal to its Original, the Image-Son of the Father, and it must not be adored in the place of the Father, but with him, in him, by the same title as him. Nonetheless, differing with Tertullian, St. Augustine allows for Christian artistic mediations that have nothing in common with the pagan idols that cause creatures to be adored in the place of their Creator. This is not without reserve or precaution. The best-intentioned artistic mediations—portraits of Christ and of Mary, of whom we have no way of knowing the human features—are only subjective fictions, acceptable as memory-aids for beginners in the faith, but dispensable for the converted. Even these "sacred images" are only venerable to the degree to which veneration does not address itself to their materiality but to the holiness of the invisible, adorable referent to which they refer. Adoration can address itself to God alone, and God is truly known only by and in his Word. Looking at holy images is not—far from it—of the same order as reading and meditating on Scripture, the true portrait of the Word. But, in the end, *it is not necessarily* a form of idolatry. This decisive nuance prefigures the doctrine of the "Bible of illiterates" of Gregory the Great in the sixth century, and cracks open the door to the immense history of Western art. The Byzantine icon, the triumph of which had been restrained or combated during nearly three centuries by equating it to the idol, would win the day much more explosively beginning with the Second Council of Nicaea in 787. There, it was recognized as having the same double nature as the Son himself.

Translated by Benjamin Storey

3

THE PAINTER'S BREATH AND CONCEPTS
OF IDOL ANXIETY IN ISLAMIC ART

MIKA NATIF

The common notion of our times has been that Islam opposes figural representation. Transfixed by the episode of the Danish cartoons of September 2005, a
Western audience has witnessed a consistent polemic about the prohibition of
imagery in Islamic tradition. The Quran, however, is silent on the use of images.[1] Where do these ideas originate, then? What impact have they exerted
on the creation and the reception of Islamic art throughout the centuries? Are
we possibly adopting a contemporary fundamentalist attitude in attempting to
portray Islam as spiritually different from or even superior to the "image–idol-
minded" West?

Historians of art and theologians have differed in their response to this
question. Some scholars focusing on art have often linked idol anxiety in
Islam to the geographical closeness to Byzantium, and to the need of early
Muslims to be different visually from their monotheistic rivals. Others sought
theological explanations that would clarify the complex attitude toward figural representation, which they saw influenced by the Jewish second commandment. Such a connection, however appealing, cannot be documented,
and there is a significant gap between textualized injunctions concerning
painters of images and the material evidence of the culture itself, which was
rich in representations. In this essay I explore the causes of tension between
modes of theology and artistic creation operating in the Muslim world. I suggest, in addition, that the attitudes regarding figural representation in Islamic
art underwent decisive changes in the ninth century. These later concerns

parallel generic problems documented for other cultures concerning concepts of truth and representation. Such ideas can be seen to have affected Islamic visuality and the way animated forms were treated in painting.

Artworks from the Muslim world reveal a cultural dichotomy in visuality. From early times, Islamic art has avoided representing living beings in exclusively religious contexts, primarily in mosques and in copies of the Quran.[2] At the same time, from the eighth century onward, we find many examples of figural painting produced by the first Muslim dynasty (the Umayyads). For example, there are large wall paintings of nude women in the Umayyad palace of Qusayr Amra, and an almost life-size sculpture of the caliph standing with his sword, as well as a floor mosaic with a ferocious lion attacking a deer, from Hisham's palace at Khirbat al-Mafjar in Jericho. There are even early Umayyad coins with the image of the Prophet Muhammad shown in a manner similar to the way in which the Byzantine emperor was represented on coins.[3]

When we turn to the Quran, whose form was finalized sometime in the middle of the seventh century, figural allusions appear in the context of the divine creative process, or the ability to form living beings. Thus God is called the Creator or the Maker (al-muṣawwir), which is derived from the same root as the word used for images and painters (ṣ.w.r). In other Quranic episodes, such as the story of the djinns (demons) who created statues for King Solomon or Jesus who formed a bird of clay and breathed life into it, another set of words is used in order to differentiate a separate creative process.[4] Nomi Heger, who studied the legalist approach to images by Islamic theologians, asserts that there is no "directive regarding human creation of any forms in general or painting in particular" in the Quran, and that concerns about committing idolatry through images and the taboo on images arose later.[5] Therefore, we may conclude that during the time of the Prophet and his immediate successors (the so-called orthodox or Rāshidūn caliphs), representations of living beings did not constitute a threat for Muslims, and their existence was not perceived as an act of idolatry.

It is only in the ninth century that we find written evidence expressing a purported earlier antipathy toward images. The historian al-Azraḳī (d. ca. 865) tells us that when Muhammad took possession of the Kaaba (the pre-Islamic temple) in Mecca in 630 he cleared pictures and statues from the old shrine and destroyed 360 idols around the sanctuary.[6] However, Azraḳī was writing in the ninth century about the destruction of idols two centuries earlier; direct evidence from Muhammad's time is lacking.[7] In Azraḳī's time, apparently, visual memory of the "old pagan faith" needed to be completely eliminated from the eyes, the minds, and the hearts of the contemporary Muslim audience.[8]

Many of these injunctions come from traditions or sayings (hadith) associated with or alluding to the Prophet Muhammad and his companions, but they are not part of the holy text of the Quran. It is in the framework of these traditions and sayings that we may find signs of idol anxiety.[9] The presence of pre-Islamic cult figurines, as well as large Christian, Jewish, and other monotheistic communities in the Ḥijāz and in the Middle East, probably contributed to the awakening aversion regarding images in ninth-century Islam, even though they were not the primary reason for the growing fear of images that developed during that time.[10]

These fears were further articulated in various hadith and in Islamic legal thought. In passages that are related to artists and the making of figures, painters are held accountable for their creations and threatened with punishment. According to a hadith transmitted by Bukhari (d. 870), on the Day of Judgment God will command artists to "make alive what you have created" knowing, however, that they would forever fail in this task.[11] Their failure to breathe life into their images would then subject them to severe punishment, since they were trying to imitate God's creation.[12]

If this were indeed the common perception regarding the fate of Muslim artists and painters who tried their hands at depicting living beings, then one would in principle have expected to find none of this art in Muslim lands. However, this is not the case, and Islam has been a culture rich in images. David Freedberg argues that the various claims for aniconism in the early stages of several religions, such as Christianity and Buddhism, "are historiographical inventions that arise from the need to claim for a particular culture a superior spirituality."[13] In the case of Islam, the claim of being "pure" and "free" from images or idols is the result of a sociopolitical power struggle, and not a religious or spiritual one. Hawting's analysis of Muslim sources from the eighth and ninth centuries regarding the seventh-century pagan Arabs in Mecca and Medina has brought welcome light to hadith studies and thus enables us to reconsider the problems that develop around representations of living beings at this time. From his work, it seems that a culture in which the existence of idols cannot be documented imagined that the pre-Islamic past had been full of them.[14]

I believe that what we witness through these hadith traditions is indeed a mirror of political tensions between the ulema and the caliphs.[15] Such situations where anti-image attitudes become an essential aspect of politics re-appear in Henry VIII's break with papal authority in England and Calvin's establishment of an independent Geneva in the sixteenth century, and find parallels in the waves of iconoclasm in the Byzantine Empire during the eight and ninth centuries. Crone and Hinds describe such power struggles in the Umayyad and Abbasid periods, between the caliphs and the religious scholars who strove to hold their status as the spiritual authority par excellence, and resist the innovation of the khalīfat Allāh.[16] The essence of the conflict was manifested in the title khalīfat Allāh, which was assumed by the Umayyad and the Abbasid rulers alike. Declaring him to be "the Deputy of God," this designation imbued the caliph with a "strong claim to religious authority."[17] The desire of the Umayyads to establish their credentials and authority as the rising leading power in the former Greco-Roman world required them to voice their status in a way that would have been familiar to and understood by other elite groups. Therefore they thought nothing wrong with minting coins with the portrait of the Prophet or the caliph on them, or with depict-ing erotic scenes in bathhouses. Hence, similar to the behavioral pattern that Hans Belting identifies regarding idol anxiety in the Christian world, when images began to gain too much popularity, or as in our case, to be identified with the court and the patronage of the caliph, it was time for theologians, or, in our case, religious scholars—or any opposition group—to put them in check.[18] It is against this historical and political background that we need to consider the hadith traditions that deal with pictures, and distance ourselves from the unfounded association with the time of the Prophet.

The tenth century also left us stories about images of the Prophet Muham-mad himself. A number of Arabic texts contain a recurring story regarding acheiropoiete (not made by human hand) portraits of Muhammad, as well as of Jesus and several figures from the Old Testament.[19] The stories allegedly take place in Byzantium during the time of Emperor Heraclius (r. 610–41). The base or core narrative tells us of a miraculous box in the possession of the Byzantine emperor in which there were pictures made by God for Adam, who asked to see his future prophetic lineage. Gaining their legitimacy through their divine Creator, the pictures were kept by other People of the Book, who through these portraits procured a preknowledge of the coming of Islam.[20] Hence, even in Muslim discourse images could serve as an "instrument of heavenly intervention," to use the words of Hans Belting, and assume the role of assisting in the process of conversion.[21]

The miraculous pictures of the prophets in the story can be regarded as part of a much broader set of image-narratives, which share the common characteristic of being *acheiropoietic* or *non manufactum* objects, and therefore they escape the fate and criticism that is usually associated with the worship of images and idolatry.[22] Such images as the Christian *mandylion* of Edessa, or Veronica's veil, make up a group of paintings that were created either by God or by other divine powers in heaven and have reached our earthly world without any human intervention. Latour further emphasizes the notion that any identifications or traces showing the marks of work of a human hand in these images would result in diminishing their power and desecrating them.[23] He phrases the issue: "to *add the hand* to the pictures is tantamount to spoiling them, criticizing them."[24]

The relationship between *non manufactum* paintings and idolatry takes on an interesting twist in the case of Mani, the founder of Manichaeism. In Islamic tradition Mani was known for his artistic genius, using pictures in order to convert people to his new faith, and he was considered to be an important link in the chain of transmission of Persian painting. His figure appears in a number of Persian texts in relation to idolatry and images.[25] In Medieval Islamic and Persian writings Mani embodies two almost contradicting qualities. On the one hand he was an infidel and heretic (*zandīk*) who set up equally powerful gods of good and of evil; on the other hand he was admired as a great painter and masterful artist.[26] In a manner similar to legends of *acheiropoiete* icons, the stories about Mani and his paintings perpetuate a strong air of "*uncertainty* about the exact role of the hand at work in the production of a mediator."[27] In one of them he made a semimagical object called the *Artang* tablet or book (*lawḥ-i artangī*), which was a piece of silk painted with images of animals, humans, and trees, which he stated was brought from heaven. By the help of these magical images Mani claimed himself to be a true prophet, and the *Artang* tablet was his proof.[28] In Firdausi's *Shahnama*, Mani supposedly argues that he is "a prophet through painting," while his opponent accuses him of being an idolater or "an image worshipper." Consequently, according to Soucek, Firdausi associates Mani's "heresy directly with his skill as a painter."[29] Some have argued that the trial and death of Mani is illustrated in a number of *Shahnama* manuscripts, perhaps as a commentary, an internal criticism or a reminder regarding the dangerous potential of images.

It is interesting to note that from the story of Mani as well as from the hadith concerning the punishment of artists, the responsibility for any misuse of such images—that is to say of committing idolatry—lies with the maker and not only with the user of the idol. From these hadith passages we come to understand that artistic creation was perceived as contending with divine creation. This dubious parallelism meant that immense power was placed in the hands of images and of their makers. Were artists of the past hailed as people with divine power? Did they enjoy a special status in Muslim society? We must read the hadith critically, since historical sources do not support these assertions. The very lack of signatures on most artworks from the Muslim world during this time and the anonymity of the Muslim artist in general raise serious questions regarding the picture depicted for us by these hadith and the actual power attributed to the hands of artists.

We do find, however, literary sources and legal documents demonstrating that images have been constantly associated with some kind of high or divine power and knowledge that could have an impact on our mental states. Testimony on this point is derived from purported actions by the Prophet himself. According to a tradition written in the ninth century, Muhammad saw Aisha's picture on a piece of silk in a dream, when a voice revealed to him that she was his wife to come.[30] On another occasion, the Prophet complained about the existence of a curtain with pictures in his home, and demanded: "Remove it from my sight, for its pictures are still coming to my mind in my prayers."[31] At the same time, he had no trouble using cushions decorated with pictures of animals.[32] Since the pillows were placed on the ground, the images on their covers were nonthreatening.

Desired and rejected at the same time, figural representation led to the creation of a unique visual language and concept of figurative art. It is therefore plausible that these notions of apprehension regarding committing idolatry through images, together with other cultural ideas, had a strong impact on the way figural art was perceived and evolved in the Muslim world throughout the centuries. It seems that the choice of artists to show human bodies as flat linear forms, to avoid naturalistic attitudes in painting, and to shun any attempt to imitate reality has its roots in such concepts. Only in the late sixteenth century in Mughal India and in Safavid Iran, these visual concepts of depictions of living beings underwent significant changes that put aside, at least for a while, the artistic tradition that partially stemmed from the image taboo.[33] At the same time, Heger observes a decline in legal interest concerning the existence of images in the post-Mongol Persian world. Her reasoning for this lack of interest is that the initial threat of idolatry in the early stages of Islam was no longer pertinent in later periods; hence there was no need to resurrect these problems.[34]

But was resentment of images ever due to strictly religious problems? Mughal India is an interesting case in point, since it comprised a minority of Muslims who ruled a largely polytheistic (Hindu) population, whose worship incorporated many images of gods. Even though Muslim theological texts castigated Hindus and urged the elimination of images, Hinduism was not perceived as a threat to Islam, unlike Buddhism which was consistently persecuted by the Muslim rulers in earlier periods. Moreover, the Mughals were interested in the old Hindi Sanskrit texts and commissioned their translations and illustrated manuscripts. Ultimately, under Akbar and Jahangir, interaction with Europeans, the Jesuits, and their religious paintings did not produce unease about images, but rather a flourishing artistic response.

The explanation of the ambivalence to imagery in the Islamic world lies perhaps somewhere between the cultural and the political—more than the pious and the religious—self-confidence of each society. Thomas Arnold mentions sources which tell us that in the Great Mosque of Cordoba there were pictures of the staff of Moses, of the Seven Sleepers of Ephesus, and of the Raven of Noah. However, he argues that this is "a circumstance unique in the religious life of Islam."[35] Was the case of images at the mosque of Cordoba so unique? Mehmed II did not destroy the figural Christian mosaics in Hagia Sophia, which he transformed into his imperial mosque in 1453.[36] When Muhammad ordered his men to cleanse the Kaaba of the statues and pictures displayed there, he spared the paintings of the Virgin and Child and of Abraham. In the museum in Tehran there is a Mughal Quran page with images of people at prayer all around its borders.[37] Furthermore, shrines, such as the one in Ardabil, had high-quality illustrated manuscripts bequeathed to their library as *wakf*s (endowments). For example, the superbly illustrated manuscript of the *Manṭik al-Ṭayr* (The Language of the Birds) at the Metropolitan Museum of Art has the word *wakf* inscribed in black ink across the tree trunk in the painting.[38]

Such evidence suggests that contradictory and ambivalent feelings operated in respect to representations of living beings and, more specifically, of the human figure as a natural organic body. Yves Porter suggests that the outcome of this attitude was that painters did not "try to reproduce a model from nature but to represent an archetype."[39] This lack of interest in imitating nature and the body as an anatomical entity in visual arts operated even in Muslim societies deeply committed to the study of medicine and natural sciences. Porter argues that the visuality of Persian painting follows Aristotelian ideas transmitted via Muslim philosophers, who viewed art as rendering "the form" of things that preexist in our imagination. He further contends that the choice made by Muslim artists to construct images far from any pictorial "realism" or nature is "a manner of defense against a taboo placed on the image."[40] Thus the emphasis was shifted to representing meaning rather than anatomical accuracy.[41] However, these two concepts, realism versus representing meaning through form, do not necessarily stand in opposition to one another, but can also be seen as choices made by artists. Porter links these concepts to Islamic mystical terms of practicing esoteric (*bāṭin*, interior) and exoteric (*ẓāhir*, exterior) knowledge.[42] Following one or another of these philosophical directions, Persian artists chose to render their images as "flat, almost transparent, without the forms of muscles, while *dīvs* are shown with heavy bodies, with muscles, hair, and genitalia."[43] I believe that Muslim visual choices were based on a combination of Aristotelian or pseudoscientific ideas and the artists' idea of what was religiously proper and appropriate.

We observe two opposite approaches to figural representation in the Muslim sphere demonstrated by two purportedly historical incidents. The first episode allegedly occurred during the Muslim conquest of Syria, when the Christian people of the area was permitted to leave their homes and join the Byzantine forces under Emperor Heraclius.[44] In order to separate the two camps, a column was erected to mark the borderline; on this column was a picture of the Byzantine emperor. Eventually, a Muslim horseman damaged the eye of the painted figure on the column while he was practicing his military skills. The Christians demanded retribution and required that the eye of the Muslim ruler—the caliph 'Umar—would be taken out from an image that they had created. The commander of the Muslim forces in the area, Abu 'Ubaydah, agreed, and thus all sides considered the matter resolved. It is interesting to note that like a number of other sources dealing with images, this later text refers back to the "pure practices" of Muslims in the seventh century. In the eyes of the text's tenth-century author, the caliph 'Umar, the commander Abu 'Ubaydah, and their entourage had no qualms about taking out the eye of the painted image. Apparently, they did not think that such an action would have any effect on the person himself. No one at the caliph's camp thought that "pictures were alive" or that "images had a power to influence human beings."[45]

In his analysis of the story about Abu 'Ubaydah and the painted image of Heraclius, Oleg Grabar remarks that the seventh-century Byzantines and Muslims did not understand each other's visual culture, since the Muslims failed to comprehend the Christians' attitude toward images, including the idea that the painting of Heraclius on the pillar assumed a much more powerful function than marking a territory.[46] Let us consider, however, the ninth-century origin of this story, a time when Muslims and Byzantines certainly understood each other's visuality all too well.[47] The author, Eutychius of Alexandria (877–940), a Christian from Egypt, provides us with specific details of Muslim-Christian conflict. Aware of the interpretation of such a story and the agenda he was promoting, he constructed a text that cannot be taken literally, but must be interpreted in dialogue with other texts dealing with images from the ninth century. In order to please contemporary Egyptians, Eutychius reminisces on a "pure" Islam that is free of images. The attitude or approach of Abu 'Ubaydah and his milieu toward images as presented by Eutychius stands in contrast to the way images were described by some Muslims, who attributed various powers to them and feared the dangerous nature of figures.

One way of exerting control over perilous objects, according to Zamakhsharī (d. 1144), a commentator on the Quran, was to separate the head from an animate figure, an action which immediately legitimized the object and made it permissible according to Islamic law.[48] Zamakhsharī's directive reveals that images were believed to have spirits, and if one symbolically severed their heads they would be robbed of life and meaning. Zamakhsharī's idea makes us ponder Mitchell's observation: "Why do [people] behave as if pictures were alive, as if works of art had minds of their own, as if images had a power to influence human beings?"[49] He cites what he calls "the paradox of the image": its powerlessness and its strength, its destruction, and its reverence.[50]

The method of neutralizing or canceling the image, recommended by the scholarly Zamakhsharī, was espoused by individual believers. In illuminated manuscripts, such as the so-called St. Petersburg *Makāmāt* (written by al-Harīrī, produced in the area of Baghdad, 1225–35), a black line was drawn along the necks of the painted figures, as if separating their heads from the rest of their bodies (fig. 3.1). We find comparable conduct by early Christians in their reactions to icons. They treated these images "like personages" who would bleed or be injured when harmed, to use Belting's words.[51] In that sense, Zamakhsharī and the person who drew the black line around the necks of the

FIGURE 3.1. Tenth *makāma, The Visit of al-Ḥārith to Abū Zayd, Who Is Guarding His Son*. Written by al-Ḥarīrī, produced in Baghdad, 1225–35. At a later time, someone drew a black line along the necks of the painted figures in order to create the impression that their heads were separated from the rest of their bodies, and thus neutralized them. From an old photograph at the University of Michigan, Ann Arbor, probably ordered/ purchased by D. S. Rice.

Maḳāmāt images, were fetishizing the pictures, attributing to them powers they did not possess.[52] According to Halbertal and Margalit, idolatry or the "error of substitution . . . occurs when a representation acquires the features of the thing represented. The mechanism of such an error involves forgetting that it is a representation and seeing it as something autonomous."[53]

In Islam, as in Judaism, theologians affirm that there should be no agent or mediator between man and God. By being fetishized, images actually acquire the power of intermediaries and even become the focus of belief, rather than mere representations. To avoid such an error, one could "kill the image" by cutting off its head before it accumulated too much power. Other Islamic scholars, however, accepted images as sources of pleasure; as long as there was no intention of idolatry, they were permitted.[54] To that extent, Khwaju Kirmani (d. ca. 1352) writes, "Not every image can be loved, but look into this painting so that you may see what meaning lies therein."[55]

Pleasure, even the seduction of beauty, was associated by some with the reflection of a higher spiritual power—of God Himself. The *naẓar* (gaze) or *shahīd* (witness) tradition is linked to the Islamic theological doctrine in which the world mirrors the divine, especially where beauty acts as a proof or a reflection of God's splendor, a position derived from Neoplatonism.[56] In poetry and prose there are descriptions of the physical beauty of the beloved—often a beardless handsome youth who is the subject of admiration, be it religious, aesthetic, or other, by older or mature men. These philosophical concepts have their roots in late antiquity.[57] Not all Islamic theologians approved of such practices, and some considered them heretical since they emphasize seeking God through sensual experience of His creation (*ḥulūl*).[58] Therefore, the practitioners of the *naẓar* occasionally were accused of idolatry, for contemplating God through His manifestations or through images rather than directly.[59] Ideas of the *naẓar* were further applied to painting, since beautiful images may reflect a deeper inner beauty that is, in some cases, to be understood as an expression of the soul and spirit.[60] It is possible to see in some pictures of beautiful beardless boys a reflection of the idea of the *naẓar*, while also acknowledging the strong homoerotic overtones that were part of such a practice (fig. 3.2).[61]

According to these ideas, the divine could be represented through the beauty of an image of a youth. However, to my knowledge, there are no anthropomorphic representations of God Himself in Islamic art. The closest to representing God in painting is probably the illustration in folio 36v from

FIGURE 3.2. *Young Prince*. Signed by Muhammad Haravi, Safavid dynasty (mid-sixteenth century). Freer Gallery of Art, Smithsonian Institution, Washington, D.C., no. F1937.8. Courtesy of the Freer Gallery of Art, Smithsonian Institution, Washington D.C.: Purchase F1937.8.

the manuscript of the *Mirajnama* (The Miraculous Journey of the Prophet Muhammad).[62] In this painting the presence of God is suggested by a series of wavy golden clouds engulfing Muhammad while he prostrates himself in order to worship the Eternal. However, this type of illustration and its subject remains a rare occurrence.[63] The complete absence of any figural representation of God in Islamic art is a result of the idea that since God has no form He cannot be expressed through it.

Muslim and Jewish attitudes to figuring God demand careful analysis. Halbertal and Margalit raise important questions concerning the ways in which God can or cannot be represented in the Jewish tradition. In Islam, as well as in Judaism, God can be described verbally but not visually. Halbertal and Margalit ask why linguistic representations of God are allowed while visual representations are forbidden.[64] Whatever the answer, we may see manifestations of this distinction in the Islamic tradition of calligraphy. According to tradition, the Arabic language and the Arabic alphabet possess a divine aura because they are the vehicles through which the Quran, the last revelation, was transmitted to Muhammad.[65] For this reason Muslim calligraphers were empowered to develop an Art of the Word which reached the highest level of sophistication and complexity, making itself visible in every medium and size. Of these various artistic manifestations of calligraphy, the calligram is remarkable for its transgressiveness. Through these calligraphed words, form becomes visible and alive, linking word and image in ways that otherwise would have been abhorrent. Hence, by inscribing the *basmala* (in the name of God Most Gracious, Most Merciful)—which is the first verse in every sura (chapter) of the Quran—into the shape of an animal, do the divine words become zoomorphic? What does it mean to have the *shahāda*—the Muslim creed or testimony that there is no God but God and Muhammad is His messenger (*lā ilāha illā 'llāh wa Muḥammad rasūl Allāh*)—written in the shape of a man in prayer (fig. 3.3)? Is it possible that this calligram has become an icon?[66] If we "read" it visually, it comes to mean that this set of holy words, which is part of the five pillars of Islam, has been composed to create a human form, or to assume the shape of a living being. Could it be regarded as God's incarnation and His assuming of a form or His indwelling in an image (*ḥulūl*)?[67] Belting calls such a paradoxical phenomenon of attempting to give form to an abstract God "making visible the invisible."[68] Such a conflation between the human form and the divine word brings great tension to the image, such that we may no longer consider it in terms of pure "aesthetic detachment."[69] Freedberg raises concerns regarding the boundaries of this art form and the fluidity of our division "between the figurative and the nonfigurative or the ornamental."[70] To demonstrate Freedberg's reservations, I would like to mention the short-lived fashion of the animated script, which was practiced mostly in eastern Iran between the twelfth and the thirteenth centuries.[71] This type of script involved Arabic letters with human or animal heads attached to their stem, hence making the words "alive" with faces, eyes, hands, facial expressions, and so on. In some cases the letters-figures appear to be interacting with one another, as if engaged in conversation, further suggesting an element of playfulness and transgressiveness.[72] Thus the creation of figural representations was no longer the prerogative of painters; calligraphers, too, touched on the anthropomorphic.

FIGURE 3.3. *Shahāda* calligram in the form of a man praying. Probably Morocco (twentieth century). From Dave Seidel, the Superluminal Web site, www.superluminal .com/cookbook/essay_many_flavors.html (accessed February 27, 2011).

If we pursue a mystical approach to calligraphy, the pen held by a human hand becomes a direct symbol of the divine *kalam* (pen); the mark it forms on paper is an image of the divine calligraphy and the cosmic book.[73] In a similar way that the handwritten word in Islamic tradition is the transformation of the word of God, the hand of the painter mirrors divine creation. And while the calligrapher will enter paradise, the painter is perceived as challenging the Eternal and is threatened with severe punishment.

In conclusion, this brief overview starts with the observation that there was no direct prohibition regarding images in the Quran. Later written traditions, however, developed a strident bias against images, far more unyielding than the actual practice or the reality of figurative art in Muslim societies. Images became problematic most frequently when a dynasty or a patronage was losing its self-confidence, and not because of religious concerns. At the same time, such anxieties fit well with Aristotelian ideas that had a strong impact on Muslim philosophy and theology. The combination resulted in a visual language that was little interested in expressing nature and realism, favoring schematic, flat, and repetitive forms. Soucek argues that in order to remove painters from any association with religious concerns regarding idolatry, authors like Nizami and others emphasized the "mental aspects of art." For that reason, their pictures of animated forms lack the notion of an organic body, and they appear to be only a memory or a "reflection in the mirror."[74] By the second half of the sixteenth century, however, these approaches change dramatically in Safavid Iran and Mughal India under the influence of cosmopolitanism, through the growing impact of Neoplatonic thought and the contact with European art.

4

IDOLATRY

Nietzsche, Blake, and Poussin

W. J. T. MITCHELL

Idolatry and its evil twin, iconoclasm, are much in the news these days. Indeed, it would be no exaggeration to say that the current Holy War on Terror is just the latest engagement in a religious conflict that dates back beyond the Middle Ages and the Christian Crusades in the Middle East, and one that centrally concerned itself with the idols worshipped by one's enemies, and with the imperative to smash those idols once and for all. While one should be skeptical about reductive ideological scenarios like Samuel Huntington's notorious "clash of civilizations" thesis, it seems undeniable that this thesis has manifested itself in the actual foreign policies of great powers like the United States and its allies, and in the rhetoric of Islamic fundamentalism in its calls to jihad against the West. The fact that an idea is grounded in paranoid fantasy, prejudice, and ignorance has never been a compelling objection to its implementation in practice. The Taliban did not hesitate to carry out the destruction of the harmless Bamiyan Buddhas, and al-Qaeda's attack on the World Trade Center was clearly aimed at an iconic monument that they regarded as a symbol of Western idolatry.[1] The War on Terror, on the other hand, first called a "crusade" by the president who declared it, has been explained by some of his minions in the military as a war against the idolatrous religion of Islam.[2] Among the most striking features of the hatred of idols, then, is the fact that it is shared as a fundamental doctrine by all three great "religions of the book," Judaism, Christianity, and Islam, where it is encoded in the second commandment, prohibiting the making of all graven images of any living thing. This commandment launches the age-old *paragone* between words and images, the law of the symbolic and the lawless imaginary that persists in numerous cultural forms to this day.

Among those cultural forms is, of course, art history. Whether regarded as a history of artistic objects, or of images more generally, art history is a field that is centrally concerned with the relation of words and images, and that one might expect to have a powerful account of idols and idolatry. Yet these topics are generally regarded as more properly the business of religion, theology, anthropology, and perhaps philosophy. By the time idols become the subject of art history they have become art—aestheticized, denatured, deracinated, neutered. Of course, many art historians know this, and I could invoke the work of David Freedberg and Hans Belting on the nature of "images before the era of art," and the more specific work by scholars such as Michael Camille (*The Gothic Idol*), Tom Cummins (studies of the Inca idol known as the "Waca"), as well as many others, who have attempted to work backward, as it were, from the history of art toward something more comprehensive, something that might perhaps be called an iconology. By *iconology* I mean the study of— among other things—the clash between logos and icon, law and image, which is inscribed in the heart of art history.

We will return to these disciplinary issues presently, in a discussion of Poussin's paintings of two scenes of idolatry, and the ways that art history has danced around the question of word and image in these paintings. As Richard Neer has noted, these discussions have been paradigmatic for the entire discipline, involving its ambivalence about the actual material objects that are so central to it.[3] But before we take up these matters, I want to approach the topic through a fundamental reconsideration of the very concept of idolatry—beginning with the second of the Ten Commandments: "You shall not make for yourself a graven image, or any likeness of anything that is in heaven above, or that is in the earth beneath, or that is in the water under the earth; you shall not bow down to them or serve them; for I the LORD your God am a jealous God, visiting the iniquity of the fathers upon the children to the third and the fourth generation of those who hate Me, but showing steadfast love to the thousandth generation of those who love Me and keep My Commandments" (Exod. 20:4–6).[4] The condemnation of idolatry as the ultimate evil is encoded in this statute with such ferocious militancy that it is fair to say that it is clearly the most important commandment of them all, occupying the central place in defining sins against God, as opposed to sins against other human beings, such as lying, stealing, or adultery. It is difficult to overlook the fact that it supersedes, for instance, the commandment against murder, which, as Walter Benjamin wryly puts it, is merely a "guideline," not an absolute prohibition.[5]

Since idolatry is such a central concept for all the adversaries in the current global conflict, it seems worthwhile to attempt a critical and historical analysis of its main features. What is an idol? What is idolatry? And what underlies the iconoclastic practices that seem invariably to accompany it? The simplest definition of an idol is that it is an image of a god. But that definition leaves open a host of other questions: Is the god represented by the image of a supreme deity who governs the whole world, or a local "genius of the place" or of the tribe or nation? Is the god immanent in the image, its material support? Or is the god merely represented by the image, while the god dwells elsewhere? What is the relation of this god to other gods? Is it tolerant toward other gods, or is it jealous and determined to exterminate its rivals? Above all, what motivates the vehement language of the second commandment? Why is its condemnation so emphatic, its judgments so absolute? Does it not seem that there is some kind of surplus in the very concept of idolatry, a moral panic that seems completely in excess of legitimate concerns about something called "graven images" and their possible abuse? Another way to say this would be to note that *idolatry* is a word that mainly appears in the discourse of iconoclasm, a militant monotheism obsessed with its own claims to universality.

When we move to the moral questions surrounding idolatry, the concept seems to spin completely out of control. Idolatry is associated with everything from adultery to superstition to metaphysical error. It is linked with materialism, hedonism, fornication, black magic and sorcery, demonology, bestiality, fascist führer cults, Roman emperors, and divination. This bewildering array of evils resolves itself ultimately into two basic varieties, which frequently intermix: the first is the condemnation of idolatry as error, as stupidity, as false, deluded belief; the second is the darker judgment that the idolater actually *knows* that the idol is a vain, empty thing, but he continues to cynically exploit it for the purposes of power or pleasure. This is the perverse, sinful crime of idolatry. Thus, there are two kinds of idolaters—fools and knaves—between which obviously there is considerable overlap and cooperation.

Much of the theological discussion of idolatry focuses on fine points of doctrine and subtle distinctions between idolatry as the worship of the wrong god, or of the right god in the wrong way.[6] The difference between heretics or apostates within the nonidolatrous community and unbelievers who live outside that community is obviously a critical distinction. But there is a more straightforward approach to the problem of idolatry, what might be called an "operational" or functional point of view. The key, then, is not to focus on what idolaters believe, or what iconoclasts believe that they believe, but on what idolaters *do*, and on what is done to them by iconoclasts, who, by definition, must disapprove of the wicked, stupid idolaters. Sometimes the question of belief converges with that of actions and practices. For instance, some iconoclasts believe that, in addition to their wrongheaded beliefs, idolaters commit unspeakable acts such as cannibalism and human sacrifice. This "secondary belief" (i.e., a belief about the beliefs of other people) consequently justifies equally unspeakable acts of violence against the idolaters, which are rationalized as an expression of the just vengeance of the one true god.[7] There is thus a kind of fearful symmetry between the terrible things idolaters are supposed to do and what may be done to them in the name of divine justice.

Another key to thinking pragmatically about idolatry is to ask not just *how* idolaters live (which is presumed to be sinful) but *where* they live. Idolatry is deeply connected to the question of place and landscape, territorial imperatives dictated by local deities who declare that certain tracts of land are not only sacred but uniquely promised to them. Indeed, one could write the history of biblical idolatry and iconoclasm as a collection of territorial war stories—wars fought over places and possession of land. As Moshe Halbertal and Avishai Margalit put it, "The ban on idolatry is an attempt to dictate exclusivity, to map the unique territory of the one God."[8] This becomes clearest when one considers the practical enforcement of the ban on images, which involves destroying the sacred sites of the native inhabitants, "leveling their high places and destroying their graven images and idols."[9] The link between territoriality and idolatry becomes even more explicit when it is invoked as an insuperable objection to any negotiations or treaties. To make a deal with an idolater, especially about land, is to fall into idolatry oneself. The only politics possible between the iconoclast and the idolater is total war.[10]

Idols, then, might be described as condensations of radical evil in images that must be destroyed, along with those who believe in them, by any means necessary. There is no idolatry without an iconoclasm to label it as such, since idolaters almost never call themselves by that name. They may worship Baal or Dagon or Caesar or money, but they do not consider it idolatry to do so; rather, their worship is a normal form of piety within their community. On the side of the iconoclasts, the idolater is generally perceived as beyond redemption. Either the idolater is a traitor to the true God (thus the metaphor of adultery and "whoring after strange gods") or he has been brought up in a false, heathen faith from which he will have to be "liberated"—one way or another.

Iconoclasm, then, betrays a kind of fearful symmetry, mirroring its own stereotype of idolatry in its emphasis on human sacrifice and terrorism, the latter understood as violence against the innocent, and the staging of spectacular acts of symbolic violence and cruelty. The iconoclastic stereotype of the idolater, of course, is that he is already sacrificing his children and other innocent victims to his idol. This is a crime so deep that the iconoclast feels compelled to exterminate the idolaters—to kill not just their priests and kings but all their followers and offspring as well.[11] The Amalekites, for instance, are enemies of Israel, so vicious and unredeemable that they must be wiped out. And the emphasis on the cursing of idolaters for numerous generations is, implicitly, a program for genocide. It is not enough to kill the idolater; the children must go as well, either as potential idolaters, or as "collateral damage."

All these barbaric practices might be thought of as merely the past of idolatry, relics of ancient, primitive times when magic and superstition reigned. A moment's reflection reveals that this discourse has persisted into the modern era, from Bacon's "four idols" of the marketplace, the theater, the cave, and the tribe, to the evolution of a Marxist critique of ideology and fetishism that builds on the rhetoric of iconoclasm. This latter critique is of course focused on commodity fetishism and what I have elsewhere called the "ideolatry" of market capitalism.[12] One of the strangest features of iconoclasm is its gradual sublimation into more subtle strategies of critique, skepticism, and negative dialectics: Clement Greenberg's kitsch and Adorno's culture industry are producers of idols for the new philistines of mass culture. The endpoint of this process is probably Jean Baudrillard's "evil demon of images," where the Marxian rhetoric rejoins with religion and veers off toward nihilism. But already in his diatribes against the Young Hegelians, Marx made fun of the "critical critics" who free us from images, phantoms, and false ideas.

The greatest break and the most profound critique of idolatry and iconoclasm is Nietzsche's late work *Thus Spake Zarathustra*. Nietzsche turns iconoclasm upside down and against its own roots of authority in the law. The only thing the iconoclastic Zarathustra smashes are the tablets of the law: "Break, break, you lovers of knowledge, the old tablets. . . . Break the old tablets of the never gay," inscribed with prohibitions against sensuous pleasure by the pious killjoys who "slander the world" and tell men "thou must not desire."[13] The only law Nietzsche will tolerate is a positive "thou shalt": he enjoins us "to write anew upon new tablets the word 'noble.'"[14] He criticizes the Manichaean moralism of the priestly lawgivers who divide the world into good and evil:

> O my brothers, who represents the greatest danger for all of man's future? Is it not the good and the just? Inasmuch as they say and feel in their hearts, "We already know what is good and just, and we have it too; woe unto those who still seek here!" And whatever harm the evil may do, the harm done by the good is the most harmful harm . . . the good *must* be Pharisees—they have no choice. The good *must* crucify him who invents his own virtue. . . . The *creator* they hate most: he breaks tablets and old values . . . they crucify him who writes new values on new tablets.[15]

Zarathustra also seems to intuit the connection between the old law of good and evil and the imperative to territorial conquest and "promised lands." He equates the breaking of "the tablets of the good" with the renunciation of "fatherlands," urging his followers to be "seafarers" in search of "man's future . . . our *children's land!*"[16]

So far as I know, Nietzsche never explicitly mentions the second commandment, but it becomes the unspoken center of his great text of 1888, *Twilight of the Idols*, a work that might easily be mistaken for a rather conventional iconoclastic critique. Its promise to "philosophise with a hammer," and its opening "declaration of war" against "not just idols of the age, but eternal idols," may sound like a continuation of the traditional iconoclastic treatment of idolatrous "ideas," like Bacon's critique of "idols of the mind" or the Young Hegelians war against "phantoms of the brain." But Nietzsche turns the tables on *both* the ancient and modern iconoclasts and the second commandment by renouncing the very idea of image destruction at the outset. The eternal idols are not to be smashed but to be "touched with a hammer as with a tuning fork." They are not to be destroyed, but "sounded" with a delicate, precise touch that reveals their hollowness (one recalls the biblical phrase "sounding brass") and perhaps even retunes or plays a tune upon them. Nietzsche's war against the eternal idols is a strangely nonviolent practice, a giddy form of "recreation, a spot of sunshine, a leap sideways into the idleness of the psychologist."[17]

The idolatry-iconoclasm complex has always presented a dilemma for visual artists who, by professional necessity, seem inevitably to be involved in violating the second commandment. Vasari opens his *Lives of the Artists* with an elaborate set of apologias for the visual arts, noting that God himself is a creator of images, architect of the universe and a sculptor who breathes life into his fabricated creatures. He dismisses the inconvenient case of the Golden Calf and the massacre of "thousands of the false Israelites who had committed this idolatry" by arguing that "the sin consisted in adoring idols and not in making them," a rather stark evasion of the plain language of the second commandment, which says "thou shalt not *make*" any graven images of any thing.[18]

The artist who comes closest to carrying out Nietzsche's inversion and transvaluation of the idolatry-iconoclasm complex is William Blake, who anticipates by almost a century the reversal of values contemplated in *Twilight of the Idols*. Blake famously inverts the moral valences of pious, passive angels and energetic devils in *The Marriage of Heaven and Hell* (1793), and he consistently links the figure of the Old Testament lawgiver with his rationalist Enlightenment offspring in the figure of "Urizen," depicted as a patriarchal figure dividing and measuring the universe, or as a reclusive hermit hiding in his cave behind the twin tablets of the law (see fig. 4.1).

Like Nietzsche, however, Blake is not engaged in a simple reversal of a Manichaean opposition of good and evil; he uses a more subtle strategy, rather like Nietzsche's notion of "touching" the idols with a "hammer" or a "tuning fork." Blake's most compelling image of this process is a plate from his illuminated epic poem *Milton* (fig. 4.2), which shows Los the artist-as-sculptor engaged in a radically ambiguous act of creation *and* destruction. We can, on the one hand, read this as an image of Los molding the figure of Jehovah out of the mud on a riverbank, as if we were witnessing Adam creating God out of clay. Or, on the other hand, we can read this as an iconoclastic act, with the artist pulling down the idolatrous statue of the father-god. The image condenses the making and breaking of idols into one perfectly equivocal synthesis of creative activity, a visual counterpart to Nietzsche's acoustical tactic of hammering the idols without breaking them. Blake's portrayal of a musical chorus on the horizon above this scene suggests that he too is "sounding" the idol, not with a tuning fork, but with the bare hands of the sculptor. As a child of the Enlightenment, Blake understood very well that all the idols, totems, and fetishes of premodern, primitive polytheistic societies were the alienated

FIGURE 4.1. Title page, William Blake, *Book of Urizen* (1794). Lessing J. Rosenwald Collection, Library of Congress, Washington, D.C.

FIGURE 4.2. William Blake, *Milton* (1804–10), plate 15, Los creating-destroying Jehovah. Lessing J. Rosenwald Collection, Library of Congress, Washington, D.C.

product of human hands and human minds: "The ancient Poets animated all sensible objects with Gods or Geniuses, calling them by the names and adorning them with the properties of woods, rivers, mountains, lakes, cities, and nations, and whatever their enlarg'd and numerous senses could perceive. . . . Till a system was formed, which some took advantage of & enslav'd the vulgar by attempting to realize or abstract the mental deities from their objects; thus began Priesthood."[19]

In the light of this genealogy of religion, which could very well have been written by Giambattista Vico, the development of monotheism is not so much a radical break with pagan idolatry as a logical development of its tendency to underwrite the consolidation of political power with absolute religious mandates. It is important to remember that Yahweh begins as a mountain god, probably volcanic since he is "hidden in clouds" and speaks "in thunder and in fire." The figure of the invisible, transcendent lawgiver whose most important law is a ban on image making of any kind is the perfect allegory for an imperial, colonizing project that aims to eradicate all the images, idols, and material markers of the territorial claims of indigenous inhabitants. The fearsome figure of Baal, we should remember, is simply a Semitic version of what the Romans called the *genius loci* or genius of the place—the god of the oasis that indicates the proprietary claims of the nomadic tribe that returns to it every year.[20] Dagon, the god of the Philistines, is characteristically portrayed as an agricultural god, associated with the harvest of grain. The veiling or hiding of the god in a temple or cave is simply the first step toward rendering him (and he is almost always male) metaphysically invisible and unrepresentable. As Edmund Burke noted in his *Enquiry into . . . the Sublime and the Beautiful*: "Despotic governments . . . keep their chief as much as may be from the public eye. The policy has been the same in many cases of religion. Almost all heathen temples were dark. Even in the barbarous temples of the Americans at this day, they keep their idol in a dark part of the hut, which is consecrated to his worship."[21] Kant simply carries Burke's observation to its logical conclusion when he argues that "there is no sublimer passage in the Jewish law than the command, 'Thou shalt not make to thyself any graven image, nor the likeness of anything which is in heaven or in the earth or under the earth.'" For Kant, the secret to the "enthusiasm" of both Judaism and "Mohammedanism" is their "abstraction" and refusal of imagery, together with their claim to absolute moral superiority over heathens and idolaters.[22]

I want to conclude with two scenes of idolatry and iconoclasm by an artist who would seem to be radically antithetical to the antinomian tendencies
of Blake and Nietzsche. The work of Nicholas Poussin, as Richard Neer has
argued in his work on the painter, is deeply concerned with issues of idolatry
and iconoclasm. But the depth of this concern would seem to be expressed, if
I follow Neer's argument, by Poussin's determination to remain firmly committed to an orthodox moral condemnation of idolatry in all its forms, at the
same time remaining loyal to the most powerful claims of the visual arts as
expressed in classical sculpture. One could put this as a paradox: how does a
painter endorse iconoclasm and condemn idolatry at the same time deploying
all the visual, graphic resources of a thoroughly pagan, idolatrous culture?

Neer takes Poussin's problem, not merely as the case of an individual artist, but as the central problem of art history as a discipline. As he notes, Poussin scholarship has made him "the most literary of painters," assuming that
"to know a picture's literary source is to know the essential thing about it.
. . . One gets the impression that he is studied more in the library than the
museum."[23] When scholars have broken away from this textually dominated
mode of interpretation to identify "visual sources," the usual conclusion is
that Poussin's numerous citations of classical imagery are "strictly meaning-
less." This "bifurcation" of Poussin into the camps of word and image "is in
fact exemplary." According to Neer: "It is, in germ, what separates 'the two
art histories,' the museum and the academy; the study of Poussin is the grain
of sand in which to see a whole disciplinary world."[24] It is as if the *paragone* of
word and image that was launched by the second commandment has pen-
etrated into the very heart of the discipline that is supposed to devote itself
to the visual arts, confronting it with a version of Poussin's own dilemma:
how does one attend to the meaning of an image without reducing it to the
mere shadow of a textual source? How does one remain faithful to the claim
of the image without becoming an idolater and descending into the abyss of
meaninglessness?

Ultimately, I want to propose a third alternative to Neer's division of the
resources of art history into the "library" and the "museum." The alternative,
unsurprisingly, is the *world* and the larger sphere of verbal and visual culture
within which paintings, like all other works of art, inevitably function, and
perhaps not merely as what Neer calls "useful evidence in . . . a cultural history," but *events and interventions* in that history.[25] But this is to get slightly
ahead of myself.

Two of Poussin's most famous treatments of the theme of idolatry are *The Adoration of the Golden Calf* (1633–36), now in the National Gallery in London, and *The Plague at Ashdod* (1630–31) now in the Louvre (figs. 4.3 and 4.4). Together, the paintings provide a panorama of the fundamental themes of idolatry and iconoclasm. The *Calf* shows the moment of idolatrous ritual and celebration, as the Israelites dance around the Calf with the artist, Aaron, gesturing toward it to urge his countrymen (and beholders of the painting) to contemplate his creation. In the darkness of the background on the left, we see Moses descending from Mount Sinai, preparing to smash the stone tablets of the law in fury over the terrible sin of the Israelites. In *Ashdod*, by contrast, we see the terrible punishment for idolatry as the panicked Philistines realize that they have been stricken by the plague. In the darkness of the left background we see the fallen idol of Dagon with its severed head and hands, and behind it the Ark of the Covenant (which the Philistines have seized as a trophy after defeating the Israelites in battle). In the story of the plague (1 Sam. 5:1–7), the Philistines bring the Ark into the Temple of Dagon, where during the night it magically overturns the statue of the Philistine's god and mutilates it.

Neer makes a convincing argument that, from Poussin's point of view, and thus from the dominant disciplinary perspective of art history, the principle subject matter of *Ashdod* is *not* the foreground tableau of the plague, but the background vignette of the Ark destroying the idol. The evidence he uses is the contemporary testimony of Joachim Sandrart as well as Poussin's own title for the painting, *The Miracle of the Ark in the Temple of Dagon*. This argument, depending on verbal evidence, goes directly against what Neer calls the "visual prominence" of the plague narrative, which would seem to undermine his insistence elsewhere in the essay that visual and pictorial elements should be primary.[26] But for Neer, Poussin is a painter whose work is governed by signs and citations that point toward an invisible and unrepresentable foundation. Like the motif of the Ark itself, which hides the tablets of the law, like the hidden God on Mount Sinai, Poussin's painting encrypts a meaning that is not evident to the eye but only to the connoisseur who is able to reverse the significance of "visual prominence" and see that the primary subject of the painting is "the hiddenness of the divine": "The miracle in the temple is the Second Commandment in action: a battle between statue and sign, ending in the literal destruction of the former," with the plague as merely its outward manifestation.[27] The failure of a beholder to see the plague as a merely secondary consequence or allegorical shadow of the real event in

FIGURE 4.3. Nicolas Poussin, *The Adoration of the Golden Calf* (1633–36). © National Gallery, London / Art Resource, N.Y.

FIGURE 4.4. Nicolas Poussin, *The Plague at Ashdod* (1630–31). Photo: Erich Lessing / Art Resource, N.Y.

the painting is thus made equivalent to the error of the idolatrous Philistines who mistake the outward image for the true meaning: "The failure of the literal-minded Philistines to 'read' the plague correctly, to *bien connoistre*, thus amounts to seeing only the Aspect of the plague," rather than the true "Perspective" in which the events and their depiction are to be understood.[28]

Neer shows convincingly that Poussin intended his painting to be an allegorical "machine" that generates a series of "rigidly antithetical" oppositions (which turn out to be reversible as well): Ark versus Idol; Imitation versus Copy; Signification over Depiction; Poussin versus the "bestial" Caravaggio. Poussin is doing everything possible to avoid falling into mere copying, mere naturalism or realism. He had an "abhorrence of reproduction, verging on mimetophobia."[29] He must constantly remind us that his scenes are staged, and are based in a kind of citational parade of classical figures. The dead mother with her babies starving at her breast is probably a citation of Matthew's Gospel that ironically undercuts the realism of its source in Caravaggio. The hidden truth of the painting, on the other hand, is *literal*; it is a straightforward *istoria*, showing a mutilated idol and an impassive Ark. Like most of Poussin's painting, it is dominated by textualizing practices if not by textual sources, planting subtle clues and citations of previous pictures that will be recognized by the learned viewer. To take the "foreground group" literally, then, not seeing it as a "citational structure" but as "the story it happens to tell," is to miss the point of the painting.[30] This foreground group is "the *allegory of the symbol of the narrative*," a phrasing, as Neer concedes, that is "otiose in a way the picture is not."[31]

I think that Neer has given us the most comprehensive professional reading of this painting we could ask for. As art history, his interpretation is unimpeachable, and as iconology it is incredibly subtle and deft. My trouble begins with his moving of Poussin's theory into the sphere of ethics, where a certain way of reading the painting is reinforced as the morally responsible and even the "pious" way of relating to the picture as a sign or symptom of Poussin's intentions. There is something subtly coercive about this move, and I want to resist it in the name of the painting itself, and perhaps in the name of that "meaninglessness" that scholars like Louis Marin have proposed. In other words, I want to ask "The Plague" (or is it "The Miracle") of Ashdod what *it* wants from the beholder, rather than what Poussin wants.[32] Since the painting outlives Poussin, and participates in what Neer calls a kind of "natural history" (as opposed to its iconological meaning), this means an unleashing of the painting from its own historical "horizon" of possible meanings and allowing it to become anachronistic.

This might be the place to admit that my whole response to this painting is radically anachronistic. I cannot take my eyes off the foreground group. I cannot help sharing in the Philistine gaze that believes this scene is portraying a human reality, an appalling catastrophe that is being reproduced in a kind of stately, static tableau, which is the only thing that makes it bearable to behold. Like William Kentridge's drawings of the atrocities of apartheid, or Art Spiegelman's translation of the Holocaust into an animal fable, Poussin shows us a highly mediated scene of disaster, of a wrathful judgment that is striking down a city and a people in an act of terror that does not discriminate between the guilty and the innocent. The center of this perception is, of course, the most prominent image in the painting, the dead mother with her starving infants at her breast. Neer sees her as a citation to the martyred St. Matthew; I cannot see her without being reminded of a contemporary image that dawned on the world simultaneously with the writing of this text: the image that emerged from Gaza, during the Israeli invasion of January 2009, of "four small children huddling next to their dead mothers, too weak to stand up."[33]

Of course there is a point of view from which this scene is, like Poussin's, merely an allegory of Divine Justice in action. The Palestinians, as we have learned recently from a leading Israeli rabbi, are "Amalekites" who deserve the disasters that are being visited on them by an overwhelmingly superior military power that has god on its side.[34] The Hamas movement in Gaza is a terrorist organization that seeks the destruction of Israel. If terrible things like civilian casualties occur, it is the fault of Hamas, which unscrupulously uses civilians as "human shields." (The fact that the fighters of Hamas actually live among and are related by blood and marriage to many of the people of Gaza does not excuse them from the responsibility to stand up and fight courageously in the open where they can be mowed down by the vastly superior firepower of the Israeli army. Instead, they are understood to be hiding away like cowards in their homes, schools, mosques, government buildings, and community centers while their women and children are massacred around them.) And if there have been injustices on the Israeli side, they will be "investigated properly, once such a complaint is received formally, within the constraints of current military operations."[35] Justice and the law are being and will be served, if only we have the ability to put this shocking picture in perspective.

Nothing I have said here invalidates Neer's interpretation of Poussin's painting. I think that it probably reflects, for better or worse, what Poussin thought about his subject, what he thought was expected of him, and what his audience would have understood.[36] My argument is that there is another, contrary perspective on the painting, one in which an "aspect" is not merely an appearance but, as Wittgenstein would have put it, the "dawning" of a new way of thinking about its subject matter and handling. This is the anachronism that disrupts the doctrine or doxa of the painting, calling into question the ethical discipline and piety that it encourages. I would argue further that this sort of anachronistic seeing is inevitable with images, which are open to the world and to history in a way that deconstructs their legibility and certainty. In short, I am on the side of Derrida's abyss and Louis Marin's "meaninglessness" in Neer's argument, not Montaigne's well-grounded faith in the invisible lawgiver. I am also on the side of Foucault's insistence, in his famous reading of *Las meninas*, that we must "pretend not to know" who the figures are in the painting. We must forego the comfort of the "proper name" and the learned citation, and confine ourselves to the "visible fact," described with "a gray, anonymous language" that will help the painting "little by little" to "release its illuminations."[37]

What happens if we follow this procedure with the *Golden Calf*? What would it mean to see this painting through the eyes of Blake and Nietzsche? Does the painting not threaten to be a transvaluation of the idol it is supposed to be condemning? Could Poussin's painting, without his quite knowing it, be *sounding* the idol with a hammer, tuning fork, or (more precisely) a paintbrush? The Calf is gloriously painted and sculpted; it is a wonder, and the festive dance around it is a celebration of pagan pleasure.[38] But up in the dark clouds is the angry patriarch, breaking the tablets of the law. Nietzsche's pious killjoy and Blake's Nobodaddy converge in Poussin's Moses.

Of course this is all wrong as art history. As iconology or anthropology, however, it may have some traction. Durkheim would have recognized the Calf instantly as a totem animal, and would have rejected the category of the idol for the ideological fiction that it is. It is important to note that totemism and fetishism play a distinguished role in disciplines like anthropology and psychoanalysis; idolatry, as a still potent polemical notion, has rarely been put to technical use by a human science.

So let's consider Poussin's Calf as a totemic image, a figure of the self-conscious projection of a community on a common symbol (totems were generally plant or animal images). Let's look at it through the eyes of Durkheim, Nietzsche, and Blake, as Poussin's attempt to "sound" the idol with his paintbrush, rather than destroying it. It is important that (in the story) the Israelites have *asked* for this Calf. They have demanded that Aaron, the artist in residence, make an idol "to go before them" as a symbol of their tribal identity. "God is Society" is Durkheim's famous formulation of the concept.[39] One could actually think of this as a kind of democratic emblem, at least partly because it seems to have been a random, chance image, flung out from the fire. As Aaron tells Moses: "I cast the gold into the fire and this Calf came out" (Exod. 32:24).

What if that was Zarathustra up on the mountain, smashing the law and joining in the fun? What if the dark clouds are Blake's Nobodaddy "farting and belching and coughing" in his cave on the mountaintop? Could it be that Poussin was (like Blake's Milton) a true poet-painter, and of the devil's party without knowing it?

DREADFUL BEAUTY AND THE
UNDOING OF ADULATION IN THE WORK OF
KARA WALKER AND MICHAEL RAY CHARLES

RACHAEL ZIADY DELUE

Troublesome Things

Spike Lee's film *Bamboozled* (2000) features Damon Wayans as Pierre Dela-croix, a television executive at the network CNS, and Michael Rapaport as Dunwitty, Delacroix's boss. Although white, Dunwitty pronounces himself "blacker" than Delacroix and commands him to produce a blockbuster by dig-ging deep into the core of his experience as a black man. Delacroix responds by pitching an idea so offensive he assumes it will get both of them fired: "Mantan: The New Millennium Minstrel Show," starring two street performers, Manray (Savion Glover) and Womack (Tommy Davidson), done up in blackface. In-stead, the show is a great success, with millions of Americans gleefully watch-ing characters such as Mantan (Manray), Sleep 'n Eat (Womack), Honeycutt, Aunt Jemima, and Lil' Nigger Jim dance and cut up in a watermelon patch on an Alabama plantation. At first appalled by the evil he has wrought, Delacroix eventually comes to defend the show and asserts belief in its social good. Even his disgusted assistant, Sloan Hopkins (Jada Pinkett Smith), finds herself ap-preciating the show's humor and the virtuoso performances of its cast. Toward the end of the film, a collective of musicians led by Sloan's brother, Julius (Mos Def), kidnaps the star, Manray, in protest. Extremes of violence ensue; both Manray and Delacroix are dead by the film's close.

In *Bamboozled*, Lee pairs the escalating success of the neominstrelsy show with a transforming Delacroix. His self-delusion and self-hatred grow apace, as marked by his own blacking up and his accumulation of black collectibles.

This amassing impulse began with Sloan's gift to him of a vintage "Jolly Nigger Bank," a mechanical coin bank whose blackfaced, big-eared, and bug-eyed subject flips coins into a grinning, scarlet-lipped mouth at the press of a lever. As the narrative proceeds, Delacroix's office brims with such objects. Piggy banks, dolls, ceramic and wood figurines, salt and pepper shakers, lawn jockeys, dartboards, children's games, ashtrays, puppets, and cookie jars assemble on all available surfaces and in every corner, an army of objects that mirrors the army of black-faced fans that crowds the tapings of the show (fig. 5.1). As with all of the objects that adorn Lee's scenes—from the African masks and posters of African-American athletes in Dunwitty's office, to the reproduction of John Singleton Copley's *Watson and the Shark* (1778) in Delacroix's, to the board game Othello in Delacroix's mother's living room—these collectibles play a decisive role in Lee's narrative and, at times, assume a leading part. Toward the end of the film, at the height of the show's success, Delacroix's mother excoriates him for putting a "coon" show on television. He retreats to his collectible-filled office only to witness the Jolly Nigger Bank come to life, its levered arm clanking back and forth as it feeds itself invisible coins. "When I thought or imagined that my favorite Jolly Nigger Bank, an inanimate ob-

FIGURE 5.1.   Spike Lee, director, scene from *Bamboozled* (2000), black collectibles in Pierre Delacroix's office. New Line Cinema.

ject, a piece of cold cast iron, was moving by itself," Delacroix says, "I knew I was getting paranoid. Did I really see what I saw? Or was I hallucinating?" Shortly after Manray's kidnapping, the Jolly Nigger Bank animates once again, but much more vigorously; its lips curve into a devilish grin and it hops up and down, rotating in place atop Delacroix's desk, the clank of its mechanical arm accompanied by the insistent rattle of coins in its belly. Delacroix screams for the bank to stop; when it does not, he grabs it and flings it to the floor. "Leave me alone! Leave me alone!" he shouts, as Lee's camera moves from one collectible in Delacroix's collection to the next, creating the impression that these too have come to life, a feeling amplified by Lee's shots of mechanical eyes moving back and forth and bobbled heads swaying on their own, their automated haunting recalling that perpetrated by the Jolly Nigger Bank featured in Ralph Ellison's *Invisible Man*, which the protagonist of the novel repeatedly fails to discard after he smashes it to bits. Enraged, Delacroix assails the objects that populate his office, sweeping them to the floor where they shatter and expire. His attempt at annihilation signals the power these things have assumed: in his life and in the lives of the other characters in the film, but also within the larger culture as shapers of and conduits for relations among humans, as the very things that establish who we think we are and how we understand and comport ourselves with regard to others. Lee's having them take on a semblance of life in his film, making them characters alongside his human ones, upsets conventional hierarchies of animate and inanimate, willful and witless, sensible and insensate. Proper human-object relations are restored only after Manray's slaying; Delacroix slumps in his office chair, cradling the Jolly Nigger Bank and pressing the lever in order to make the bank's arm move. Sloan's parting words to Delacroix—"You made me do that"—uttered after she mortally wounds him with a gunshot to the gut underscore the message of this series of scenes, as does the parade of seemingly self-animated toys, figurines, and puppets that accompanies the film's credits: that inanimate objects can behave and compel as if living, their power over us superseding our intentions and will.[1]

I spend time with the objects featured in Spike Lee's *Bamboozled* in the context of an essay on Kara Walker and Michael Ray Charles because it strikes me that the work of Walker and Charles similarly animates historical or collectible images and objects and does so precisely so as to make them, as with the Jolly Nigger Bank and its comrades, infinitely troublesome. By the latter I do not mean only that Walker and Charles stage a critique of racist imagery and stereotype in their work by appropriating offensive material and replaying it in altered form for present-day audiences. Nor do I intend to suggest that the goal of these artists consists solely in shocking their viewers into self-reflection or political action. Rather, I am interested here in the manner in which Walker and Charles make their imagery behave as would things not altogether lifeless and inert, as with the objects in Lee's film. If that description sounds like the hedge of a bet, it is. What I am trying to characterize here is the way in which the cut-out silhouettes of Walker and the painted characters of Charles are at once inanimate, of course, and filled with life—an impossibility, yes, but a potential state of being with which these images force us to contend. The idea of their animation, as I explain in the pages that follow, comes by way of an excess of representation that fashions brute matter into a set of qualities associated with life and volition. To be sure, the stuff of Walker's and Charles's art is not alive, but the conditions of its manipulation and presentation bestow on it the semblance of the living, a lifelikeness crucial to its operations and effects, the chief characteristic of which is agency, what one normally associates with a living, sensate being. Following Bill Brown, Lorraine Daston, W. J. T. Mitchell, and Barbara Stafford, among others, who variously construe objects or images as agents of a sort, my interest lies in the procedures by which the things fashioned by Walker and Charles come to act on their own or at least argue that they can.[2] Again, I do not claim that these things do in fact speak, move, or act, but that they take on the qualities of bodies or beings that do.

As I argue in the succeeding sections, beauty in excess constitutes this gesture toward life. Given the depraved content it serves to adorn and the impossible relation viewers are thus asked to establish with such a diabolical pairing, beauty also claims responsibility for making the things brought into being by Walker and Charles so vivaciously troublesome. These things provoke worry, I argue, because their lifelikeness, along with the power they threaten to wield over us, akin to that exercised by the collectibles in Lee's *Bamboozled*, pushes them toward a category of object relations already vexed and fraught: that of idolatry. Because they are so captivating and seemingly full of life and because their makers give them idol-like qualities such that they call to be worshipped after a fashion, the things with which Walker and Charles present us compel a form of viewing that approaches veneration. These things are of course not idols in the classic sense of the term, that is, images of God. As I will argue, however, the features with which their makers invest them and the response that they provoke in their viewers make them idolatrous in the sense described by Mitchell, following Francis Bacon's formulation, where an idol can be an image but might also be a word, idea, opinion, or concept.[3] And while it is not incorrect to ascribe aspects of the fetishistic to these things—I do so myself toward the end of the essay—my interest here is in the manner in which the productions of Walker and Charles *surpass* their materiality and approach the status of the sacred: not spiritual sanctity but a sacrosanct character derived from the quality of being prohibited or taboo. In other words, and I will have more to say about this later on, because it is so vile and because of its association with violence at its absolute limit, the imagery deployed by Walker and Charles has accumulated over time an aura of untouchability that inspires a kind of negative reverence. This is a condition of thrall that hinges, not on the transfer of desire or relationality to an object or group of objects— that is, one that relies on the translation of the subjective into the objective— but, rather, on the ascription of special subjectivity to a set of images and artifacts, special in that this subjectivity is of a nonhuman, even inhuman sort: not God's superhumanity, but slavery's and racism's traumatic breaching of human limits. As I see it, the lifelikeness through beauty-in-excess that attends the images under discussion, in that it connotes or instantiates but never fully constitutes a subjective state, figures this nonhumanity. And this lifelikeness generates a perceived consciousness or agency—again, not unlike but not the same as the objectified force or power of a fetish—that transforms viewing into a form of exchange, a back-and-forth between bodies that collapses the adoration of the idolater and the revulsion of the iconoclast into a single experience, something that mirrors Delacroix's response to the objects that plague him, which he exposes as mere matter by shattering them to pieces even as he continues to invest in their inhuman subjectivity, pleading with them to let him alone. As such, idolatry configures as a double bind in Walker and Charles, as an untenable position that the viewer—as if an idolator simultaneously transfixed and disenchanted—must nonetheless occupy.

Ugly Beauty

In *The Emancipation Approximation* (1999–2000), installed in the nineteenth-century hall of sculpture on the second-floor balcony of the Carnegie Museum of Art in Pittsburgh during the Carnegie International (and rendered in slightly altered form as a series of large-format silkscreen prints), Kara Walker scattered silhouetted figures cut from black or white paper across a series of white or slate-gray grounds. The installation evoked the successive scenes of a moving panorama, the subdividing pilasters of the architectural setting enhancing this sense of serial flow (fig. 5.2). Typical of Walker's art, many of the figures are grotesque hybrids—little girls with animal tails, men with cock feathers, women sprouting wings, swans sprouting human heads—and many engage in lascivious or murderous acts. A kneeling woman fellates an unmistakable George Washington; a swan sodomizes a flying female figure; a little girl stomps on what is either a stillborn fetus or the afterbirth of the newly born infant standing next to it; a young boy wields a shiv-like branch over a baby that he and another male figure kick back and forth; and a girl suckles the breast of a woman she holds aloft. Bodily excretions figure largely—feces, breast milk, blood, semen, tears, and the aforementioned afterbirth are either visible or implied—and their flow and spread often serve as connective tissue between one figure and the next. Past and present collide in this work. Allusions to characters from

FIGURE 5.2. Kara Walker, *The Emancipation Approximation* (1999–2000). Carnegie International, Carnegie Museum of Art, Pittsburgh. Courtesy of Sikkema Jenkins & Co.

minstrelsy shows, nineteenth-century literature, and vintage children's stories and toys, including artifacts that would feel right at home in Delacroix's collectible-filled office, along with the silhouette format, the moving panorama, and the neoclassical setting embed the installation in a time before, while Walker's fantastical distortions and their eruption in an exhibition of contemporary art signal the now. This makes it impossible to locate and fix what we see in time and space, an effect compounded by the impenetrable and depthless gray or white in which all of the shadowy figures hover, unmoored and phantomlike, with no foreground, middleground, horizon zone, or vanishing point in sight.

Beauty, understood for the moment as a quality of form, serves both to alleviate and to exacerbate the inscrutability of *The Emancipation Approximation*. The work possesses a lyrical quality and a rhythmic, one-after-another pace, a sweeping and epic flow that seems almost cinematic. The arched back and uplifted arms of a male figure shielding himself from a cascade of feces-like white evokes the recoiled body of a woman in the next panel which in turn echoes the point-counterpoint pairing of the infant-kicking men; this same sway emerges in the semicrouch of a pigtailed and hoop-skirted girl and her formal double, the carpetbag-carrying man whose twisting form continues in the billowing loops of an airborne net in the next scene. The interplay among black, white, and gray accentuates this point-counterpoint effect while playful, interwoven contrasts of light and dark create a delightful frisson; the gray on its own evokes the lush softness of down or rabbit fur, adding the pleasure of touch to the mix. Critics have rightly pointed to the sheer beauty of a work like this one, here constituted by the aforementioned lyricism as well as a general and pleasing fitness or coherence of form and emblematized by the gracefully writhing swans, attributes of Aphrodite and Venus. In combination with the virtuosity of Walker's technique, this beauty compounds the frustration of our inability to define the pictures temporally or spatially or to attach a reasonable, fitting narrative to the scenes she conjures.[4] That Walker hands us her vile content by way of such beautiful form rattles and jars all the more. Her *American Primitives* (2001), a series of small-scale works on paint board that feature silhouetted figures inserted into landscape settings, vividly colored and exquisitely rendered in gouache, embodies this discomfiting disconnect, as does Walker's affixation of decapitated heads to the necks of the aforementioned swans in *The Emancipation Approximation*, making them hybrids of classical beauty and degraded flesh. As Thelma Golden has said, "She is a virtuoso. Her process . . . is phenomenal. . . . I also find that some of

Kara's images that are most conceptually disturbing . . . are often the ones that are most beautiful. Any of the various images of the little nigger wench as she wreaks her havoc are some of the most lyrical passages in her work."[5]

In his series of paintings entitled *Forever Free*, Michael Ray Charles presents the viewer with an analogous amalgam of virtuosity, inscrutability, and ugliness. Like Walker, Charles draws on images from the past—most notably characters or types from popular entertainment, advertising, and product packaging (Sambo, Aunt Jemima, and the like)—and transforms these images so as to create a new cast of characters, hybrids of past and present, old and new, familiar and unfamiliar. In one particularly powerful grouping within the *Forever Free* suite, Charles renders the disembodied and ghoulishly grinning head of a grossly caricatured black man; in each image, his lips and teeth take the form of a watermelon slice, bones criss-cross behind his visage, and a coin slot cuts into his bald pate to reveal a hollow interior. As with many of Charles's paintings, these assume the look of vintage advertising posters—for a circus, say, or a minstrelsy show. Old and worn, their edges are tattered and a two-fold crease divides each image into fours. The crease resembles the cross hairs of a rifle scope, the sight smack dab between the grinning ghoul's eyes, and serves to articulate a major theme of these works: the violence perpetrated by looking at any person through a stereotyping, racist lens. In *Hello, I'm Your New Neighbor*, in the series *Forever Free* (1997), the head and bones hover in front of a light green circle which in turn overlays a bright red square, contributing to the targetlike feel of the ensemble (fig. 5.3). In the upper register of the image sits a grass-covered hill and on this hill two huts; from each hut extends an arm with a white-gloved, Mickey Mouse–like hand. The hands clasp tightly as they meet above the face, an emblem of good will between neighbors (one arm is black, the other white), a ludicrous proposition when juxtaposed with the sneering mask of fear and hate.

It is hard to imagine an image more vile than this one, yet we may find it difficult to look away from it, not only because of the heinous nature of what we see, but, perhaps, because it feels good to look at it, a sensation that results from the peculiar and paradoxical beauty of the scene. There is no red more luscious than that of the watermelon lips, a transparent wash or stain that calls to mind the soaking, sticky sweet of that fruit's juice. Set next to the green of the backdrop circle, this red glistens and gleams all the more. The impossible, dripping grin appears to figure the exuberance with which Charles renders the scene as a whole: audacious, striking color too vivid for the putative

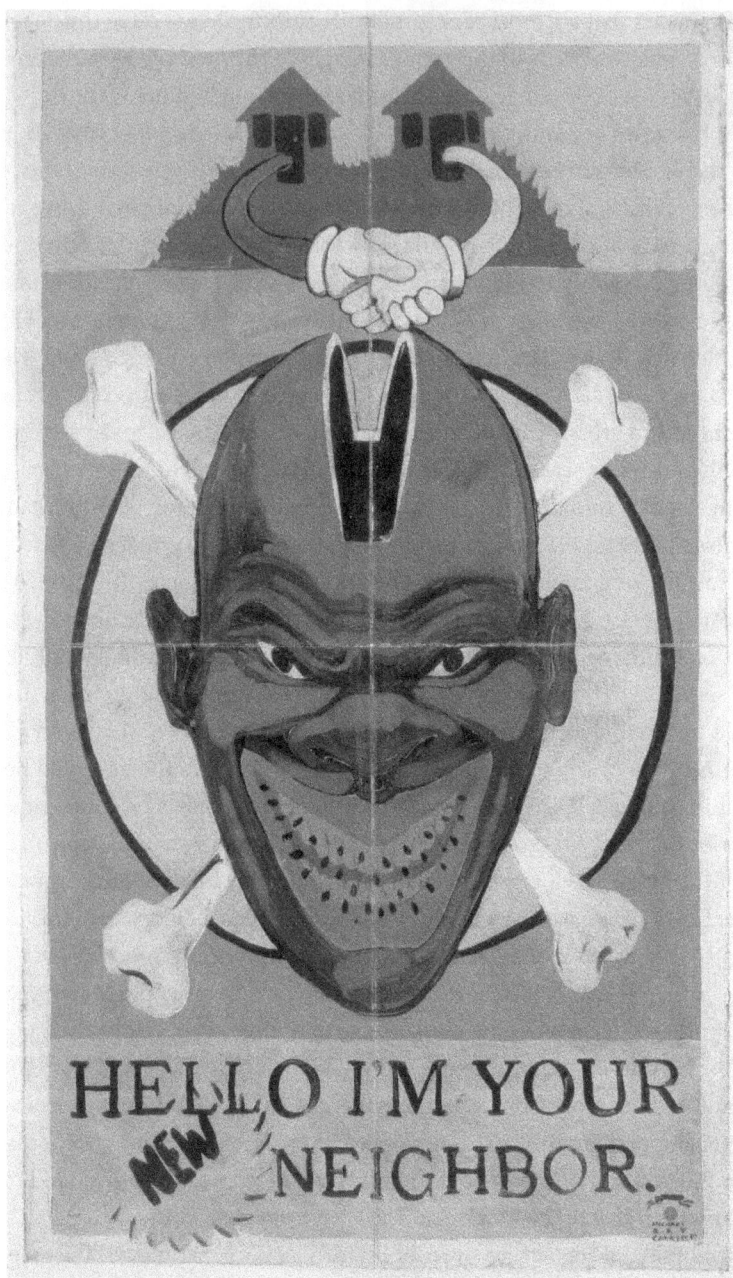

FIGURE 5.3. Michael Ray Charles, *Hello, I'm Your New Neighbor*, in the series *Forever Free* (1997). © Cotthem Gallery and Michael Ray Charles. Courtesy of Cotthem Gallery.

age of the object; thrillingly strident brushwork; an exquisite choreography of rhyming or resonating forms (crease/bones, circle/square, mouth / outstretched arms, huts/nose, coin slot / blackened windows and doors); and a face so caricatured, distorted, and violated it exceeds by far the imagery of actual stereotype and thus evokes an artist gleefully and giddily piling it on. What one might call the work's pseudo–trompe l'oeil effects—the crease, the tattered edges, the flaking color, all of which result from actual acts of folding, tearing, and sanding but still produce only the illusion of age—signal the pride taken by their maker in creating something that appears so close to real that it might be mistaken as such. The upshot is an impression of an artist bringing into being his creation with loving care, with great affection for his medium and motifs, a feeling bolstered by the air of nostalgia that envelops these scenes, described by one critic as "an alluring patina" that entices and seduces.[6] This effect constitutes something like a wistful fondness for things old and worn, enjoyed and then folded and hidden away in hope chests or tucked into bottom drawers, or perhaps discovered in grandma's attic or at a favorite antique store; the connection to the collecting impulse portrayed in *Bamboozled* is clear. As Charles has said, "I'm very attracted to worn surfaces, especially those that expose the different layers of paint chipping away. I think that's beautiful"; and, "I'm a nostalgic person—I like old things. I like the idea of things that appear to be weathered, that have lived through time, that have existed through a period of time. Those things communicate their existence just by looking. There's a certain amount of beauty that I find in that."[7] The fact that these works are paintings, as opposed to some other more typical contemporary artistic form—assemblage, say, or installation—and thus evoke centuries worth of virtuoso production in that medium further underscores their status as the products of a devoted and meticulous hand. Yet, as with Walker's fantastical scenes, Charles's tableaux discomfit precisely because they combine beautiful form with deplorable content. The pleasure we take in looking, which recapitulates the artist's pleasure in making, runs up against figures that allow only partial recognition and classification: they register by way of our familiarity with history's most noxious stereotypes and slurs even as their hybridization and beautification renders them recalcitrant, resistant to any taxonomic labeling. They exist, says Charles, "in a time frame that's neither here nor there."[8] Iconographic analysis, for which these paintings seem cater made, fails and knowing stalls, if temporarily, at the level of exuberantly elaborated and beautiful form.

Adulation

Charles's paintings, in which beauty encodes as exuberance, skill, and nostalgia, are not beautiful in the same sense as are Walker's images, but they are alluring all the same. Thus they present a conundrum similar to that offered up by *The Emancipation Approximation* and others of Walker's works. In *What Do Pictures Want? The Lives and Loves of Images*, W. J. T. Mitchell stipulates that it is not enough for an account of pictures, "understood as complex assemblages of virtual, material, and symbolic elements," to ask of them what they mean or do. We must, he says, consider pictures as living beings of a kind, asking "what they *want*—what claim they make upon us, and how we are to respond."[9] Critical and art historical accounts of Walker and Charles have adequately and compellingly described the general themes and investments of their work. This critical literature, in characterizing and parsing their technique, iconography, and source material, thus offers a basic understanding of artistic intent, an interpretation of what Walker and Charles hope to convey and the means by which they choose to do so. There exists no great need, then, to rehearse what others have already and satisfactorily written regarding the meaning of Walker's and Charles's production: that through their strategies of appropriation, which involves recourse to and transformation of past forms (silhouettes, song lyrics, novels, minstrelsy shows, advertisements, product packaging, collectibles, and the like), they aim to cast light into history's shadows and repressions and also to explore the presentness of the past, the manner in which the images, ideas, and experiences of an earlier time subsist in and constitute the representations and realities of today, particularly those having to do with identity, race, and racism. At the same time, Walker and Charles seek also to show that no imagery stands fully adequate to the task of representing the past and its traumas, or the power that memory wields over the present day.

The art of Walker and Charles of course means things other than this, but my summary description paints a fairly accurate general picture of their work and does so without misrepresenting what other scholars have already and more eloquently had to say. What this work *wants*, in the end, from its viewers—the demands it makes on them as distinct from the meaning it conveys—and how this work imagines these viewers responding to these demands as they interact with it, remain far less clear (though not, of course, unaddressed; that Walker's installations, for instance, compel viewer participation and thus implication, has been pointed out on numerous occasions if not deeply explored, and some of the best writing on Walker takes affect into account).[10]

We know what Walker and Charles are saying, or at least we have a pretty good idea of this, but we find it difficult to fully fathom how we are meant to feel when faced with the vehicle of this message or meaning. Looking at these pictures entails confronting at one and the same time intense beauty and exuberance in making and a deep, haunting ugliness, the latter as constituted by supremely offensive subject matter—fellated founding fathers, murderous pickaninnies, demonic minstrels, and blackfaced buffoons—and, also, by our own attraction to the sheer beauty of these things as rendered by Walker and Charles. Put another way, our shudder comes close on the heels of our swoon. The very idea, courtesy of Mitchell, that a picture can desire at all—that an inanimate object can exert a more-than-metaphorical power over its audiences—might be met with raised eyebrows and a healthy dose of doubt. Yet, as I see it, the confusion, discomfort, and/or anger felt by many viewers when faced with the imagery of Walker and Charles—what underpins the ongoing and vigorous debate over its appropriateness—arises from the manner in which this work, through its beauty and exuberance and our response to these things, seems to exceed the intentions of its makers, even if this excess is, paradoxically, intentional. The work troubles because it lives a life of its own, because it stands as an embodied presence, a *thing* that puts itself in relation to us as would another human with whom we are forced to interact and to whose desires we are compelled to attend—much like Delacroix and company are made to dance to the tune of the lifelike and automatistic collectibles in *Bamboozled*—not least because these desires, given the visual allure of the work, are often also our own.[11]

Relation is the key term here, as it is for Mitchell, who appoints the relationality of image and beholder as his field of investigation in *What Do Pictures Want?*[12] For the images of Walker and Charles, if they insist on anything, it is that we enter into a relationship with them, one deeper than that constituted by a quick glance in a gallery or museum and more akin to the bond established between an icon and the faithful that venerate it, an attachment or engagement evoked by the descriptor "idolatry." That a veritable movement has arisen calling for the eradication of work such as theirs, in large part because this work (Walker's especially) has inspired such critical adulation, further evidences the appropriateness of idolatry as an interpretive framework or elucidatory term. But it is not simply the fact that for whatever reasons, innocent or otherwise, these artists inspire a particular sort of critical worship or that they compel idolatry's counterpart, iconoclastic critique, that suggest idolatry as an explanatory concept here. As I see it, both Walker and Charles deliberately and strategically create the conditions particular to and compel the practices associated with idolatry, as understood in its most basic sense as worship of a graven image for its perceived extra- or superhuman qualities, and as distinct from but not unrelated to the invention of a fetish object, which is invested with human-only qualities and relations.

How so? As many critics have noted, Walker's installations compel participation and thus complicity. They do so by adapting the format of the cyclorama or circular panorama to the gallery space such that we exist inside of what we see; we thus confront images but we also engage a physical, material space. Walker involves us materially also by evoking, through narrative vignettes and carefully wrought characters, the feel of history past and present, suggesting a span of time and an ongoing series of events of which we are a constitutive part. Similarly, Walker's projection works, such as *Darkytown Rebellion* (2001), where she casts colored patterns across her silhouette-adorned walls, make the viewer, whose body intervenes between light source and screen and thus distorts what is on view, a literal part of the scene. Both Walker and Charles fashion recognition as a vehicle of participation by anticipating their audience's familiarity with the historical imagery that serves as their artistic starting point and by counting on the cultural conditioning that predisposes a viewer to recognize certain visual cues or forms as pleasing or beautiful. We are constitutively engaged with Walker's installations and Charles's paintings because what we see in them is already part of our lived existence and perceptual set. A structure of give-and-take or perceived connectedness particular to idol-worship thus displaces a more detached optical scrutiny, for the exchange that occurs between image and beholder occurs at a level other than the purely optical. Such a form of relation arises because we share our memories and collude in knowing with the imagery on view, one upshot of this being the bestowal of a kind of consciousness on the part of the art object, a capacity to know and act attributed only to the most special (or diabolical) things. Extra-optical engagement that entails the establishing of a relation as if between two corporeal beings happens also because what we see takes its form from images but also from things; both Walker and Charles allude to past and present images but they also incarnate, if two-dimensionally, past and present objects, among them Jolly Nigger Banks, cookie jars, wood or ceramic statuary, string puppets, and children's toys. Our seeing of an image created by Walker or Charles thus comprises consciousness of and consequent association with the thing of its origin, what contributes to the visceral nature of our experience of their work and presses that experience toward the domain of object-relations and thus idolatry.

Both Walker and Charles execute false images of the sort proscribed by society, at least in theory—caricature and stereotype—and, as I have begun to argue, render them such that they inspire pleasure and devotion on the part of those who view them, gestures that also serve to align their practice with that of idolatry. This, of course, is not the sort of dissolute, drunken, and bodily pleasure depicted in paintings of the Israelites worshipping the Golden Calf, from Lucas van Leyden's famous representation of this subject to Emile Nolde's early twentieth-century interpretation of it, but rather its analog at the level of vision or, more properly, viewing; "visual interchange" may be the best way to describe the image-beholder relationship here, given what I have described as the manner in which viewing this work entails shared knowing and remembering and carries the potential for corporeal co-presence.[13] To be sure, viewers do not become mad with delight and revel with abandon when beholding the art of Walker and Charles, or, possessed by religious fervor, imagine this art to manifest bona fide supernatural powers. Of course not. Rather, I want to argue that Walker and Charles make their art beautiful because they want their viewers to look at it in such a way that the ensuing sensory stimulation—the pleasure taken in looking—pushes them to fall into a sort of visual, as if precognitive, adoration, one that can make them blind to the subject depicted, even if for a mere moment or two (Walker) or for a split second (Charles), such that beholding momentarily transfigures as the feel of idol-worship, with the images assuming a subjective-like presence in excess of their inanimate condition. Walker and Charles surely anticipate that such adoring blindness will occur in a space—a gallery or museum—itself not unchurchlike, what with the objects on view displayed as if sacred things and the requisite, even ritualistic behaviors that occupying such a space entails (pay entrance fee, check coat, use restroom, enter gallery, decelerate gait and soften voice, view art, cluck with praise or disapproval, visit gift shop, exit). With many of his motifs drawn from product packaging, including the yellow shout of "New" in *Hello I'm Your New Neighbor*, Charles of course also calls to mind, with a nod to Andy Warhol, that modern-day cathedral, the supermarket. He thus comments on consumerist excess and the commodification of the black body in American culture, while also locating his images in yet another ritualistic space. Indeed, both artists appear to capitalize on these particular practices of viewing and conditions of display when compelling their work to assume idol-like qualities.[14] And they do this precisely so that this work can wriggle free of their control and take on a certain kind of autonomy—a set of behaviors and qualities that seem in excess of intention—with this autonomy being a prerequisite for becoming an idol, a human-made object or thing that assumes the capacity to compel veneration on its own, that *desires* this veneration, apart from human intervention. Like the collectibles in Delacroix's office, which, once acquired and amassed by him, come to move on their own, the images created by Walker and Charles, once made, exert a pull so intense—a magnetism associated with overabundant charisma—that it can seem as if they long and pine for us to be in their thrall.

As I have already stated, beauty plays a leading role in this seduction. I am not the first to point out the beauty of Walker's work; that Walker skillfully combines ugly content and beautiful form so as to generate a productive structure of cognitive dissonance has become a critical commonplace, if not the subject of detailed or sustained analysis, and she herself has commented on the manner in which beauty and seduction serve a strategic purpose in her art, where, as she has said, "a kind of beauty" and "violent lust" intertwine. "I think that when I work out the large pieces," she explained in a dialogue with Thelma Golden in 2002, "I'm half conscious of keeping a sort of balance, even if it starts off in a skewed place, so that if some of the actions are ugly or ambiguous or not in keeping with a progressive view of ourselves, then I try and at least make the gesture beautiful, and ultimately the form is beautiful." In another interview that same year, she stated, "Working with such loaded material as race, gender, sex, it's easy for it to become ugly. I really wanted to find a way to make work that could lure viewers out of themselves and into this fantasy. Seduction and embarrassment and humor all merge at a similar point in the psyche—vulnerability. That's a tough thing to achieve from a stationary object."[15] It may seem a stretch to call the faux-poster art of Charles beautiful but, as explained above, beauty encodes as exuberance, skill, and nostalgia in his paintings and serves a centrally strategic purpose therein, a vital function akin to that in Walker's pictures; more than a formal quality, beauty initiates and drives the basic procedures and processes of both of their work. I thus see beauty as centrally strategic within the operations of the art of both artists: as that thing that fashions their creations into venerable idols and, consequently, produces such anxiety on the part of their viewers, onto whom is forced an immensely problematic and intensely strained image-beholder relationship.

Following Elaine Scarry, who has written eloquently on beauty, I do not pretend to define beauty as such, as apart from the objects in which it is perceived to reside. Indeed, my understanding of beauty arises from a consideration of object relations—what transpires between a thing and its maker/viewer/consumer—and locates beauty, again following Scarry, in/as the experience of an encounter, one that, for my purposes, engenders a particular sort of response to objects that bear the attributes of "beautiful" as culturally and socially defined, including certain aesthetic as well as associative forms, namely those I have identified in Walker and Charles: languid lines and rhyming shapes, say, or the marks of loving wear (the latter might also belong to the category "picturesque" as defined in the eighteenth century by William Gilpin and others).[16] Beauty in the work of Walker and Charles troubles because, as I said, it compels reverence or awe in front of despicable or horrific imagery, what I have described as a pleasurable, precognitive swoon. Their art thus raises philosophical questions, none of them wholly new, concerning how we comport ourselves in regard to beauty, how we conceive of or establish what Susan Sontag has called "the proper relation to the beautiful," and it does so in part by allowing us, despite our longing, no easy or proper relation to what we see.[17] As Scarry has described, beauty induces a desire for more of the same: "it seems to incite, even require, the act of replication." Not only this, beauty "brings copies of itself into being," forcing us to reproduce it through imitation or articulation. "The generation is unceasing," Scarry writes.[18] It goes without saying that to desire more of the particular beauty on offer in Walker and Charles presents a relational predicament, visual but also moral. Stanching this desire helps, but the threat of proliferation persists, not least because attraction originates in something that is itself already a kind of copy: a work of art constituted by appropriation and quotation, by replicating and reproducing already-present forms so as to beget even more, some of these far worse—copies in transformative excess—than what preceded them, offspring more hideous than their already-monstrous progenitors. That Walker and Charles themselves initiate the procreative process—and that Walker does so by cutting and pasting silhouettes, a process that evokes mechanical reproduction despite the fact that she creates hers by hand; and that both artists repeat figures and motifs among multiple works, as if to signal a genealogical line—only serves to deepen the threat of an unceasing onslaught of seductively dangerous forms. Scarry identifies worry over just such a "contagion of imitation," and no speculative stretch is required to imagine that the detractors of the strain of art promulgated by Walker and Charles see it as potentially pathological, inclined to spread, viruslike, in the same manner that the craze for Mantan and his fellow neominstrels infected an entire, fervent nation as depicted in Lee's *Bamboozled*.[19] The even-for-a-split-second rapture (Walker might call it giddiness) inspired by Walker's and Charles's work could easily inspire a thirst for such visual ecstasy to propagate and persist, a yearning that precedes full comprehension of pleasure's source. What is more, as potentially autonomous creatures—representations that seem at a certain point to generate themselves (more on this below)—these works can seem as if they might just decide to replicate on their own.[20]

In the made-ness of the work—in the radical visibility and materiality or one could even say the *celebration* of this made-ness—lies another part of the problem. No "acheiropoietic" images these; they are, like idols, manifestly made by human hands. We know this to be the case by way of the worn and worked surfaces of Charles's canvases—the manner in which they show us paint as exuberantly as they offer up blackface, stereotype, and caricature—as well as by the manner in which both Charles and Walker do more than simply appropriate and quote previous images and text, creating their own, idiosyncratic casts of characters and superfluous stereotypes, figures so beyond the pale that they have to be the products of their maker's imaginations, even if history's repertoire of racist images provided the initial inspiration.[21] To make matters worse, certain of Walker's projects incorporate a form of self-portraiture (to use a term inadequate to the complex iterations of subjectivity in her art) by way of the alter-ego "Negress," including, for example, *Gone, an Historical Romance of a Civil War as It Occurred Between the Dusky Thighs of One Young Negress and Her Heart* (1994); *Presenting Negro Scenes Drawn upon My Passage Through the South and Reconfigured for the Benefit of Enlightened Audiences Wherever Such May Be Found, By Myself, Missus K. E. B. Walker, Colored* (1997); and *For the Benefit of All the Races of Mankind (Mos' Specially the Master One, Boss) An Exhibition of Artifacts, Remnants, and Effluvia EXCAVATED from the Black Heart of a Negress I* (2002). As with Albrecht Dürer's hubristic *Self-Portrait* (1500, Alte Pinakothek, Munich, Germany), Walker's images rejoice in their human origin (although, as Joseph Leo Koerner points out, Dürer's image associates its maker with the miraculousness of self-portraits of Christ).[22] By way of a signature, Charles affixes shiny copper pennies to his canvases as if to ensure, by dint of their alluring glint and gleam, that his viewers know that what they see is a product of his hand, as manifest in the material, sculptural presence of the coin as well as the literality of its being affixed with glue to the canvas surface. As Charles has said, he prefers painting to printmaking because the latter precludes "the ability to physically touch each one" of the works as they are produced.[23] It is not, then, merely the presence of offensive images that irks, that has made so many viewers anxious and irate. The fact that Walker and Charles so lovingly conjure and craft images as abominable as those I described above is what disturbs; Walker herself has said that she sometimes struggles to confront her own images and the ideas that are their impetus: "I am sometimes horrified by the thoughts that come to my mind and am occasionally blinded by them."[24] Rather than imitate or quote historical or contemporaneous sources and then reconfigure them so as to blunt or co-opt their force, Walker and Charles invent abominations far in excess of the originals. As long as Christ paints himself, his image may stand; as long as an artist simply ventriloquizes or positively transforms a racist past, his or her images may stand as well. When a human hand is discovered to have concocted images that so fiercely offend, well, that is another, more sordid story altogether.

Renunciation

Yet things are more complicated than this. Accompanying the manifest madeness of Walker's work is a certain renunciatory quality—a refusal to admit authorship as well as a resistance to the idea that her images are pictures and thus available as idols at all—one brought into being by virtue of the very things that announce Walker as maker: the "Negress" persona, which serves to displace Walker as author; the mining of historical sources such that history itself becomes the artist-scribe; and the lyrically beautiful silhouettes which, like shadows or ghosts, shapeshift and mutate before our eyes, at once presence and absence, the very definition of the silhouette form. As Walker has stated of such an object, it is "both there and not there." This makes her forms and figures seem living beings that, once wrought by the artist's hand, slip free of her grasp and generate narratives all their own. Their undifferentiated whiteness or blackness presents a perfect blank slate and their twofold departure from history—they are not traces of actual profiles, as are conventional silhouettes, and they do not imitate but rather excessively elaborate or transform extant imagery and stereotypes—wrests them even more from authorial or interpretive control. Here is Walker, again, speaking of one of her installations: "They all jumped into life—waking life—without my really controlling them."[25] That the silhouettes over time or in response to climate changes sometimes break free of their adhesive bonds, fidgeting and twisting against their flat grounds, seems a perfect if serendipitous metaphor for the autonomy I describe. *Strewn-seeming* is Darby English's wonderfully apt term for characterizing the manner in which the silhouettes create the effect of having alighted at random or, perhaps, haphazardly chosen their own positions and locales—yet another disavowal of what we know to be the careful craft and choreography that put them where they are.[26]

Such renunciation—what Lisa Saltzman has called, in reference to the artist Glenn Ligon, "painterly iconoclasm"—might also be attributed to Charles.[27] His paintings seem like found objects—posters, sheet music, and product labels, among other things, that have been worn, torn, dog-eared, creased, folded, and faded. By producing simulacra of these end products of age and use, Charles posits time itself as the author of the paintings. One could even say that these effects of wear put forward these objects as having made themselves, their passage through history and the lives that they lived being those things that made them what they presently are. As with the animated Jolly Nigger Bank in *Bamboozled*, these objects come to seem as if living entities, the exigencies of their existence, the traces of their travel through time and space worn into and borne by their flesh. The pseudo-trick-the-eye effects of Charles's canvases discussed above underscore this ontological confusion, for they blur the boundary between similarity and identity, one of the central concerns of iconoclasm; Charles's *Hello I'm Your New Neighbor* causes anxiety, as do all of his works, in part because it appears to be at one and the same time a representation of a thing, created exuberantly, and that thing itself, its creation thus disavowed.[28] Spike Lee zeroes in on this confusion or doubleness by including one of Charles's paintings in *Bamboozled*'s visual cataloging of Delacroix's black collectibles: a 1997 work from the *Forever Free* series, itself titled *Bamboozled*, that depicts a children's game but assumes the identity of the game when shown alongside the other collectibles under filmic review. The viewer has no way of knowing, as the image flashes by, that it is in fact a work of art, and thus takes it for the real thing. The chimeras and hybrids that populate each artist's work—human-animals in Walker's, Nike-clad minstrels and Aunt Jemimas outfitted as Wonder Woman in Charles's—embody this simultaneity, this status of being fabricated and seamlessly real all at once. When Delacroix's collectibles come to life in Lee's film, they clank and click and jingle and knock, their chatter making them seem to speak; Charles's paintings are of course mute, but they chatter after a fashion as well, chock full as they are with words, as evidenced by the following examples from *Forever Free*: exclamations ("Please! Be Careful Sir"); queries ("Can I Be of Any Assistance?); declarations ("Hello I'm Your New Neighbor"); advertising copy ("New," "Service with a Smile"); quotations ("'Good Night Ma'me'"); explanatory captions ("The Greatest Blow on Earth"); ditties ("You Can Be Like This or You Can Be Like That"); and cryptic phrases ("'Mo Money, Mo Money'/ Ideal"). This half-speech, this talking, talking, talking at us without producing sound, appears designed to signal the idea of just such a doubled state, a sense of hovering between animation and representation, life and art.

So Walker and Charles instantiate a double bind: an art that induces image worship even as it clamors for its own unmasking. Put another way, they make idols and then they tear them down. They compel their images to become sui generis objects or things, as opposed to high art, by iterating the possibility of their nonmadeness and by allowing them to speak and act on their own, as if apart from a human interlocutor, or at least creating the illusion that they can do so. This does not aim at convincing viewers of their sanctity and worth (as the argument for the validity of images has gone) but rather endeavors to suggest that, as products not of the artist's studio, gallery, or museum, these things—denizens of supermarkets, kitchen shelves, toy chests, and bottom drawers—are just that: things. Thus Walker and Charles play all parts in a historical drama of image worship, one staged on gallery and museum walls. They are at once the idolaters and the iconoclasts. They erect images for adulation in the very spaces that have sanctioned modern forms of image veneration and they seduce viewers with the beauty and exuberance of their forms. Then they shatter these images at the adorers' feet. Destruction takes the form of putting these images in their thingly place, demoting them by making them only objects, and mortal ones at that, marked as they are by history and time and constituted by their existence in the material world, as evidenced by their seeming loquaciousness and mobility. If they can talk and transmute, if they can speak and write and image themselves, they must be like us, and if they are like us, they must be as brute in their materiality as we are. Consequently, and despite their beauty and allure, they are anything but powerful, transcendent, or divine.

Walker's and Charles's images, then, work to strip away any historical gloss or sheen that might numb us to the ugliness of history's images and forms or, worse yet, make us love this ugliness all the more. Through an excess of beauty they warn against the very practice that their images enact: what Walker has called the romanticization and what I would also term the fetishization of historical forms, the making of them beautiful and thus powerful by virtue of loving them or hating them too much (here is where the fetish and the idol cross paths). Walker and Charles also seek to problematize the gesture by which one might substitute their objects for actual human relations, allowing the prohibition-cum-reverence of images to masquerade as a coming-to-terms with America's traumatic past and the persistence of its effects in the present.[29] Walker and Charles put these images on a pedestal in order to knock them off while never ceasing to insist that we keep them in view, that we look at them squarely, without the veiling and muting patinas of history, collecting, or kitsch. Elaine Scarry has described such a fall from grace. Realization that one has made an error in attributing beauty, she writes, "is so palpable that it is as though the perception itself (rather than its object) lies rotting in the brain . . . the perception has undergone a radical alteration—it breaks apart (as in breaking plates) or disintegrates (as in the festering flower); and in both cases, the alteration is announced by a striking sensory event, a loud sound, an awful smell."[30] The slice of Walker's scissors and the rips, scrapes, and tears wrought by Charles might be taken as an analogous renting asunder, the bodily fluids that course through Walker's scenes and the dripping, sickly sweet watermelon juice of Charles's as equivalent to Scarry's rotting pile, or to what Walker has called "Muck."[31] But it is our visual and perhaps bodily rapture that stands as the striking event that brings us to our senses, first by way of a bewitching and then through dint of a betrayal, our faith dashed to bits before beauty unmasked.

Both Walker and Charles call to mind forms of entertainment that involve images or bodies in motion, Walker by evoking the moving panorama or phantasmagoria format (and perhaps also Civil War reenactments), Charles by way of advertisements for circuses, minstrelsy shows, and other forms of revue. The fact that the figures they depict stand motionless—Walker's immobilized by the adhesive that binds them to gray or white grounds, Charles's embedded and embalmed in paint—is not simply a symptom of the nature and limits of their chosen media. Immobility here connotes fatality, idols debunked and put to death. Sometimes Walker uses pins to attach her sil-

houettes to their grounds, a gesture that evokes tacking a botanical or en-
tomological specimen to a display board, thus driving home the idea of her
creatures' expiration; even the silhouettes that Walker does set into motion, as
with the stick puppets featured in her films *Testimony: Narrative of a Negress
Burdened by Good Intentions* (2004), and *8 Possible Beginnings; or, The Creation of African-America, a Moving Picture by Kara E. Walker* (2005), wind up
looking more flattened and dead than those that remain silent and still.[32] No
mere critique of images this: what these artists aim for is a wholesale recon-
figuration of the manner in which we interact with and consume racist iconography as well as a recasting of beauty as an aesthetic form. By compelling
their viewers to enter into a relationship with works of art that is strained to
the point of breaking—how else to describe the seduction by things so beauti-
fully vile?—they point up the untenability of any such relationship, challenging us to scrutinize the nature of our attachment to or interest in the racist
imagery that they make the subject of their work. As Mark Reinhardt has
pointed out, the pleasure we take in pictures such as Walker's can resemble
that inspired by the "political pornography" of nineteenth-century abolition-
ism, and Walker has said something analogous about Civil War reenactors,
calling their worship of history (or what passes as history) fanatical and the
outcome of their "Civil War games" absurd. Comprising a fetishistic devotion to things—period uniforms, weapons, and foodstuffs—more so than a
critical engagement with the past, these pageants fashion their participants as
obsessive, panting idolaters. "Historical accuracy," Walker has said, "panders
to subjective, even corrupt desire."[33] Racist imagery, but also history itself:
Walker and Charles skewer our idolatrous attachment to the stuff of the past,
our veneration and repetition of narratives that purport either to recount history dispassionately or to condemn the past even while exulting in its horrors. This may have been what Walker was getting at when she controversially
hypothesized that all black people in America wished to be slaves just a little
bit, or when she stated, "I think really the whole problem with racism and its
continuing legacy in this country is that we simply *love* it. Who would we be
without it and without the 'struggle?'"[34] If Scarry is even partially or condi-
tionally correct in claiming that beauty, as an aesthetic attribute, can exert
pressure on us to act fairly and justly in part because it attracts and holds our
regard, the loathsome allure of what Walker and Charles conjure in their art
and the attentiveness thus inspired—what comes by way of beauty's radical
redefinition, what Thelma Golden has called "a more radical approach to its

use"—might manage to make us see in a way that before we could not, with eyes ultimately undimmed by devotion, fantasy, or desire.[35]

What, then, does this work want? It wishes to be beautiful so as to be looked at and desired, to be looked at and desired so as to be seen, to be seen so as to be disavowed, and to be disavowed so as to create a space for deliberative thought, what the extremes of idolatry and iconoclasm refuse to allow. One could even say that the vile beauty of the images fashioned by Walker and Charles posits itself as a new language, an artistic idiom that acknowledges the monumental evils and injustices of the past but stops short of claiming this past to be unrepresentable, a stance these artists would surely call a dodge.[36] Their art, instead, assays the present usefulness of beauty itself by rewriting it *as* grotesque and depraved, precisely so that the limits of representation and the boundlessness and sublimity of history might pictorially align and so that our desires might finally find their proper object and place.

6

ICONOCLASM AND REAL SPACE

DAVID SUMMERS

The valley temple of the pyramid builder Chephren has bases for twenty-three statues, presumably all diorite like the only one that survives. As this example shows, images, as works of human art, have made their way to us in fragments, and in small numbers. Perhaps it is the expectation that things might or should be otherwise that most needs to be explained. This expectation is closely related to the inclination to think that if images do not last forever they can only have come to a violent end. There are historical reasons for this inclination, and, as is well known, iconoclasm has been part of Western history in some of its most crucial episodes.[1]

The second commandment (Exod. 20:4–6) forbids the making of any "graven image, or any likeness of anything that is in heaven above, or that is in the earth beneath, or that is in the water under the earth; you shall not bow down to them, or serve them."[2] This prohibition is straightforward, but it is difficult to fix the limits of its effects. The second commandment justified the destruction of religious images in Byzantium and again in northern Europe, but this destruction was also the prelude to (for example) centuries of white-walled Protestant churches, bearing the implication day in and day out that images *should* have been excluded from the space of worship, that they are precisely *not* sacred. Since the worship of images is often coupled with "whoring" in the subsequent chapters of *Exodus*, it is hard to tell how the conspicuous absence of images might have affected attitudes toward images in general. Iconoclasm, in short, has had institutional effects contributing to the historical development of attitudes toward images reaching far beyond their actual destruction.

As I have suggested, exclusive interest in iconoclasm tends to conceal the quieter life and death of many images. If images are treated as if "alive," it is also possible to think they have died, and that any power associated with them has simply come to an end. And even if they have not completed a lifespan whose nature we do not know, images are used; they wear out and are replaced, and they are disposed of, sometimes with ceremony, sometimes without. In India, a religious image might be laid to rest in a stream; and in the midst of his defense of images, John of Damascus, citing authorities to show that it is not the material of an image but rather its prototype that is venerated, reports that "when the character has been smoothed away leaving bare wood, we burn up what was once an image."[3] The "character" makes the image recognizable and when the image has been handled to the point that its identity is no longer evident, or its appearance is no longer appropriate, the remains of the image can be burned without anxiety.

To take another example, sub-Saharan African sculpture, which is carved from wood, is prone to decay and destruction by termites.[4] Westerners have been inclined to preserve these images, but Africans have not, and have not been since time immemorial. If these images have short lives in the spaces of use for which they are made, and are expected to disintegrate with time, the motivation of those who make and use them is hardly iconoclastic. The Pende, the group in question, believe that images are places where the spirits of ancestors can be invoked by their descendants, and the actual lives of images might be seen to coincide with the span of time for which human beings still "see" their forebears in memory and dreams. When there are no longer those who remember, and no new images of newly departed family members, the spirits pass into the realm of the ancestors as their images crumble. If these images were made of permanent materials, then their spirits could not join the ancestors, and there would be spirits to whom proper respect could not be paid.

Different as the images themselves may be, these African sculptures are not so different in function from family photographs. Photographs of parents, grandparents, and great-grandparents are displayed to recognition, sympathy, and a kind of deference. Great-great-grandparents, indispensable as they might be in the chain of lives leading to our own, assume a kind of distance, and so also become "ancestors." Photographs are very slight, chemically fragile, technically datable, and at a certain point they vanish (if they are not also preserved in museums) to join the billions of now-nameless once photographed. The poignant Fayum portraits were placed over the faces of the mummified dead, and the finished mummies stood upright in homes. They were given offerings and included in celebrations, and must have been status objects in their own right. After some time, however, perhaps again the hand-span of the length of the memories and dreams of their descendants, they were simply buried, almost as if discarded. As the centuries passed, mummies were ground into medicine and pigments, recycled into paper, even thrown into the fireboxes of locomotives. The point to be made is that mortality goes on and on, generation upon generation, and the life of images may acknowledge this. The large-eyed images placed as offerings in the sanctuaries of Sumerian temples had to be removed and buried in the foundations of an enlarged temple structure as their numbers mounted. Was this iconoclasm? Offerings must continue to be made for the living, and the dead must finally join the ancestors.

Recognition

The first part of the Mosaic prohibition against images might be understood to say that the appearance of everything in creation—everything to be seen in heaven, earth, and the waters beneath the earth—should not be imitated, and that any result of doing so—any image—can only be a fatal temptation, both for those who see it and for the one who made it. Those who recognize it are tempted when they think that it possesses life and power, and the one who made it has dared to imitate God in making what seems to have life but does not. True creation is the creation of life. In the Islamic hadith, God challenges the image maker to breathe life into his images; when he cannot he is cast into hell. Or, as most abstractly stated by Western medieval theologians, the creature cannot create.[5]

The Greek word *eikon* means image, similitude, or likeness—most simply, a portrait. In the discussion to follow, I will use the word *icon* a little differently.[6] An icon is typically a single sculpture or painted figure, although it might be a small group, a Virgin and Child, for example, or a Crucifixion with Mary and John the Evangelist.[7] Any icon raises the question of presence in the real space shared with an observer (or observant; icons are objects of worship).

Icons are to be distinguished from *narratives*. The representation of narratives entails *virtual* space, whereas icons minimize virtual space. Christianity is a narrative religion, in that the Gospels recount an exemplary life. Christian *icons* were justified in large part by the Incarnation, and they were distinguished from idolatry by the argument first made by St. Basil, that "honor paid to an image passes to its prototype."[8] This is a culturally specific variation of the much more widespread idea that icons have another dimension, that they are animated, or able to be animated.

Plato (who seems first to have called the imitation of appearance *mimesis*) remarked in passing that painters "make imitations which have the same name as real things."[9] This claim is not as simple as it seems. We may say of Henry, and of his portrait, "That is Henry." If we have never met Henry, we might say, "That is a portrait of an unknown man," with the implication that there is or was such a man, that he had a name, although we do not know it. In the same way, however, we might come to the conclusion that, because there is an image of a centaur, centaurs must exist. We have named the image, but the name is not the name of a real thing. Centaurs are of course fictitious, but they must be labeled as such. What might be the basis for this credulity with respect to images?

The hypothetical example of simple recognition I am about to describe must be admitted to be far in the past, in something like the Paleolithic past, but it might also explain something as simple as why we are reluctant to throw darts at photographs of our friends. If images are considered from the standpoint of recognition by an observer rather than from that of likeness to a model, then a crucial ambivalence in images begins to come into view. *Recognition* is in important respects the recognition of living things, and when an image, a likeness encountered in the space of one's experience, is recognized *as* something, its movement and life are *anticipated as recognition occurs*. In evolutionary terms, recognition is certainly much older than images, and the basic survival value of recognition is obviously very high. The threshold for recognition is also much lower than that for resemblance, and we may, for example, recognize a smiley face as a friendly face.

As I have described it, the anticipation that occurs with recognition is primarily perceptual, and it provides the possibility of a range of reactions. When a recognized image does not move, it may be thought to have failed a basic test, in which case it can be disregarded. Then again, it might simply be seen as communication and information; someone who made the image *was* here, and so perhaps was what is depicted. But it is also possible to think that the image *does* have a life, or that it is itself a manifestation of life, or that it may be brought to life. This range of possible reactions, in short, tells us nothing about the nature of images "as such," but rather presents possibilities, not only for individual reactions to images but for cultural choices and their institutionalization. Once a cultural choice has been made, and behavior with respect to images has been institutionalized, then one or another treatment of images becomes routine, part of shared culture.

Worshippers often report movement on the part of images, as if in immediate fulfillment of anticipation, but it is more important that images are used in social spaces, and in the context of ritual, important times and places in which the life implied by likeness and recognition may be invoked and addressed. It must be supposed, however, that the other possible reactions to images are always at hand. An image fully animated in ritual, for example, might still be seen by some as no more than the materials from which it is made, or as a display of a craftsman's skill.

If the "life" that images may seem to possess is specified and established in the social spaces, the ritual spaces, of which they are part, then iconoclasm must involve more than the destruction of images; their places must be destroyed together with them. Before modern times, images were centered; that is, they were closely identified with groups, their places, and thus with their origins, identity, and continuity. Images of any size were extraordinary, and their very existence was an indication and even a justification of the power to gather the materials and to command the skills necessary to have them made. And again, these images were an integral part of religious, political, and civic places. When Moses finally ascended Mount Sinai for the second tablets of the law, God told him that he and his people would be victorious over all who stood between them and the Promised Land. Not only would they defeat these peoples, they must eliminate the temptations posed by their gods. "But ye shall destroy their altars, break their images, and cut down their groves" (Exod. 34:13). That is, the sacred places in which images serve as substitutive presences should be destroyed, not just the images themselves. (It may be noted that from the standpoint of any center, all *other* deities worshipped may be seen to be false, much as, from the standpoint of monotheism, *all* images worshipped are false.)

The Golden Calf

The story of the Golden Calf is the archetype for all iconoclasm, told in the midst of the account of God's pronouncement of the law, including the Ten Commandments. Three months after their departure from Egypt, the Israelites camped in the wilderness near Mount Sinai, a sacred precinct entered on pain of death. Moses was called to the mountain, where God told him that his people had been chosen, and that they should prepare for his appearance. Moses was given the tablets of the law, in God's own hand, "that thou mayest teach them." After forty days and forty nights, however, the people gave up on Moses (32), "the man that brought us up out of the land of Egypt," and they asked Aaron to make them gods "which shall go before us." Aaron took their golden earrings, from which he cast and engraved a calf, and the people said, "These be thy gods, O Israel, which brought thee up out of the land of Egypt." Aaron, a willing participant throughout, built an altar before the calf. The next day was a feast, at which the people ate and drank and "rose up to play," dancing naked, "unto their shame to their enemies." God knew that the people had "corrupted themselves," and told Moses he would destroy them. Moses objected, God relented, and Moses started down the mountain with the tablets. When he saw the calf and the naked dancing, Moses himself became angry and broke the tablets. He pulverized the calf, sprinkled the powdered gold on water, and forced the people to drink it. Moses commanded that three thousand men be killed. He then asked God to forgive the people, God promised only to punish the guilty, and a plague followed. Moses ascended the mountain a final time, and there he was given the second tablets of the law.

In this story, the word is the law (or the law is the word), and the image—the Golden Calf—is contrary both to the word and to the law. God, Moses, and the Golden Calf are all referred to as having brought the people out of Egypt, but certainly the point of the story is that the Golden Calf is absolutely *not* the god that delivered them, and the people are grievously mistaken. Moses and God are harder to differentiate. Only Moses talks to God, reasons and bargains with God, and he is the sole bearer of the law, who is also able to punish in the name of the law.

The late (first century B.C.E.) Alexandrian Book of Wisdom, often called the Wisdom of Solomon, was included in the Septuagint and the Catholic Vulgate, but was rejected from the Jewish canon and is not included in Protestant Bibles. Its mixed philological history notwithstanding, Wisdom was often cited in the Western Middle Ages, and figured prominently, for example, in the iconography of the Virgin Mary. A hefty central section takes up the question of idolatry. There we read that "the worship of infamous idols is the reason and source and extremity of all evil. For they either go mad with enjoyment, or prophesy lies, or live lawlessly or lightly forswear themselves. For as their trust is in soulless idols, they expect no harm when they have sworn falsely. But . . . justice shall overtake them" (14:27–30).

If images are addressed, they are dumb and cannot reply. The mute image is antithetical to the spoken word, and, more than simply false, it sanctions "either childslaying sacrifices or clandestine mysteries, or frenzied carousals in unheard-of rites" (14:23). The worship of idols not only breaks the second commandment, it is absolutely *contrary to the law taken as a whole*; it "unleashes all evil, murder and adultery, theft and guile, corruption, faithlessness, turmoil, perjury, disturbance of good men, neglect of gratitude, besmirching of souls, unnatural lust, disorder in marriage, and shamelessness" (14:25–27).

"Solomon" also provides an account of the origins of images. In the beginning there were no images, and images were not created, otherwise God must have created them. The only image was man and woman, made in the image of God and his companions. Images made by human beings are trifling exercises of human freedom. The woodcarver makes useful implements, then whittles a likeness "of a man" or some "worthless beast" from the scraps. A potter turns from his work to mold a likeness from leftover clay. Moreover, images are insubstantial in themselves, and, like their makers, they are "vain," essentially empty. Like their makers, they deteriorate, and can be burned and broken to pieces.

The woodcarver not only made an image, he distinguished and enshrined it. "He has (13:14 ff.) daubed it with red and crimsoned its surface with red stain, and daubed over every blemish in it. He makes a fitting shrine for it and puts it in a wall, fastening it with a nail." This gives the image an appearance and space of its own, and thus gives it another status, so that "he prays about his goods or marriage or children, he is not ashamed to address the thing without a soul."

A modern, post-Freudian reader of this argument might ask why the (idle) hands of the carver or potter turned to making such images, and, as if the same question occurred to the author of the Book of Wisdom, this example leads to another explanation of origin, which is also another dimension of "vanity" (and an amplification of the ambivalence of recognition). As substitutes, images offer the false hope of a remedy for death. "For a father, afflicted with untimely mourning, made an image of the child so quickly taken from him, and now honored as a god what was formerly a dead man and handed down to his subjects mysteries and sacrifices. Then in time, the impious practice gained strength and was observed as law, and graven images were worshiped by princely decrees" (14:15–16). In this sequence, the possible, hoped-for life of the image became immortality and deification with compulsory worship, then reproduction and distribution. The image not only defeats death, it overcomes a second basic condition of human spatio-temporality, the impossibility of being in more than one place at a time. At the same time, the ubiquity of the prince's image is an extension of rule, and an assertion of the power to have such images made. For the pseudo-Solomon, of course, this is vanity built upon vanity.

The original, Byzantine iconoclastic dispute began in 726, when Emperor Leo III ordered the destruction of religious images, and it continued into the ninth century. (The much more thorough suppression of Buddhism in China followed closely in the ninth century, near the end of the once cosmopolitan Tang dynasty.) John of Damascus defended the use of images in worship with theological arguments that are repeated to the present day, and, although John opposed the emperor's policies, the example of the *imperial* image figured prominently in his arguments. His third treatise on the defense of images ends with the quotation of a text in which it is stated that the image of the emperor, whatever its material, is equally honored by everyone. "And one who slanders either kind is not acquitted as if he had only spoken against clay, or judged for having disparaged gold, but for having shown disrespect to the emperor and lord himself."[10] The identity of the emperor and his image could even be used to clarify the loftiest mystery, of them all, relations among the persons of the Trinity.[11] And we read that "the image of an absent Emperor fulfils the place of the Emperor, and rulers venerate it, not looking at the wooden plank, but at the figure of the Emperor, who is not seen to be present by nature, but is depicted by art."[12] It would not be surprising, then, if the iconoclastic controversy involved both the destruction of religious images by iconoclasts and the destruction of imperial images by iconophiles. Again we read that "he who abuses the image of the emperor suffers punishment as if he had dishonoured the Emperor himself, even though the image is nothing other than wood and paints mixed and blended with wax, in the same way he who dishonors the figure of someone offers an insult to the one whose figure it is."[13] The insult borne to the emperor's image entails insult to the emperor himself. That is, the image of the emperor is once again an extension of rule; it is equivalent to the presence of the emperor, with the full force of law. We may also consider the duplication of images on coins. "Whose image is this and whose inscription?" Jesus asks the Pharisees (Matt. 22:20). It is Caesar's, they reply. "Then repay to Caesar what belongs to Caesar and to God what belongs to God."

Displacements

As I have said, icons raise questions of real and social spatial presence, and so make demands of observers quite different from those made by narratives. Presence entails some form of *substitution*. As we have seen in several examples, icons are usually meant to make a presence accessible in a designated place and in response to specified behavior, and it is usually necessary to invoke that presence, to please or flatter it, by prayer, song, or offering. Innumerable examples might be given of practices in which icons are treated as if affording access to spiritual powers, whatever those powers might be thought to be, from the spirits of the dead, to tutelary deities, to saints, to the creator of the world. Since they are embedded in ritual, it should be noted, it is not surprising that those unfamiliar with the behavior appropriate to them treat images as nothing, or as potentially dangerous.

I wish to return to the question of why images are preserved. Icons have been essential to culturally central practices in many times and places, and they are a principle means for collective memory. (These same factors, however, might justify both preservation and destruction.) Rather than being destroyed, images have also been carried off by conquerors, either to augment the power of their own centers, or to show domination, or both. But images may also be valued and preserved as *art*. If we quickly trace the course of art in Western modernity (which, not incidentally, saw the rise of secular subject matter), we see that images were treated less and less like icons, that is, as mediations between individuals and the transcendent. Beauty, in the long Platonic tradition, signals transcendence, participation in the higher, and this might be seen as the possible life of an image at its most abstract. Religious icons may have been made to be beautiful precisely in order to articulate the sacred, but these qualities may also be separated from their images as "aesthetic." It is more important, however, that, as art itself was separated from representation altogether, images were preserved because of the "vision" of the artist who had made them. The idea of autonomous art took shape together with ideas of authenticity, of real contact with the hand and unique controlling spirit of the artist. The transcendent, in short, was displaced from the image to the artist, the genius, whose traces were to be seen in the image as "work," which became a "creation," a "Michelangelo" or a "Rembrandt." In these terms, it is hard to know if modern "iconoclasts" are attacking the Virgin Mary with a hammer, or the *Night Watch* with a knife, or if they are attacking "Michelangelo" and "Rembrandt." They could even be attacking "art" itself. Even derangement might be expected to take modern forms.

There is yet another displacement of transcendence, which answers the question of why, for example, the *malanggan* of New Guinea are bought by Western curators and collectors and taken away to museums, to the utter bafflement of their makers and original users.[14] These elaborately carved funerary images were meant to be discarded after the event for which they were made, not to stand indefinitely—forever, in principle—in a protected world of climate control. Such impermanent works from many parts of the world were first regarded as curios and marvels, then more thoroughly collected and installed as specimens in museums of natural history and ethnography. The next displacement, which gave these artifacts an entirely new status, can be understood by considering the amplification of the idea of style. Style was originally individual style (the basis for the first displacement), but in the nineteenth century it expanded to collective style, thus to become the expression not of an individual but of a culture. All art became the expression of spirit, a possibility of the human imagination, significant as form, and therefore absolutely worthy of preservation, regardless of the reasons for which it was made. "Form," which is pre-representational, became the lingua franca of all cultures. To be sure, there was resistance to the canonization of "primitive" art, but lack of appreciation for images from New Guinea, to keep to that example, simply set a new goal for education in the formal and visual.

Daedalus

If the idea of iconoclasm descends by various historical routes from the second commandment, the implicit or anticipated life of images developed in quite different ways in the early Greek tradition. Daedalus, the archetypal Western artist, was said to have made statues that move, implying that human art could in fact bring images to life. It may be noted that in this case the images in question are not sacred. Homer described automata hurrying in and out of the workshop of Hephaestus, but, although they serve the gods, they are not yet images of the gods themselves.[15] Aristotle observed that such mechanical workers might one day end the human institution of slavery.[16] But just as there were no illusionistic images of the kind Homer imagined on the shield of Achilles, there were also no such automata. On the contrary, Greek painting was far in the future when Homer sang, and the Daedalic phase of Greek sculpture is early archaic. The eventual blossoming of Greek painting and sculpture in the fifth and fourth centuries was accompanied by stories of works of art that, more than simply imitating appearances, were like automata in blurring the distinction between art and life. There are painted grapes to which birds fly to feed, their painter lamenting that, had he painted the boy carrying the grapes with the same skill, the birds would have been frightened away. The great Apelles painted horses at which real horses whinnied, and love brought Pygmalion's virginal statue to life.[17] The ideal of the actual attainment of life as a limit of art returned with full force in the Renaissance, soon to be reinforced by the rise of new technologies. In pursuing his radical doubt (and imagining his mechanistic universe), Descartes considered the possibility that the people in the square outside his window might be automata bundled up in winter coats.[18] His doubt was prophetic.

The displacement of animating spirit from image to artist (and viewer) corresponds to the adaptation of the traditional liberal and mechanical arts to the new purposes of "fine art" and "technology" in the eighteenth and early nineteenth centuries. Art was not so easily sundered, however, and the artificial imitation of life has proceeded apace, becoming more closely identified with "popular" than with "high" art. And, to get a little ahead of myself, electricity closed the gap between recognized images and their anticipated lives. Seen in these terms, the contemporary world is the fulfillment of an ancient Western dream. There are apparently living images everywhere, and the desire to make them even more lifelike drives both technological ingenuity and consumer appetites at a rapid pace.

The Daedalic strain in Greek culture is related to the mostly Platonic assumption that appearances are intrinsically deceptive and that the *imitation* of appearances is doubly so. Plato's distrust of sense may seem overdrawn, but it is compatible with the beginnings of Greek natural philosophy, which are also the beginnings of Western natural science, now of world natural science and technology. This epoch-making enterprise at its beginnings was based on the notion that things are not what they seem, in the sense that beneath appearances there is really water, or fire, or a combination of elements. In parallel, Socrates interviewed a contemporary painter and a sculptor, getting them to agree that the imitation of the visible movements of the body is also the imitation of the movements of the invisible soul, so that once again appearance indicates more than we see.[19] Both the physical and the psychological truth of things are so to speak concealed in appearances, but the implication—and this is continuous with the Daedalic enterprise—is that what is hidden by appearance is there to be understood, and, when understood, to be imitated in its own right. Defining the physical and psychological, and sorting out the relation between them, has been one of the millennial intellectual projects of the West.

Plato also wrote in response to the rise of the art of rhetoric. One need not embrace his solution—transcendental "ideas"—in order to share Plato's misgivings about rhetoric, or sophistry, which for him was the paradigmatic art of appearances and their manipulation. Plato compared rhetoric to painting. Both are imitative arts, and the sophist, like a painter, makes "spoken images of all things."[20] In order to understand this comparison it is necessary to recall that in Greek, the first meaning of *chroma*, which we translate as "color," was "skin" or "surface" (in Latin, *superficies*). It must also be recalled that a sense of the visual nature of language runs very deep in the Western classical tradition, in which there was no hard opposition of word and image. We need only think of *ut pictura poesis* (a poem is like a painting), often put together with the words of the poet Simonides, that a poem is a speaking painting, a painting a mute poem.[21] The goal of the rhetorical exercise of ekphrasis was to write with the vividness of the works of art being described.[22] The terminology of rhetoric itself, its "figures" (shapes) and "tropes" (turns; we prefer "straight talk") and "colors" (we distrust "purple prose") is fundamentally visual.

Aristotle wrote that the art of rhetoric had achieved its goal when the matter had been set before the eyes of the listener.[23] The "eyes" to which he refers must be inward eyes, by means of which we apprehend the images of imagination (*phantasia*, of which more soon), and "see" what we continually remember or imagine. The vividness of the actually present to sight (also *phantasia*) was, however, clearly regarded as a kind of ideal limit.

Rhetoric was psychagogic, that is, it led the mind, and the purpose of the art was to lead minds where the artful speaker wished them to go. Rhetoric was the art of persuasion, and "persuade" is closely related to *suavis*, sweet. This might seem to be a strange accident of linguistic history until we recall that "sweet talk" is still a synonym for seduction and beguilement. Rhetoric could also be demagogic; it could move the people, all of the people, this way and that, changing minds by an appeal to sense, imagination, and feeling, rather than convincing them by an appeal to reason.[24] For Plato, the stakes in this distinction could not have been higher. Rhetoric played an important part in the civic life of Greek city-states, and decisions of peace or war might be made on irrational rather than rational grounds. There must have been many eager to learn and use such an art.

Rhetoric painted *mental* images, *phantasmata,* and mental images played an essential role in the psychology of Aristotle, whose *De anima (On the Soul)* is the founding document of the Western science of psychology. Aristotle set out the principle that there is no thought without a *phantasm,* that is, a mental image.[25] The word *phantasm,* he tells us, is from *phos,* light. The act of vision is an abstraction—a drawing away—of form from matter, like the impression of a signet ring in wax. As I have just said, however, *phantasia* was also the power of the mind to recall these images, the basis for a kind of inner vision, and, confronted with the problem of how we remember what is not present without confusing it with what *is* present, Aristotle also turns to the analogy of painting. A picture painted on a panel may be called by the name of what it represents, and it is also an image. Similarly, we may call mental images (*phantasmata*) to mind and consider them as such, but we may also think of them as representations, like paintings, in which case they are aids to memory, or more emphatically, they make memory possible.[26] As we have seen, rhetoric stands on the same metaphoric foundations, and what if the speaker painted new paintings in the memory? Or repainted the memories already there?

There is a third essential function of *phantasia.* It is essential to animal movement (including human movement). For Aristotle, the soul was a life principle, which makes each thing grow and move according to its kind. Plants have a vegetative soul, which guides them through their life cycle, but they cannot move. Animals do move, and these movements are driven by appetite (*orexis*). Appetite is a fundamental life force, a kind of movement in itself. When appetite moves, the animal moves, but the animal cannot move without sense and *phantasia,* that is, without mental images. At the very least, an animal must be able to form some notion of what it seeks, and recognize what it seeks when it finds it. In human beings reason operates in a variety of ways, with and against appetite.[27] But motivation is always linked to *phantasia,* and to return once again to rhetoric, what if the speaker paints only the most simply and immediately desirable images, even desirable images of the harmful, before the mind's eye?

Video

Rhetoric developed alongside another powerful visual tool, the *science and imitation of sight itself.* Geometric optics began to take shape in the same place— Athens—and at about the same time that debate raged over the use and abuse of artful language, and the origins of optics are closely connected with the illusions of theater. We are all familiar with "point of view," which is a familiar echo of geometric optics in everyday language. The word *point* implies pure geometry, but optics always had a physiological dimension, and it was recognized that in some sense vision actually occurs on a surface of the eye, from which it is transmitted to the brain. The atomist Democritus is said to have thought that the tiny image reflected on the eye's outer surface was in fact the act of vision, an argument Aristotle rejected because it could not explain why nature, which does nothing in vain, made the eye so complicated. For Galen, writing in the second century C.E., the crucial surface was the crystalline humor, perhaps because vision could then be explained without an inversion of entering images (which was considered impossible on the face of it). Early modern anatomy showed the crystalline humor to be a lens, and around 1600 Johannes Kepler finally located the "seat of vision" (as it was called in the Middle Ages) in the retina (where the image is in fact inverted).[28]

Whether vision occurs at a point in the eye or on one of its surfaces, geometric optics was based on the observation and assumption that the light reaching the eye travels in straight lines, unless it is reflected or refracted. In antiquity, nothing was known about light itself, but light rays travel in straight lines, and this premise held through the centuries, and thus, from the beginning of geometric optics, any two-dimensional representation made according to its principles shows things not so much as they appear as in approximate proportion to the image on the surface of an eye at a certain location in light. Greek optics continued to develop in the Islamic world, and the optics of Ibn al-Haytham provided a theory of light according to which the relation of any body in light to the eye may be described. Ibn al-Haytham figures in the early history of the camera obscura, and, to race along, photography fixed the image in the camera obscura, cinema brought a rapid sequence of indexically vivid photographic images to apparent life. As I have mentioned, electricity introduced a crucial new element to the imitative project I am describing, a continuous animating flow analogous to conscious life itself. This finally brings us to television, a "live" medium, vision at a distance, at any distance.

As a further compression of the optical tradition I have briefly outlined, and as a transition to a new set of real spatial issues, we may consider the *TV Buddha* of Nam June Paik (fig. 6.1), made in 1974, after which it became the theme for several variations.[29] An under life-size wooden Buddha—an icon in present terms—is seated on a plain white surface. Judging from the gesture of his right hand, this is Sakyamuni, shown at the moment of enlightenment, when he appealed to the earth. He faces a television monitor. The monitor is bubble-shaped, very much of its time in design, rather like an eyeball, or like an astronaut's helmet (in which case the facing transparent surface would be a visor, through which an astronaut sees). Just behind and above the monitor, also on axis with the facing Buddha, is a television camera. The arrangement is so simple, or minimal, that the few elements change meaning when only slightly rearranged. One such variable is the distance of the Buddha figure from the camera and monitor. The gaze of the meditating Buddha is lowered, and if the image is close to the monitor, then he seems to face into it. If he is farther from it, then the "gaze" of the camera does not quite clear the top of the monitor, partly occluding his image on the screen.

The *visual* geometry of the installation is as clear as that of the crisp surface upon which its parts are set, and with which they are all aligned. The lens of the camera collects rays of light from the Buddha directly before it and immediately transmits their pattern to the monitor. The *TV Buddha* is sometimes compared to Narcissus, who fell in love with his own image reflected

FIGURE 6.1. Nam June Paik, *TV Buddha* (1974). Closed circuit video installation with bronze sculpture. Photo credit: Digital Image © The Museum of Modern Art/ Licensed by SCALA / Art Resource, N.Y.

on the planar surface of a quiet pool. There are, however, crucial differences between *TV Buddha* and Narcissus, adding up to the conclusion that this is not a Narcissus at all, that it is in fact a kind of anti-Narcissus. (Certainly a component of narcissism is anxiety about one's own image.) To be sure, there is a reflection involved. The convex surface of the television monitor must also collect the light rays before it, a "view" that includes the Buddha, but also a good many other things in the room, such as museum goers. The reflection is a shifting narrative, a floating world, in which, however, the icon is central. Any reflected image can only obey the inflexible geometry of light and surface, and, precisely because it *does* obey this geometry, the reflected image would be small and reversed. This is the way Narcissus would have seen himself in the pool, and this is the way we see ourselves in mirrors, however important that image may be to us (or however much anxiety may be attached to that image).

The visor is not only reflective, it is transparent, and its slight, fugitive image is reversed in the televised image "inside" the monitor, which faces the Buddha as another person, or as if the Buddha were seen by another person. It is essential throughout that the Buddha (and so of course his televised image) is meditating, his eyes downcast, because, if the two Buddhas "see" one another, the images must be internal. And it is just as important that the televised image shows him as he could not see himself in a mirror.

As long as the power does not fail, the image on the television monitor is a "live" image. The Buddha, however, is not doing anything. He and the image he faces have their own right and left. If the arrangement is so simple, and the geometry of light is so consistent with that simplicity, what is at issue? I would argue that it is point of view. We cannot see what the Buddha might "see" both because the image is inward and because he occupies the point from which we might see it. We can only imagine ourselves doing that. Even the slight reflection on the bubbled surface of the monitor can only be seen from the same point. We also cannot see the Buddha as the television camera "sees" him simply because the camera is where it is, and, if we stand beside the camera, we cannot see the image on the television screen. Is the Buddha we see from beside the camera and from behind the monitor the same as the one "seen" by the camera? Are we like the mechanical, electrical eye? Does the Buddha face himself, or another, or the ungainly, quasi-anthropomorphic apparatus that makes it possible for us to entertain both possibilities?

Not only are we unable to occupy the points of view established by this arrangement, we are made to "survey" this arrangement of artificial vision as if it were a table sculpture. We look over the whole thing, and what we are made to see is the arrangement of artificial vision itself. If *TV Buddha* is itself a meditation on point of view, our own "point of view" is established outside the geometry of facing and gaze the work states.

Quite reasonably, *TV Buddha* has been related to Buddhism. Such interpretation of course runs the risk of "speaking for others," but perhaps these suggestions can still be usefully, if provisionally, extended. In another version of *TV Buddha* the television monitor is set in a small mound of earth. A stupa is a large earthen burial mound, beneath the centers of the earliest of which the ashes of the Buddha were said to have been placed, beginning long, broad traditions of both architecture—stupas and pagodas—and religious observance. The idea that there are *two* Buddhas present—not simply the reflection of one—is consistent with the suggestion that *TV Buddha* recalls the conversation of the Sakyamuni and Prabhutaratna, the Buddha of the Future, a sign of the universal possibility of buddahood in all places and times. The idea of such universality might lead to another dimension, Vairocana, the Buddha of Universal Light, which, with a short leap of imagination, might take us to the medium of television. Self-contained as *TV Buddha* might be, with a few adjustments, which have become more possible with advancing technology, the image of the Buddha on the monitor could be broadcast throughout the world, and in principle all of the televisions in the world might show it, so that countless millions of people might face what the stone image of the Buddha faces, and in no case would this be a mirror image of the viewer. It would be as if all viewers had become the meditating Buddha.

Whether or not it reflects Nam June Paik's own thoughts, this interpretation may serve as a vivid illustration of the contrast between the earlier world of images represented by the stone Buddha and the world of images in the electronic age. For Nam June Paik, television—or "video", that is, "I see"—was so pervasive and fundamental a part of modern life that it was an inevitable and continuing theme of his art. As I have just characterized his *TV Buddha*, it is what might be called an ironically hopeful dream of the possibilities of television, and the uses to which the images broadcast by this new medium are actually put relate more obviously to the ancient distrust of rhetoric than to the prospect of general enlightenment. In general, electronic media have made images of entirely new kinds available in near-infinite density and profusion, and the real spaces of modern images, and of characteristically modern images, are utterly different from those that have defined iconoclasm. The world knew at once of the destruction of the Bamiyan Buddhas. To be sure, the old disputes have not gone away, but it is most important to adjust their terms to present reality. The effects of the incessant, circumambient chaos of images, all of them in imitation of vision, their immaterial flow like consciousness itself, are by no means understood.

·   ·   ·

There have been centuries of debate over the proper use of figured language, that is, of primary appeal to sense and imagination. It was generally agreed to be appropriate to the education of young children (nursery rhymes, for example), but not appropriate to theological discourse, except after the fact, that is, after more rigorous progress in thought has been made by higher means. There has also been perennial controversy about the appropriateness of rhetoric (and more generally of the use of images) in natural science. We obviously cannot be persuaded to come to scientific conclusions; rather, we must be convinced by observation, repeatable experiment, and mathematical proof. We may consider the important case of one of the pioneers of modern empirical science, Francis Bacon. Bacon argued that Plato had overstated the case against rhetoric, but he also drew a hard and fast distinction between "invention" in word and thought, and discovery governed by things. "I . . . dwelling purely and constantly among the facts of nature, withdraw my intellect from them no further than may suffice to let the images and rays of natural objects meet in a point, as they do in the sense of vision."[30] This empiricist credo exalts external vision and observation, but just as significantly, it characterizes the internal world as a world of *false* images—"idols"—that, by impeding direct observation, impedes the restoration of an Edenic state like that in which Adam named the world and was given dominion over it. Reality exists in the mind as a false reflection, whereas mind and world should coincide. The contents of the mind should be entirely replaced by the directly experienced. The human mind is a kind of attic of mental images, or better, of golden calves, all of which must be subjected to systematic doubt and criticism. Are these idols necessary? Have we in effect simply been persuaded of them?

For Bacon, the study of nature had the goal of the control of nature for human purposes, and the "idols" of the mind prevented this study, and therefore prevented the institution of a new world order. The characterization of the contents of the mind not just as images but as "idols," false images in urgent need of breaking, was truly and simply revolutionary. Bacon's "idols" are not only mistaken or conventional beliefs, they are personal and collective prejudices and still deeper, innate predispositions of the mind to systematize. The late eighteenth-century and then pervasively modern idea of ideology grew from this reduction. In these terms, "iconoclasm" assumes new meanings, familiar modern meanings.

In modern revolutions, political images are at obvious risk, and, as assertions of power, will be destroyed and replaced. From the materialist point of view of modern revolution, religious images may be regarded, like religion itself, as an essential part of the old order, not so much because religious institutions were allied with political institutions (which they have often been) but because (to keep to the terms of the Western iconoclastic tradition) there simply is no transcendental prototype to which such images refer. In the most powerful modern views of history, transcendence survives only in variants of eschatology, myths of providential progress and the "invisible hand" on one side, and dialectical socioeconomic process on the other. These latter-day quasi monotheisms are inclined to treat images implying other transcendence as false and reactionary. The Bolsheviks burned icons, and the Red Chinese scourged Buddhist Tibet. This is not to say that modern revolutionaries have dispensed with images. Jacques-Louis David invented images of "martyrs" of the French Revolution and designed new spectacles for new holidays in a new calendar. Lenin's tomb is a reliquary and a shrine, and huge images of Mao tse-Tung as the sun rejoin the oldest iconography of empire and divine kingship. In general, socialist realism has turned to the tested patterns of religious art as a means of indoctrination and instruction, rejecting the avowedly revolutionary art of aniconic modernism, in intention the beginning of the construction of a new visual and spatial order, as reactionary.

Before ending these reflections on the breaking of images, I will briefly consider the changes undergone by the terms of the discussion in the modern world. In intellectual circles, the hyperaristocratic world-historical iconoclasm of Nietzsche's "philosophizing with a hammer" in the "twilight of the idols," in anticipation of the "transvaluation of all values," has enjoyed broad currency. In more common parlance, it is now a term of praise to call someone an "iconoclast." This posture might be called Baconian, always with the potential to assume the significance of ideological critique in its later forms. Such "iconoclasm" usually has nothing to do with images, and such "iconoclasts" may simply think or act "outside the box," in opposition to prevailing assumptions, conventions, and attitudes. Iconoclasm may have a programmatic political dimension, but marching to a different drummer is also compatible with ideas of creativity, originality, and self-realization. If we accept (as we do) Rousseau's opposition of culture and individual nature, then the iconoclast, by questioning everything and assuming nothing, achieves a kind of liberation, and however indifferently targeted a blanket iconoclasm may be, it demands the ongoing justification of any status quo. Iconoclasm may thus stimulate desirable social and political changes, and, like the "breaking of taboos," contribute to innovation. The problem then becomes that of choosing the desirable.

The words *idol, icon,* and *image* have all assumed powerful cultural meanings that have very little to do with the old religious disputes, at the same time that they present problems of their own. Popular "idols" and "icons" may still be objects of worship, and their relics may still be collected, but this is a slight connection. "Images" themselves are now likely to be perceptions manipulated by public relations experts through mass media. Power is now centered in the control of media able to present images everywhere as if in the flow of consciousness itself.

HOW MANY WAYS

CAN YOU IDOLIZE A SONG?

ROSE ROSENGARD SUBOTNIK

In the beginning, in his essay "The Work of Art in the Age of Its Technological Reproducibility," written between 1935 and 1939, Walter Benjamin created the notion of "aura."[1] By Benjamin's account, unavoidably simplified here, certain objects that are venerated or beautiful project an effect of distance, which separates them from everyday life.[2] The power of this effect, which Benjamin calls "aura," comes from its physical uniqueness, which links it to both a specific history and an actual location.[3] This notion offered insight into how, in a secularized world, sculptures and paintings might have retained something of the power once associated with idols or other objects of cultic worship.[4] At one point, Benjamin links this secularized power to the fetishistic aspects of collecting.[5]

Unfortunately, such a notion was not so helpful in the case of music. One of Benjamin's few allusions to music here suggests that he thought of live performance as a musical entity that could project aura.[6] Benjamin doesn't push the analogy between live performance and a cultic object very far. And indeed it is difficult at first glance to see how a musical performance could become an object of worship: a service, after all, even if its name is *Parsifal*, is not quite the same thing as an idol. What would you worship? The music being performed? The person performing it? The act of performance? Although it turns out that since the German Romantic elevation of music to a quasi-sacred status all three possibilities have been tried, the relevance of Benjamin's notion of aura to music does not seem to be self-evident.

Fortunately, Benjamin's musings caught the attention of just the right man to redirect them toward music: Theodor W. Adorno. I will confine my attention here to one of at least three works by Adorno inspired by Benjamin's essay: Adorno's 1938 essay "On the Fetish-Character in Music and the Regression of Listening."[7] By couching his response to Benjamin in terms of fetishism, Adorno introduced the perfect imagery through which to reflect on the relation between music and idolatry.

Alongside a typology of musical fetishists, Adorno lists numerous parameters of music that have been objects of fetishism for the public.[8] Some are people (singers, instrumentalists, conductors, and for one moment even composers). Some are sources of sound (golden voices, brand-name instruments). Some involve composition (hits, famous themes). Some are phenomenological (moments of recognition and other kinds of moments, a sense of immediacy or culinary satisfaction, which Adorno links at one point to collecting) or even abstract (e.g., perfection).

What all of these elements have in common is a disconnectedness from any significant musical or psychological context. Sometimes Adorno lumps them all together as part of a "[totalitarian] star principle."[9] But most important for present purposes is the plethora of explicitly religious images through which he describes these various fetishes. Thus he writes, for example, of "sacramental moment[s]" in which music listeners think they are "having a good time"; of capitalized song titles (in sheet music) from which false values emerge "like an idol"; and of overplayed favorites that become "vulgarized . . . like the Sistine Madonna in the bedroom."[10]

Now it is true that Adorno's notion of "fetish" is explicitly economic and social rather than religious or psychological. He defines it in terms of Marx's concept of "commodity fetish" and integrates it into a Marxist critique—unorthodox to be sure—of society.[11] "The specific fetish character of music" in current society, he argues, lies in the replacement of use-value in music with exchange-value. By appropriating virtually all aspects of musical experience, the culture industry produces illusions of immediacy or usefulness that the public can fetishize as musical.[12]

Benjamin likewise aims in his essay at a social critique that is specifically, albeit naïvely, Marxist. But despite their common frame of reference, and their common purpose of trying to demystify art, Benjamin and Adorno come to opposite conclusions about the ramifications of aura. Benjamin welcomes a decline of art forms that project aura, such as painting, in favor of mechanically reproducible ones, such as film, that allow anyone to become an expert through an attitude of distracted attention (as opposed to concentration).[13] Adorno, by contrast, sees in Benjamin's "distraction" the loss of a capacity by listeners to engage with art without succumbing to their own economic and social exploitation. Thus Benjamin can present distraction as a superior alternative to "contemplative immersion," which he sees as a "breeding ground for asocial behavior," for which the "theological archetype" is an "awareness of being alone with one's God."[14] For Adorno, on the contrary, the "inattentiveness of . . . listeners" is inseparable from a situation in which, faced with "the theological caprices of commodities, . . . consumers become temple slaves."[15] Both essays have proven remarkably prescient with respect to the character and effects of postmodern technology. What neither offers is an alternative to Marxism as a framework in which to think about the relation of music to idolatry.

Wilfred Sheed

I am now going to discuss, very briefly, three books that do suggest some alternative frameworks. None exhausts the possibilities offered in its own generation; yet each seems representative of a group sufficiently large to merit attention. The first is a 2007 book by the novelist and critic Wilfrid Sheed, called *The House That George Built*.[16] On the surface, Sheed's idols are the composers of the American classic "standards," sometimes called the Great American Songbook. Sheed sees them as magical figures who pull great songs out of the thin air. From time to time, he muses about a few performers—notably Fred Astaire, Bing Crosby, and Frank Sinatra.[17] But mainly what Sheed enshrines are songs. Not only does he embed page after page with song titles; he also studs his text with excerpts from lyrics, which he doesn't always mark with quotes. Who did he think would recognize them in 2007?

From one perspective, Sheed exemplifies Adorno's fears about popular song fans and about Benjamin's hopes for such people. Adorno disdains a taste for popular songs as being culinary; Sheed admits to being a glutton for melody (not to mention a song addict) and further boasts that he and his friends could be called melodic connoisseurs and even snobs.[18] Adorno once dismissed songs as "a subordinate form" because they cannot get beyond their initial idea; Sheed relishes their brevity.[19] Adorno scorns the moment when the fan first recognizes a song; Sheed delights in it.[20] Adorno cannot get beyond the worthlessness of song lyrics; Sheed cheerfully advises the listener to "turn off the switch that tells you what words mean. Forget you know English altogether if you can."[21] Adorno disdains successions of "moments"; Sheed, with a collector's passion, loves simply "to recite the titles and start the tunes spinning in one's head, beginning anywhere on the list and ending up anywhere else."[22] Indeed, Adorno pities the would-be individualist who "whistles [his songs] at the world."[23] Sheed laments the passing of the day when men of all classes whistled on their way to work and in public toilet stalls.[24] He even puts an entry on "whistling" in his index to his book.

Furthermore, where Benjamin can imagine value in developing a group response to painting, Adorno dismisses the American notion of *"having a good time,"* which he takes to mean "being present at the enjoyment of others." To Adorno, "good times" like this are as phony as "the auto religion [that] makes all men brothers in the sacramental moment [when] the words [are uttered], 'That is a Rolls Royce.'"[25] Although Sheed starts his book with the observation that "the proper medium for studying the American song . . . is the sing-along and . . . the bull session," he rarely describes group listening.[26] Yet the assumption of a shared intensity is crucial to his passion for popular song. In 1947, at the age of sixteen, in New York, Sheed encountered the Irving Berlin songs in the film *Top Hat.* At that moment in the movie theater, he tells us, "what Norman Mailer has called the little capillaries of bonhomie began to go off everywhere like firecrackers." From then on, it appears that he thought of America as his imagined song community. That same year, in a brief exchange with Hoagy Carmichael at the London Stage Door Canteen, he confirmed his belief that songs represented America at its best.[27] Now Adorno had good reason to fear unreflective group loyalties. What makes Sheed's patriotism interesting is the fact that he wasn't originally American. He was an Englishman who had had two extended stays in the United States before settling there permanently in his late twenties. For Sheed, American popular song connoted the possibility of a community that one could imagine not just from the inside but from the outside as well.

A similar dynamic emerges from what Adorno might dismiss as an inclination on Sheed's part to identify with what he fetishized.[28] Near the start of his book, Sheed describes an epiphany when he realizes that in writing a book about songs he has been writing a memoir.[29] Proust contended, at age thirty-four, that when we recall our childhood pleasure in reading what pleases us is not the memory of what we read but the memory of ourselves reading.[30] For

Sheed, writing in his late seventies, this view is half right. "Songs are circumstantial," Sheed writes, "in ways that headlines can never be."[31] There are so many places, he asserts, that he would not recall "without the illumination of melody, which still turns on like a bedside reading lamp when [he] feel[s] like remembering something."[32] News accounts of recent brain research suggest that we forget where we learned most of what we know; we suffer from "source amnesia."[33] This is not so for Sheed and his songs.

And yet, Sheed tells us incomparably less about his youthful listening self than he does about the songs he loved. Unlike the books of Proust's childhood, the songs Sheed remembers mean no less to him now than they did sixty years ago. Rather than folding those songs into some sort of autobiography, he prefers to melt himself into those songs. Listeners, he says, took in such songs through a kind of automatic memorization—a process that would have confirmed for Adorno the listener's servitude but bears a certain similarity to Benjamin's distraction.

Sheed collected. Looking into his own mind, he finds that "songs had lodged themselves in every hole and corner of [his] memory."[34] This image recalls the complaint of the critic Joseph Bottum, in the year 2000, that with the loss of a common culture Americans' heads have become "silted up" with "something shared" that "doesn't mean anything": "the lyrics of American popular song."[35] But consider also the loss of an internalized culture that Socrates feared as writing replaced memorization.[36] The Russian poet Osip Mandelstam carried a copy of Dante's *Divine Comedy* wherever he went in the 1930s, so he would have it on him if arrested. He carried Dante twice into prison.[37] What if the second time his guards confiscated the book? Ten years later a young German Jewish woman memorized every poem and joke that she could in order to have "something [that] no one could take away if [she] was ever put into a concentration camp."[38] Sheed's repository of memories served a happier outcome. "Writing this book," he tells us, "I must have sung a couple of hundred songs to myself. . . . I hope it's contagious."[39]

Yet "the standards," he goes on to say, "were not just about [his] private history, but about the whole country, concerning which they provide maybe the most trustworthy record we have. . . . When you hear a George Gershwin tune," avers Sheed, who was born in 1930, "you are hearing not only the 1920s, exactly as they were, but the atmospheric difference between . . . say . . . 1924 . . . and 1926."[40] Likewise Irving Berlin's World War II songs convey "exactly the sounds [Sheed] remembers from [*his*] streets."[41] Thus, even as these songs fuse with his sense of who he is, the significance Sheed ascribes to them turns him outward, toward the world.

As does his very choice of songs. Most are no doubt love songs; and Sheed draws on song aficionado Jonathan Schwartz to suggest that "almost all great love songs are written either for nineteen-year-olds or for . . . people who re-member nineteen all too well and only wish they could do it over again."[42] Sheed turned nineteen at the end of 1949. Most of the standards, he notes, were written from 1925–50, though the "official" end of the genre did not come until the late 1960s;[43] his book mentions songs from as late as 1977, when Sheed was approaching fifty.[44] Even by current standards of perpetual immaturity, that would constitute an awfully long youth.

Actually, the period that mesmerizes Sheed starts before his youth, indeed, before his birth, as far back as the second decade of the twentieth century. When he mentions the "speakeasy . . . tingle" that once attached to songs, he is speaking of the Prohibition Era, which ended when he was three years old.[45] The songs he mentions from the 1930s are not the kinds of childhood songs that Adorno (or D. H. Lawrence in his poem "The Piano") associates with re-gression to infantilism.[46] In all these cases the songs that Sheed idolizes come not from his own youth but from the youth of his parents (about whom he has written a well-regarded memoir).[47] Some were favorites of his grandmother;[48] some weren't even about youth. "All Alone (by the Telephone)," says Sheed, was "written in [Irving Berlin's] mother's last years," and "remains the last word on old age and loneliness."[49] By his own description, Sheed belongs to "a sturdy little betwixt-and-between generation [that] . . . fell in love with the standards just as they slowed to a trickle, and then stopped altogether."[50]

At the end of World War II, he goes on, "just like that, the magical coin-cidence of quality and popularity was over."[51] Sheed continued to learn new songs from film, records, and radio. But he was departing from the tastes of his peers when he and his friends came upon a copy of the *Rodgers and Hart Song Book* and played through it at the piano, an occasion they found so mo-mentous that some fifty years later they celebrated it with a party.[52] The *Song Book* was published in 1951, but its songs dated from 1925–42. They belonged to the young years of Sheed's parents—as did the piano playing. Increasingly, thereafter, Sheed engaged in what the composer Cy Coleman would one day call "selective deafness":[53] he tuned out all the songs but his own kind.

As a member of the so-called "Silent Generation," Sheed probably repre-sents the last era of young Westerners, or at least Americans, who felt com-

fortable identifying unselfconsciously with the songs of their parents. And the
values that emerge in his account of these songs point toward a certain lack of
self-absorption that would have served young people well during the Depres-
sion and World War II—for example, an admiration for no-nonsense action
coupled with self-restraint. "In the 1940s," he writes, "the worst thing that you
could be was a hotshot or a big deal."[54] Heroism, for Sheed, was personified
by the decision of the song composer Jimmy Van Heusen not to let the public
know, between 1942 and 1944, that he was test-flying military airplanes.[55] And
Sheed thought that Bing Crosby emerged from World War II as America's "ultimate entertainer" largely because, as song-guru Alec Wilder put it, Crosby
seemed like "the first guy you would send for if your theater was on fire and
you wanted everyone to keep calm."[56]

As a listener geared to radio intimacy, Sheed did not seem to need the
vividness of live performance or any associated aura. Sheed could envision an
entertainer as someone who "whispers a private message [into a microphone]
and a million people swear it's for them."[57] He resisted any noise that might
"break the spell" of music on the car radio "by either waking the driver or
putting him all the way to sleep."[58] The singer's restraint reinforced Sheed's
primary allegiance to the song and thereby his inclination to sanctify his
songs as others once sanctified Romantic *Lieder*: by canonizing them.

At bottom Sheed came to the song as an entity he admired from without,
for qualities that he imagined as inhering within it, qualities that seem human.
His favorite adjective for praising a song is an abstract one, *gorgeous*; but even
when he calls a tune "haunting," or says it "whines classily," he is speaking not
of the listener or the performer but of the tune. "The emotion in the sobbing
[of a Johnny Mercer lyric] is genuine," says Sheed, "if you listen to the subtext,
which is the same in all Mercer's songs. 'Isn't this a goddamn beautiful tune?'
is what they're saying so passionately. 'Can you hear what I hear? Please love it
as much as I do.'"[59] This is also the subtext of Sheed's entire book.

Benjamin claimed that "the ritualistic basis [of art], however mediated it
may be, is still recognizable as secularized ritual in even the most profane
forms of the cult of beauty."[60] The kind of outer-directed aesthetic veneration
that Sheed brings to bear on the songs he describes has something like the
force of a secular religion. An Irving Berlin song, he grants, may sound today
like "housebroken jazz."[61] But his is no plea for a so-called "Mondegreen"—for
the acceptance of some cherished childhood mistake about a song. Rather,
Sheed goes on to convey with conviction the force that such songs had even

before his birth. For "fresh young geniuses" of the postwar 1920s, he tells us, such songs constituted "the light at the end of Gatsby's dock"—a kind of aesthetic and possibly even moral ideal glowing somewhere in the dark distance.[62] And even after the genre fell out of favor, decades later, Sheed could celebrate the appearance of occasional new songs that he deemed "celestial."[63] Indeed, for Sheed, the Great American Songbook seems to function as a song-studded firmament that preserves the aesthetic, cultural, and behavioral values that he idealizes.

Rogan Taylor

The second book I wish to discuss is anything but secular in its tone or imagery. This is *The Death and Resurrection Show: From Shaman to Superstar*, a lavish book, written by Rogan Taylor and published in London in 1985.[64] Taylor, born in 1945, is today a football scholar at the University of Liverpool. He once did a doctorate on primitive religion, at Lancaster University.

Like Sheed, Taylor starts his story before his birth. About twenty-five thousand years before. But whereas Sheed's chosen block of time seems stable, except for the fall from grace of his songs, Taylor's calls to mind Wagner's account of history, in which all roads culminate in Wagner himself. Taylor does not share Wagner's megalomania. But he does convey the sense that the history of shamanism is of interest chiefly because it culminates in a handful of 1960s pop stars. The clues are many. The most telling, perhaps, is his description, as he nears his peroration, of the 1960s as a "time-out-of-time"—surely the view of an early Baby Boomer.[65]

Taylor's musical argument is far more compressed than is Sheed's. He does not zero in on music until his penultimate chapter, which includes discussions of Louis Armstrong and Bessie Smith. His general thesis—that the concomitant decline of religion and rise of science produced an urgent need for the shamanistic effects of theater—while thought-provoking, seems sweeping and impossible to prove. But this is not important. The purpose of his first fourteen chapters, as I read his book, is to provide the imagery needed for understanding the one chapter that really matters, chapter 15, the one on musical stars of the 1950s and 1960s.

Taylor's vision centers on the figure of the shaman. The shaman, as Taylor describes him, is a magical figure who transports his audience to other worlds, especially hell, and eventually heals them.[66] In the process of moving between worlds, the shaman typically undergoes transformations of identity, often through drugs, suffers death and dismemberment, and is eventually restored to wholeness and health—not just of the body but above all of the soul. Taylor sometimes calls this process "a healing séance," where "everybody is sick" and *everybody gets better.*[67] Songs, especially of two types called "lyric" and "epic," play a powerful role though they do not exactly belong to the shaman; if anything, the shaman belongs to them.[68] Typically they somehow come into the shaman from outside—from a guardian spirit or another world.[69] The shaman himself, according to Taylor, is ill with a sickness he can never fully banish; thus he is compelled to perform again and again to heal not just his audience but himself.[70] At bottom the shaman is inseparable in his journeys from his audience.

Taylor seems driven by concerns that he could well have derived from Adorno although Adorno would have recoiled at Taylor's solution, which amounts to an antirationalist call for a massive remystification of society.[71] Taylor's argument is rooted in the erupting Western youth culture of the 1950s, which Taylor sees as a response to manipulation by the culture industry on the one hand and the terror of the bomb on the other. Young people of that decade, he argues, desperately sought the reinfusion of something that could be called a "soul" into their society. Certain musical stars of the 1950s advanced this search by introducing elements of shamanistic power into their performances. And the quest triumphed in the 1960s when a handful of superstars presented themselves as full-fledged shamans, and were received as embodiments of soul on a level that was openly acknowledged as religious.

Among both groups of stars, Taylor identifies attractions that fit readily into Adorno's list of fetishes. The voice figured prominently in the 1950s. Little Richard, says Taylor, gave an "almost unaccountable impression of having *more* voice than he need[ed]"; "when he shouts," Taylor adds, "the spirits move."[72] In the 1960s "a guitar became the vehicle for [Jimi Hendrix's] ecstasy, in exactly the same way," writes Taylor, "that the shaman's drum operates as a transporter of the spirit of the shaman . . . [into] Hell."[73]

Songs in themselves have only a modest importance for Taylor. Just as Sheed displays a passing disdain for the rock music that supplants his repertory, Taylor reduces Sheed's songs to vehicles for rhyming "moon" with "June."[74] In fact, he shows a sustained interest in specific songs only in the 1960s, when stars begin to double as songwriters and performers, and songs can be viewed as a function of performance—shamanistic performance.

Already in the 1950s, writes Taylor, Little Richard combined an "androgy-nous [stage presentation]" with "macho vocal power" to offer the spectacle of "a frenzied, near-lunatic stage presence. . . . Belt[ing] out . . . songs like a man pos-sessed," Little Richard came across as "a veritable wild man . . . a jigging, jiving, howling witchdoctor of rock'n'roll."[75] Starting in the 1960s, Jimi Hendrix and then David Bowie expanded on this act.

David Bowie's shows featured "*the transformation of the hero into a fan-tastic spirit-form,*" featuring an "explosion of [sexually indeterminate] person-alities," and feats of flight into other worlds.[76] Jimi Hendrix took his listeners "into psychic hinterlands they hardly knew existed. [Hendrix] led his séance like a black wizard, and his shows often included a fiery sacrifice."[77] Clearly we've come a long way from Bing Crosby calming the audience when a theater catches on fire.

The function of the song in a shamanistic performance was to deliver "hot-from-the press accounts of ecstatic experience."[78] But whereas 1950s songs, which "celebrated the shared experience of adolescence," appealed to a group, songs of the 1960s tried to "carry the listener down with the singer into an otherwise pri-vate and highly individualized world."[79] In stressing this fusion between singer and the individual listener, Taylor recalls two themes from Benjamin's essay. On the one hand, as "modern attempts to *democratize* out-of-the body experiences and dream states," 1960s songs expanded the possibility of expertise to all listen-ers.[80] And on the other hand, technologies of mechanical reproduction allowed an unprecedented individualizing of the listener's experience. Paradoxically, although the 1960s song experience, as Taylor describes it, drew its power from the performer, the listener no longer had "to see the superstars to get the full ef-fect."[81] He or she could simply "remain at home, eyes closed and mind opened, with head pressed close to the speaker of the record player," and be transported away from "anywhere specific" to "a no-man's land" that was "located in the mysterious realm somewhere between performer and audience."[82]

Taylor stresses the increasing sophistication of 1960s lyrics as essential to the new circumstances. But what clearly differentiated the 1960s listener from Wilfrid Sheed zoning out to his car radio was drugs. By Taylor's own account, the most fundamental bond between singer and listener in this period was not the performing of music but the taking of drugs.[83] In a situation where everyone is taking hallucinogens, "*anyone,*" writes Taylor, in Benjaminian fashion, "is likely to become a performer if they find themselves possessed of the spirit(s) of the occasion."[84] Someone listening to a record at home through a haze of drugs very well might not notice the loss of any aura associated with live performance. For Benjamin, who first tried hashish at the age of thirty-five, such a possibility might have been intriguing, though it would not have been attainable.

Both Sheed and Taylor practice selective deafness: again, the "rock'n'roll" that Sheed avoids is the very music Taylor venerates. Both pull song into a kind of worship by way of memory. But unlike Sheed's outer-directed credo, Taylor's way of fetishizing music seems self-referential, pointing back not to himself personally (he tells us nothing autobiographical whatsoever) but to the youthful experience of his own generation. Although one can well imagine why this experience of performers and performances, which Taylor sometimes calls "the magical puberty show," seemed sacred to its celebrants, it is far less easy than Sheed's tune-bank to store in one's head, retrieve, and share. By 1985, as memories lost their edge and technologies aged, a devotee with scholarly skills might well have wanted to enshrine this generational experience in a book as elegantly produced as the Taj Mahal.

If Sheed's cult of song glorified a spirit of "can-do," "whine with class," and sometimes even "get-happy-damn-you," Taylor's exuded narcissism.[85] The quality is unmistakable in Taylor's account of how one of his two shamans-in-chief, Bob Dylan, broke out of the 1950s mold by writing a drug-inspired song about a "*shaman-figure*," "Mr. Tambourine Man," that is often taken to be "the eulogy of a drug pusher," and that more generally embodied a 1960s turn toward "intense introversion."[86] Yet Taylor's cult also offered a nonmaterialist, spiritual idealism that was utterly foreign to Sheed's, most notably in Taylor's candidate for "the quintessential song of the shaman," a 1971 song by his other shaman-in-chief, John Lennon: "Imagine."[87]

Carl Wilson

The last book I will discuss, by the Canadian critic Carl Wilson, *Let's Talk About Love: A Journey to the End of Taste*, appeared in 2007 (like Sheed's), when Wilson was close to forty (like Taylor).[88] Of the three books, it is the shortest and by far the most autobiographical. Yet the cult of song worship that Wilson describes, which is associated with the French-Canadian singer Céline Dion, is explicitly not Wilson's own.

The principal idol of this cult is Dion's voice, which is of a kind that Adorno deplored quite specifically as a fetish. "Today," Adorno wrote, "the material [of the voice] as such, destitute of any function, is celebrated. . . . To legitimate the fame of its owner, a voice need only be especially voluminous or especially high."[89] Wilson describes Dion's appeal in very similar terms. "Whether [people] like [Céline] or not, they'll acknowledge her vocal ability, but the word you hear most often is 'pipes'—as if she were a conveyance system, a set of tubes to pump music through, more a feat of engineering than a person."[90] The effect is impersonal. It is also felt as larger than life, even superhuman or "saintly," to the point where it seems to be "somehow *real* magic, a kind of vocal sublime."[91]

Of course, Dion's voice projects itself by way of songs, primarily songs with sentimental lyrics. The most famous is the Oscar-winning theme song from the 1997 film *Titanic*, "My Heart Will Go On." It is one kind of "power ballad," a genre that Wilson traces to a 1970s recovery by arena-rock of schmaltz after the latter's ten-year exile from mainstream popular music. The power ballad has been prominent in contexts as disparate as heavy metal and musical theater. It also plays a large role in the theatrical form that for Wilson constitutes Dion's roots, the talent show. Wilson invokes *American Idol* as his archetype.[92]

Wilson wrote this book in hopes of discovering why "millions upon millions of other people adore" a musical experience that he himself finds repellent.[93] His answer points to class differences that Adorno could readily absorb into his theory of exchange- and use-value. Wilson in a sense turns Adorno's theory on its head, attributing authenticity to the masses of ordinary people rather than to a handful of critical thinkers. Drawing on Pierre Bourdieu, among several sociologists, Wilson notes a sharp difference in the way that the less privileged and the more privileged classes—my demographic terms here are not scientific—describe what they value in music. Poorer people's tastes are "pragmatic": they want music to be "entertaining, useful and accessible."[94] The "middle classes and up," by contrast, choose music that will "[reflect] their values and personalities" or "add to their cultural capital"—if possible through the discovery of works that are not yet widely known. In other words, Wilson quips, poorer folks want music that "taste[s] good," whereas richer folks want music "in good taste."[95] Taking Adorno's culinary image to an extreme, educated people tend to fancy themselves not as snobs but as musical "omnivores."[96] The quest to be cutting-edge may encourage this stance: at some point, the sheer exhaustion of "trying to know who the next-big-thing is" could find some relief in what Wilson calls an "anything-goes eclecticism." People with good taste become people who like just about every kind of music—as long as they can exclude something as beneath them.[97] Enter Céline Dion.

Adorno not only discounted as social delusion listeners' reports of pragmatic satisfaction with music itself; he doubted altogether that people could give trustworthy responses to questions about their tastes.[98] Wilson proposes to take such responses seriously. He has no objective touchstone for testing their validity. What he can offer is the credibility of acting against his own self-interest, specifically, of asking with an open mind why he looks down on what ordinary people seem to like about music—for example, sentimentality and loudness. Wilson contends that members of his demographic—Generation X—actually apply a double standard to such qualities.

In art that is pretty, Wilson says in effect, sentimentality has been spurned among the educated "for a century or more [as] the cardinal aesthetic sin," in a word "kitsch," appropriate only for "the art of religious dupes, conservative apologists and corporate stooges."[99] But "you could say," Wilson counters, that "punk rock is anger's schmaltz."[100] Why, he asks, is "excess in the name of rage and resentment [morally more laudable] than immoderation in thrall to love and connection"?[101] The standard academic answer, that one serves "quiescent" goals and the other "subversive" ones, he rejects as suspect because it flatters the vanity of academics and their fantasies of "revolutionary play-acting."[102] He would agree with Richard Taruskin's recent argument that idealizing transgressiveness encourages an old "aristocratic disdain for ordinary people," while in the process producing its own "misdirected sentimentality."[103]

Likewise for loudness. "To supposedly more refined, educated ears," Wilson asserts, "being a 'showoff' is the height of tackiness."[104] So when critics describe performers as "bulldoz[ing]," why are they praising the Ramones, a punk group, but condemning Céline Dion?[105] Could it be because they perceive Dion's voice as "nouveau riche"?[106] "Mastering one's emotions," asserts Wilson, is "a time-honored upper-class imperative."[107] (Here, of course, he is treading on Sheed's values.) "There's a [social] reason," Wilson concludes, that "cool is called 'cool.'"[108] Could it be the same reason that "oversinging" such as Dion's is considered "uncool"?[109]

Once ensconced in this self-critical mode, Wilson speaks out for the Céline Dion cult on a more general level as well. Rather than discrediting the fervor of her fans on the Adornian grounds that it is not actually directed at music, Wilson credits her fans for responding to music as a function of life. In this way, he claims, they keep faith with "one of the laws of motion" that, although "minor," "make the world turn": "People need sentimental songs to marry, mourn and break up to, and this place they hold matters more than anything intrinsic to the songs themselves."[110]

But what Wilson does most memorably is mount a defense of what Adorno might call the culture of affirmation. Either unable or unwilling to attempt a logical refutation of the negative culture Adorno prizes, Wilson argues for affirmative culture mainly through a series of rhetorical questions—questions, often laced with obscenity, that have considerable power. After some time with a Dion believer, for example, he asks himself, "What was the point again of all that nasty, life-negating crap I like?"[111] And: "Is [Dion's] soundtrack-to-your-life approach [to music] more 'self-indulgent' than James Joyce's multilingual word games?"[112] And my personal favorite: "What [should we make] of the fact that it is hard to imagine a male performer today having a hit by singing about his mother, at one time a regular occurrence in popular song? Is that topic inherently less artful than singing about fucking?"[113]

Wilson presents a sympathetic case for the cults surrounding Céline Dion and *American Idol*. In the process he sheds even more illumination on the status of song worship within his own Generation X, and a similar demographic right behind it. Wilson can never fully put himself in the camp of Dion believers.[114] His demographic is as militantly opposed to that sort of fetishizing as Adorno was. If the demystification that both Benjamin and Adorno sought in art was incompatible with Sheed's brand of secularism, and antithetical to Taylor's shamanism, it has come fully into its own in Wilson's world. But this doesn't mean that young educated people today lack a capacity for song worship. On the contrary, Wilson implies that the vehement rejection of Céline Dion's music may come from a thwarting of the religious impulse that the Romantics had once hoped to salvage through art. We "antireligionists," writes Wilson, "who have turned for transcendent experience to art . . . react to what our reflexes tell us is bad art as if it were a kind of blasphemy."[115]

Music has never been so ubiquitous as in the past decade (although Adorno complained as early as the 1960s about its excessive presence).[116] Back in 2000, Joseph Bottum predicted that there were babies being born who might "never know an unorchestrated moment in their lives."[117] Today, people armed with an iPod and earphones—typically young people—can get through an entire trans-Atlantic flight without glancing at a printed page. In 2007, an American student told a Boston reporter that "right now I mainly listen to music on my cell phone, because my iPod died. The quality isn't that bad. Well, it is that bad. But I'm willing to make the trade. I need to have music with me at all times."[118] While omnivorously seeking the cutting edge, the authentic, all the qualities that would seem to immunize them from musical fetishism, many of Wilson's philosophical comrades and descendents are carrying their electronics with them everywhere, as if they were household gods.

Members of my generation (the Silent Generation) may see the infatuation with exploding technological possibilities as a sign that musical fetishism today, outside the domains of Céline Dion, has replaced songs with technology as its object of worship. More likely what is happening is that the whole concept of the song is transforming itself through an interaction with technology. There has surely, after all, never been a more widespread interest in writing songs, especially to satisfy an infinite variety of autobiographical urges. But perhaps there has also never been a situation in which people, for all their claims to be omnivores, did more "selective listening," that is, walked around within a greater number of parallel universes of song. What then will become of shared musical memory?

▪ ▪ ▪

There is a reason that shared memory allows song to resonate with an almost religious significance for people—a reason that Adorno's Marxist account does not accommodate. David Lowenthal has noted that "the impulse to preserve is partly a reaction against the increasing evanescence of things and the speed with which we pass them by. In the face of massive change we cling to the remaining familiar vestiges."[119] Memories stored up in one's head and shared with others provide a bulwark against the inevitable erosion of all that we hold dear in life.[120] That bulwark can be especially strong when our memories encompass our parents and can be passed on to our children. In an age that no longer provides religious guarantees of permanence in the cosmos, bulwarks of this kind have a compelling existential value.

Shared memories are what allowed Sheed and Taylor to construct a kind of religion around song—and I want to stress that Sheed, Taylor, and Wilson constitute but three of many possible such enterprises. In Sheed's case, it was the shared memory of songs. In Taylor's case, it was the memory of shared musical experiences. Will shared musical memory play a comparable role for the younger generations today? I hope so, though it will certainly be in ways that I cannot imagine. Today you can hire a service that "selects and sequences the perfect songs" to give, say, to an exlover.[121] This service conjures up the possibility that when it comes to songs, the new generations are already outsourcing the kinds of memories that earlier generations accumulated automatically, or at least took for granted.

But people of my generation should not overesteem our past modes of song worship. In the end, songs cannot stave off our essential aloneness. No one has brought home more starkly the existential limitations of songs than the Irish columnist and author Nuala O'Faolain, whose death in 2008 at sixty-eight inspired an editorial tribute in the *New York Times*. After she learned that she had terminal cancer, O'Faolain "confessed that she felt shattered by the pointlessness of it all. . . . Beauty, she said, meant nothing; she didn't believe in the afterlife [nor could she find any consolation in the mention of God]. . . . 'I know loads and loads of songs,' she said, 'and what's the point of it all? So much has happened, and it seems such a waste of creation, that with each death all that knowledge dies.'"[122]

What songs she had in mind, I cannot say. Nuala O'Faolain was born in March 1940. Her tastes, I'm sure, were a lot less square than mine. Still, she ended up sharing an adopted country with Wilfrid Sheed. It would be nice to think that in 1951, when she was ten or eleven, she had a moment of fun hearing "the whole laid-back essence" of her future country that Sheed claims "can still be found in the multiple cool" of the song "In the Cool, Cool, Cool of the Evening"—the "epic" song that Sheed avows " clinched . . . once and for all" for Carmichael (and Mercer) the "mythical title" of "the great American songwriter."[123]

ICONOCLASM AND THE SUBLIME

Two Implicit Religious Discourses in Art History

JAMES ELKINS

This essay is partial, and tentative. It is assembled from other projects that are themselves works in progress, all united by my sense that some of the interpretive discourses in contemporary art history are implicitly religious, and that their implicit nature matters. I am aiming at a general account of some current art historical writing: I want to say it is articulated as an echo, an analogy, or a metaphor of interests and concepts whose provenance is the history of Christian theology. Some of art history, in this way of thinking, is a shadow discourse. It wants to say things about transcendence, the sacred, the spiritual, and the religious, but in an academic setting—and for many reasons that continue to confuse and fascinate me, it feels it cannot.

This is not investigative journalism in search of a sensational hidden truth. I do partly intend to practice the sort of textual criticism that demonstrates unnoticed features of texts, but not because I think that it makes sense to begin reading *The Art Bulletin* as covert theology. It seems a long time ago that I argued, in *Our Beautiful, Dry, and Distant Texts: Art History as Writing*, that accounts of scholarly writing that attempt to reveal hidden subtexts can end up being less interesting than the texts they excavate.[1] So my point is more that I find myself reading art historical accounts as muffled reports of meditations—many unarticulated, and perhaps uncognized as such—on religious questions, and I wonder what would happen if those apparently historical texts, which have no open allegiances to religion or belief, were temporarily reassigned to their original sources in religious and theological writing. Some texts in art history are about religious art, and those texts can often have more or less covert interests that can sometimes be read between the lines. I am not so much interested in that phenomenon as I am in two slightly but importantly different phenomena: first, art historical writing that pursues apparently nonreligious themes but puts those themes to religious uses; and second, art historical writing that pursues religious themes but applies them to nonreligious works. An example of the first is the discourse of the postmodern sublime; an example of the second is the discourse around iconoclasm.

Here are the principal concepts and discourses in art history that I think occur in historical and theoretical writing on art, where they function as versions of concepts and discourses that belong to religion:

1. The discourse of the sublime, as it has been received from poststructural scholarship by Thomas Weiskel, Neil Hertz, Jean-François Lyotard, and others.

2. The concept of art history as a melancholy discipline, in part as it has been recently formulated by Michael Ann Holly, but also as it is implicit in Walter Benjamin's writing.[2]

3. The concept of the aura, again partly from Benjamin, but more pervasively from the many interventions and versions of Benjamin's essay, which are in a kind of endless circulation in the art world.

4. The concepts of iconophilia, iconoclasm, idolatry, and iconophobia, and the idea that Western painting can be approached as a question of the ongoing history of iconoclasm.

5. The concepts of the unrepresentable, unpicturable, and inconceivable, and in general "ultra-avant-garde" attempts to destroy all images, following on modernism's turn away from naturalistic representation.[3]

6. Talk of materiality, matter, medium, and substance, principally from the revival of Georges Bataille in art history in the 1980s and 1990s, exemplified in books by Georges Didi-Huberman and Rosalind Krauss.[4]

In this essay I will talk only about the first and the fourth of these. My general claim is that these six concepts and discourses function as the final interpretive goal of scholarship, the purpose toward which the machinery of historical explanation tends. The indirectness of that goal—its hidden nature, half-revealed by the secular and secularized discourses of historical writing—

only increases its power. Even the historian's choice of subject matter, which is putatively a result of many converging interests, can come to seem to be a strategic aid in the search for these concepts and discourses.

Before I explore the two topics, it may be helpful if I explain the background of my interest. A few years ago I wrote a book called *The Strange Place of Religion in Contemporary Art.*[5] It was motivated by the absence of what might be called committed religious art in the international art market. With a few exceptions, recent art that engages religious themes and is also widely seen in international venues is either critical of religion, or broadly skeptical, or ambiguous about the institutions of the church. I had become aware of the tremendous quantity of committed, sincere religious art that is being produced worldwide, and its absence from the art world. Broadly speaking, the book is an attempt to weave the discourse of contemporary religionists together with ways of talking about religion and spirituality that are more common in academic writing. The book has introduced me to a new world, because I now receive invitations to talk to Christian institutions. In many cases I had not even been aware that those institutions existed—for example Westmont College in Santa Barbara, Lipscomb University in Nashville, and Biola University in Brea, outside Los Angeles. Those engagements have led to a number of further conversations and symposia, but so far only one invitation has been initiated by a secular institution; it was from Caroline Jones at MIT, for her conference "Deus e(x) historia," in April 2007.[6] Getting to know some of the many careful and reflective people who write about religious art from outside academia has made me sensitive to the absence of personally engaged conversations about religion (as opposed to historiographic, philosophic, or sociological conversations) in academia. The excellent scholars of religion who are themselves religious, and value their scholarship principally as a way to enrich their religious experience, have shown me a different way of reading art history. To them, some texts in art history are indirect, in that they explore religious issues without identifying them as religious.

The themes of this essay are the mirror reflection of those experiences. Visiting Biola University and other institutions, I was for a while "inside" religious communities, looking out. In this essay I am "inside" art history and its concerns; I am not primarily concerned here to write with religionists in mind, but rather to historians and philosophers of art, to see how far these themes might make sense from the points of view acknowledged and embodied by recent art historical writing.

The two subjects I will touch on here, iconoclasm and the sublime, are not connected except by the fact that they both appear in art theory and art history as secular discourses. A larger account, one I hope to build, would bring the six themes together in an analysis of what I would like to call art history's uses of crypto-religious discourse. I will introduce iconoclasm and the sublime in turn, and end with a brief conclusion.

Iconoclasm

For this first section I will be borrowing from two unfinished projects, the book series *Theories of Modernism and Postmodernism in the Visual Arts*, and in particular the final volume of that series, *Last Experiences of Painting*, by Joseph Koerner;[7] and the book series *The Stone Theory Institute*, and in particular the second volume of that series, edited by Maja Naef and James Elkins, *What Is an Image?*[8] Both books, I think, are exemplary moments in the recent articulation of the concept of iconoclasm (and related ideas) in art history.

I am wary of the relatively sudden ascendance of iconoclasm, idolatry, iconophobia, and other concepts in art historical scholarship. It is unarguable that these concepts are among the most influential conceptualizations of religious images in Western societies, but I am not yet persuaded by the extended claim that these concepts make up optimal starting places for any interpretation of modern and postmodern fine art in general.

Some very thoughtful work by Joseph Koerner—especially his contribution to the exhibition and book called *Iconoclash*—set the tone for this resurgence of interest in the last decade.[9] In a book from the Iconology Research Group based in Leuven, several scholars write about the fundamental nature of iconoclasm and how it is indispensable for any investigation of the represented body in art.[10] The book as a whole takes as its theme the relation between representations of the body and religion, but the contributions center on themes of iconoclasm. I would not claim that iconoclasm is as specific to twentieth-century scholarship as words like *liminal, parergon*, the *BWO*, the *uncanny*, the *abject*, or any number of other concepts current in the art world: but it may be premature to say that the discourse of iconoclasm, iconophilia, and other such concepts can be generalized in such a way that it is useful for understanding images in general. My experiences at Christian institutions have also made me sensitive to the relatively wide gulf between belief and scholarship about belief. Like most of my friends in academia, I am an iconophile: I love images with a moderate love. I would not kill or die for images, or even risk being injured for images, unlike some of the people who first engaged in iconoclasm and idolatry. An interest in iconoclasm is an interest in a passion stronger than one that we ourselves possess, and that may cause us to mistake it for a fundamental category of imaging.

Iconoclash, the book that did more than any other to impel the new interest in these terms, is heavier than Arnason's *History of Modern Art*, and larger than Rem Koolhaas's *Harvard Design School Guide to Shopping*.[11] It was the bane of my existence the six times I carried it with me on a flight across the Atlantic, trying to read it in economy-class airplane seats (it fit on the tray-tables, but I couldn't easily turn the pages). This behemoth of an exhibition catalog was the *Fragments for a History of the Human Body* for the first decade of the twenty-first century. Like that earlier book—which was, incidentally, even larger, at three volumes—*Iconoclash* samples a number of widely divergent approaches and ideas around a concept of pressing importance. At the time of *Fragments for a History of the Human Body*—and again with the Iconology Research Group—the concept was "the body." In *Iconoclash*, the concept is the power of images of all sorts and the desire they incite to destroy or multiply them.

There are essays in *Iconoclash* that can, if they are read by themselves, comprise a good introductory survey of iconoclasm as it is documented in art history and anthropology. A recurrent theme is the ambiguity of the concept of iconoclasm. "Simple" iconoclasm is revealed to be forever split from itself, forever in anticipation of itself, or forever wedded to its opposite. The three possibilities are blended in many essays, but also distinct. First is the claim that iconoclasm is split from itself, that "iconoclasts' hammers always seemed to strike sideways, destroying something else."[12] Then there is the idea that iconoclasm seems to anticipate itself, redouble onto itself, repeat itself. Pierre Centlivres, for instance, notes that the Buddhas in Bamiyan were intentionally faceless, which folds the Taliban iconoclasm onto an originary one and connects the sculptures to the early aniconic phase of Buddhism.[13] And third, iconoclasm is also wedded to its opposite. A long and somewhat wandering essay by Dario Gamboni argues mainly that modernist images are "indestructible" because they spring up after innumerable iconoclasms, blending the two motivations.[14] Gamboni, Bruno Latour, and others note that iconoclasts, "theoclasts," and "ideoclasts" have produced "a fabulous population of new images, fresh icons, rejuvenated mediators: greater flows of media, more powerful ideas, stronger idols."[15] In other words, iconoclasm is always already its opposite.

Most of the intellectual work on the ambiguity of the concept of iconoclasm takes place in the introduction by Bruno Latour, in a long and beauti-
fully worked essay by Joseph Koerner, and in a short contribution by Caroline
Jones. Koerner's text is nothing short of brilliant. He puts the central ambiguities of iconoclasm quite succinctly: "Long before the hammer strikes
them," he writes, "religious images are already self-defacing. Claiming their
truth by dialectically repeating and repudiating the deception from which
they alone escape, they are, each of them, engines of the iconoclash that periodically destroys and renews them."[16] The central insight, and the moment
of highest abstraction, comes midway through the essay. Koerner considers
the claim, often made in "image wars," that iconoclasts are secretly idolaters.
In a sense idolatry is only a fiction, because no one is an idolater in the way
that is implied by iconoclastic gestures. "If idolatry is indeed but an accusation made by iconoclasts to caricature certain uses of pictures, if . . . it is less
a belief than a fiction of naïve belief, what function is served by accusing the
accusers of their [own] accusation?"[17] The answer leads Koerner to the idea
that "believers in belief"—that is, in this case, iconoclasts—"do not confuse
representations with persons (the idolater's imputed error). Rather, they confuse representations with facts. Imagining that iconophiles know the wood
falsely (as God, not wood), they hit the wood but instead strike representation. . . . No wonder the critical gesture rebounds."[18] This is an abstract but,
I think, very cogent argument. It can stand as an ur-explanation for the ambiguities in iconoclash that are played out throughout the book, because the
"wood"—the material and substance of the icon—is always representation
in the discourse of iconoclasm, and it repeatedly becomes explicitly representation, and therefore liable to further attack, each time it is seen as "spe-
cious." Iconoclasts' hammers strike "sideways," and scholars' arguments veer
into ambiguities. The resurgence of icons following iconophobic attacks is
interesting and in need of explanation, all because the real *Bildersturm* takes
place within and periodically against the emergence of representation as an
explicit theme.

Koerner ends by saying, very boldly, that an interest in religious iconoclasm, in "the impulse to pass beyond representation" or to do without representation altogether "entraps us in a world that is only representation: religion
as nothing but what people customarily do."[19] It is a bold admission because
it means that the entire subject of iconoclasm tends, by minuscule degrees
and without our notice, away from the religious truths that it seeks to un-

derstand.[20] How much more interesting and honest art historical scholarship would be if it could find a way of acknowledging that truth whenever it turns its attention to religious images.[21]

Iconoclash is a starting point for further thinking about iconoclasm, or it should be. Two other texts I want to mention in this regard are the following. In anticipation of the book Last Experiences of Painting he has contributed to the series Theories of Modernism and Postmodernism in the Visual Arts, Koerner gave a lecture in Ireland; after the lecture he participated in a seminar that was taped and transcribed for the book. Here is an excerpt in which the subject is the position of the art historian, as iconophile, studying iconoclasm.

> JAMES ELKINS: Let me introduce another such term: iconophile. Some of the
> allied terms—iconoclast, idolater—have historical lineages, but icono-
> phile has an interesting place in the literature, and in your writing. There
> is a passage in the introduction to your Reformation of the Image in
> which you say that in the exhibition Iconoclash, "We were neither icon-
> oclasts or iconophobes," which would seem to leave open the question
> of what you were. There are other passages in Reformation of the Image
> in which iconophile would be a reasonable term for you, as a narrator. I
> mean to ask that in light of what is perhaps the most widespread sense
> of the word iconophile, Tom Mitchell's sense of it, in which it means ap-
> proximately "all of us who like images." It means academics, in other
> words: people who would be prohibited by definition from being icono-
> clasts or idolaters.
>
> So that's another example of a very slight difference in terms, which
> could effect a change in the way history, and historians, describe them-
> selves. Like the terms you have been discussing, "noncontemporaneity"
> and unzeitgemäss, iconophile would enjoin a split chronology.
>
> JOSEPH KOERNER: It's true; it's a very interesting question. Just to get back
> to the Iconoclash question: I suppose we were not collectively iconophile
> or iconophobe, because some of us may have been iconophile and some
> iconophobe, so we balanced each other out. The most obvious case of that
> was that Bruno Latour felt the whole function of Iconoclash was to say
> you can't get rid of images, particularly in science, but Peter Weibel pro-
> ceeded, again and again, to embody everything Bruno Latour thought
> was wrong about twentieth-century art—that is, the ultra-avant-garde

claim to have destroyed all the images. Weibel kept showing the "destroyed" images, saying, "There they are!"

I have a pretty strong sense that *iconophile* is there in the earlier literature about Restoration history, so that it would be there long before Mitchell utilized it.

J.E.: That sounds very plausible, but that would still place it in a context of historical observation, and therefore a kind of detachment. Iconophilia, in that sense, could be seen as a theme within the historical reception of iconoclasm.

J.K.: Yes, I think the association of modernity with the critique, and therefore of modernity with image destruction, is something which I have naturally always assumed; but it may not be a well-theorized topic.

J.K.: If you try to do a show, like *Iconoclash*, in which you trace the aftermath of Protestant iconoclasm, and if you are slightly easygoing about how iconoclasm is described, then what you get is a canonical representation of twentieth-century art. *Every* twentieth century artist who makes his way into a textbook, every one of them, from Malevich and Duchamp and Picasso onward, marching through the whole history, is an iconoclast. That was what was so surreal, from a practical perspective, about organizing the show. For the "art section," all we had to do was transfer the modern art gallery; that was what Peter Weibel did. He just moved the ZKM [Center for Art and Media, Karlsruhe] collection into the exhibition. He didn't even have to make choices. There was not a single exclusion. (No one could think of an example of iconophile art. We had to commission one, and then we rejected it.)

The second unpublished text I want to bring in is from the book *What Is an Image?* which records a week of seminars, with thirty-five participants, that took place in Chicago in July 2008.[22] One of the five faculty who led the seminars, Marie-José Mondzain, is arguably one of the most provocative scholars of the image; her specialty is Byzantine iconoclasm but she also writes widely on modern and contemporary art.[23] Her texts adopt an intensive, unwavering focus on the problems of representation in a theological context. Even so, our conversation that week rarely turned to theological debates, and rarely strayed into any of the six categories I listed at the beginning of this paper. We talked extensively—for a total of thirty-seven hours over the course of the week—about representation, denotation, notation, language, semiotics, graphs, diagrams, ontology, digital images, the public and the private, painting, what counts as an image and what is outside images, and many other topics, but none of us except Mondzain had much to say about iconoclasm, idolatry, or the entire history of Western images and Christianity. Here is a sample of what was said when our conversation *did* turn to religion and the sacred. (In this passage she is talking with W. J. T. Mitchell and Jacqueline Lichtenstein, one of the foremost scholars of seventeenth- and eighteenth-century French painting.)

> JAMES ELKINS: Here is a theme that we have not raised this week, because even our very lengthy conversations are limited. It is the difficulty of connecting two discourses about the image: one that insists, with the full weight of the history of art and anthropology behind it, that images have been ritual or religious objects in all cultures; and another that places images within a secular discourse. Examples of the former are endless: they include the whole tradition since Christianity, including the very intricate themes Marie-José Mondzain has explored, replete with terms like *homoousia, homoiosion, homoiōma, skhésis, skhéma, prototypon,* and many others, and continuing up to the present in themes of incarnation, iconophobia, and iconophilia. Examples of the latter are historically bounded, but they include widely divergent accounts—from philosophers like Peirce and Goodman to modernist and postmodernist art historians to historians of science and technology. Among the fifteen Fellows at this event, there are texts where you would have to work hard to find elements of what Marie-José would rightly insist are questions of representation that have ultimately to do with incarnation and other religious themes.
>
> I think this subject is difficult because it is so easy to decline to accept the existence of fully secular discourse. Let me propose as an opening example Tim Clark's intransigent line in *Farewell to an Idea*: "I will have nothing to do with the self-satisfied Leftist clap-trap of 'art as substitute religion.'"[24] Let me just take that to epitomize one form of the deliberate rejection of religious discourse.
>
> JACQUELINE LICHTENSTEIN. Sorry, I don't understand: for you Tim's sentence is an example of nontheological discourse?
>
> J.E.: It proposes itself as nontheological. Tim knows these histories very well.
>
> J.L.: Because for me it has nothing to do with the difference between theological and nontheological. It is a reaction to an idea that was developed in the nineteenth century, the idea of religion as art. For me, the passage is more a critique, or opposition, to a familiar way of thinking that includes

a certain interpretation of Nietzsche, Baudelaire, Huysmans, and what is called *la réligion de l'art*.

J.E.: I take that point in relation to Tim Clark, but that is one of the reasons this is such a hard question. Tim's discourse *is* secular, at the very least in that his points of reference are Hegel, de Man, Benjamin, and many others—writers whose pens were soaked in religion, to adapt Benjamin's phrase, but who did not write using religious concepts. Compare Tim Clark's texts, for example, to Marie-José's wonderfully concise observation that "the story of the incarnation is the legend of the image itself," or the assertion that "only the image can incarnate."[25] Or to Jean-Luc Nancy's meditations in "The Image—the Distinct" that "the image is always sacred" if by that word is meant "the distinct," "the separate, what is set aside, removed, cut off. . . . It is there, perhaps, that art has always begun, not in religion . . . but set apart."[26]

Perhaps those contrasts capture what I mean a little better.

Tom Mitchell: But somehow the idea of art as a substitute for religion . . . I would first want to divide the concept of religion from the sacred . . .

J.L.: . . . and from theology.

T.M.: Yes. I'm not sure how that would go, but I would be really surprised if there was anyone in this room who thought that art was a substitute for religion. But almost everyone would say art is an issue in religion, and not just art, but the role of the image.

J.E.: Right, but would everyone say that their interest in images is usefully informed by a discourse on religion?

T.M.: Yes, that's quite a different thing.

That is where our conversation ended; then we turned to other subjects. That kind of dead end happened several times during the week, and I think it suggests the presence of a kind of unspoken rejection of the very idea that a discourse of belief or commitment can sensibly coexist with a discourse about belief or commitment. Lichtenstein, Mitchell, and others did not reject the idea of talking about beliefs (including, in this example, the belief that art is a substitute religion), but they did not feel the need to adopt the languages of iconoclasm and idolatry, as Marie-José Mondzain has done, in order to articulate what they think about images. Mitchell, Lichtenstein, and a majority of the thirty-five scholars and artists in the seminars talked widely about religious images, and when Mondzain was leading seminars, they also talked about iconoclasm and idolatry. Many of them, including Mitchell, have written about those concepts. But at our seminars, Mondzain exemplified a different discourse, because for her the crucial terms of politics and economy, together with the problems she was pursuing in her own work—the meaning and action of hatred, the rise of racism, the construction of community—were soluble in terms of theological questions. Political questions dissolved into questions of resurrection, incarnation, and the icon, and those questions precipitated back into politics. Many of the other scholars at our table, who represented a very wide range of historical, philosophic, and critical perspectives on images, did not participate: they knew what kinds of conversations they did not want to pursue.

I would like to draw two provisional conclusions from these two excerpts. First, regarding iconophilia: it seems that even though there have been iconophiles in a literal sense in the past—as Koerner says in the conversation—we do not use the word in that sense in our own scholarship. The root *philos* in *iconophile* behaves more like the *philos* in philosophy: it names a person who takes great pleasure in his or her subject, but not a person who would strike a sculpture or painting, or a person who would put him or herself in danger protecting a sculpture or painting. Iconophiles like me very much enjoy discussing images in seminars and conferences, and writing about them in essays and books. I feel this somewhat simple observation is a good starting place for discussions of the *historical place of our interest in iconoclasm*. Our place, that is, at the beginning of the twenty-first century, after a century of committed iconoclasm in fine art, and after several decades of sometimes ruthlessly secularized art criticism. Some of these terms, I think, are subtly transforming themselves in our relatively gentle and dispassionate writing.

Second: it seems to me that *if* iconoclasm and its allied concepts are to occupy a central place in the interpretation of images, we should try to discover what limits we wish to put on their applicability. In the Stone Theory Institute seminars, it was clear that Mondzain's thinking on the subject of iconoclasm has an unprecedented richness, and many of us knew Joseph Koerner's work, Georges Didi-Huberman's writing on representation, and work by others on *acheiropoietai* and other kinds of miraculous images. It remained unresolved how far each of us might want to go in following Mondzain's expansion of themes from their original Byzantine contexts to the ongoing problems of Western art.[27] The themes around iconoclasm are not limited to religious images, but it is not yet clear when it makes sense to invoke them.

The Sublime

The second subject I want to address is the sublime, and here again I will be borrowing from work in progress.[28] The essay in question is the result of a long interest in the sublime, which has turned into a long dissatisfaction. Here I will confine myself to two arguments.

First, the sublime is not well used as a transhistorical category: it does not work comfortably when it is applied outside particular ranges of artworks, most of them made in the nineteenth century. Second, in contemporary critical writing the sublime is used principally as a way to smuggle covert religious meaning into texts that are putatively secular.[29]

The first of my arguments is that the sublime is an historically bounded term, not a transhistorical concept that can be applied to art or science in general. The sublime, as elaborated by Kant, has a specific historical context, which makes it appropriate mainly for the interpretation of artworks in and around Romanticism and its descendants. The postmodern sublime, first in Jean-François Lyotard's formulation, and then in its many later forms, is primarily an outgrowth of philosophy and literature, and has no clear brief in the visual arts aside from individual authors' interests.[30] The most prominent visually oriented formulation of the sublime, Mark C. Taylor's, has a clear application, but to a very limited range of work and for a specific set of interpretive possibilities.[31] He remains a minority interest even in regard to the artists, such as Anselm Kiefer, whom he privileges. Aside from those moments, the Kantian sublime and the different postmodern sublimes run nearly exactly against the current of poststructuralist thinking, in that they posit a sense of presence and a nonverbal immediacy that short-circuits the principal interests of theorizing on art in recent decades, which are nearly all concerned with mediation, translation, deferral of meaning, miscommunication, and the social conditions of understanding. References to the sublime bypass that literature—in some cases, it would be appropriate to identify that literature with poststructuralism in general—in favor of meditations on the possibility of direct access to pure and immediate presence. Very few authors—George Steiner might be the only widely visible example, with his book *Real Presences*—have attempted to reinstate notions that depend on pure presence within a poststructural context.[32]

If I were to adopt an ahistorical stance, I would be able to speak more freely about the sublime. I could in effect count as sublime any image that points outside itself. A landscape painting points beyond itself simply by showing us objects that cannot be fixed—trees with swaying branches, clouds that move. An oil painting refers to things beyond itself with every gesture of the painter's brush. Following those widening gyres, the sublime could grow to encompass the entire history of images. It could even appear as if the sublime were the central problem of representation itself, as the philosopher Jean-Luc Nancy has suggested, or at least the crux of modern painting, as Jean-François Lyotard says.[33]

A philosophic approach has its advantages, but it is open to historical objections. Still, the sublime is not purely an historical artifact. It is not a relic of the past, cut off from what seems true about pictures. More than other subjects, the sublime slips in and out of history in a bewildering fashion. Lyotard's lack of focus—his slurring of Fuseli and Friedrich, Mondrian and Onslow-Ford—is an intentional strategy: his sense of the sublime includes an awareness of its history as well as a conviction that it is an unavoidable element of experience. Part of the truth of the sublime, Lyotard might say, lies in the very broad tradition called "Western metaphysics" (that part can only appear true), and part lies in individual historical movements. Hence some of Lyotard's points are philosophical and others are historical.

These slides in and out of history have been analyzed by Peter De Bolla, in a book called *The Discourse of the Sublime*. De Bolla distinguishes between a discourse *on* the sublime and a discourse *of* the sublime. The former includes texts that inquire into "the forms, causes, and effects of the sublime": books on the subject of the sublime, we might say.[34] The authors of such books tend to cite "external authorities," and to divorce themselves from their analyses as far as possible. In the discourse of the sublime, authors produce sublime effects in their writing: the books themselves evoke and create the sublime. For the discourse on the sublime, the sublime effect is mostly out there, in the world; for the discourse of the sublime, it is found in "the interior mind."

For an art historian or art critic, writing about the sublime is nearly always a matter of history—it is a discourse on the sublime. In art history, sublimity is known as a term applied in retrospect to Caspar David Friedrich and a number of later Romantic landscape painters in Germany and France; and it is a term found in art criticism beginning with the abstract expressionists. Applying the sublime to other movements means taking increasing license with historical sources. It is historically inescapable that the sublime is a current critical term, and even if I wouldn't go as far as Lyotard and claim the sublime "may well be the single artistic sensibility to characterize the modern," or that aesthetics is completely dominated by the sublime, it is indispensable for any serious account of contemporary images.[35] No matter how little sense references to the sublime may make, and no matter how little light they shed on the artworks that are said to embody them, the sublime is in the lexicon of contemporary art discourse. It would be artificial to exclude the sublime altogether—as artificial as omitting words like *representation, realism, image*, and any number of other terms that are arguably just as poorly defined.

There is another, possibly deeper reason why the sublime matters to a contemporary sense of pictures, and why it is so important, so vexed, and so often opaque in literary theory. Talking about the sublime is a way of addressing something that can no longer be called by any of its traditional names, something so important that words like *art* would be crippled without it: the possibility of a truth beyond the world of experience (and not merely beyond the world of articulation, or representation).

In past centuries, some of the ideas now contested under the name *sublime* were known more directly as religious truth or revelation. Today words like sublimity, transcendence, and presence, shrouded in clouds of secular criticism, serve to suggest religious meanings without making them explicit. For many reasons, the sublime has come to be ones of the places where thoughts about religious truth, revelation, and other more or less unusable concepts have congregated. An example that is often cited is from Thomas Weiskel's influential book *The Romantic Sublime: Studies in the Structure and Psychology of Transcendence* (where the word *transcendence* is used in a philosophic sense). Weiskel says, all at once (and only once) that "the essential claim of the sublime is that man can, in feeling or speech, transcend the human." A "'humanist sublime,'" Weiskel thinks, "is an oxymoron," because the sublime "founders" without "some notion of the beyond." At the same time, he will not write about the religious aspect of his subject. He closes the subject peremptorily: "What, if anything, lies beyond the human—God or the gods, the dæmon or Nature—is matter for great disagreement."[36] That is at the beginning of the book; afterward he keeps quiet about religious meaning.

I would not be quite as silent about religious meanings as Weiskel, but it is a matter of knowing when to speak and how much to say. For example, it is important not to assume that the sublime, presence, or transcendence, are philosophic masks that can be removed, revealing a hidden religious discourse. They *are* that discourse: they are taken by authors like Weiskel to be the only remaining ways in which truths that used to be called religious can find voice within much of contemporary thought. (Outside "secular" thought, and therefore outside the sublime, a writer like Weiskel might argue that it is possible to go on thinking and living with religious ideas, and many people do: but that is a different sphere of experience, a different discursive field.) In one sense the dozens of twentieth-century books that discuss the sublime are interrogating the possibility of religious experience: but in another sense—the only one available for reflective writing—they are not addressing religion but only asking about the coherence and usefulness of the sublime.

This permeable veil between two kinds of thinking has been a trait of the sublime from Kant onward. Longinus talks uncertainly of divinity, Kant is adamant about the separation (he protests too much), and Weiskel permits himself the one apostrophe. The same veil comes down in front of religious writers when they look across at the sublime from theology and religious history. Rudolf Otto's book *The Idea of the Holy*—famous partly because it introduces the wonderful word *numinous*—skirts the sublime, as if Otto is unsure whether the sublime is part of the holy. His book is one of the best places to study the twentieth-century vacillation about the sublime and religious writing. At one point he calls the sublime a "pale reflection" of numinous revelation; five pages later he says the sublime is "an authentic scheme of 'the holy.'" Otto is a neo-Kantian, and he sees Kant's aesthetics as unmoored talk about the holy. There is a "hidden kinship," Otto concludes, "between the numinous and the sublime which is something more than a merely accidental analogy, and to which Kant's *Critique of Judgment* bears distant witness."[37] What an odd phrase, "something more than a merely accidental analogy," especially in a book devoted entirely to a systematic reappraisal of Kant: it is entirely typical of the tenuous alienation that still obtains between religious vocabulary and the sublime.[38]

Otto says that thought can never articulate the numinous; in his doctrine it forms the nonrational half of the concept of the holy.[39] (Doctrines and dogma form the rational half.) Otto is partly under the spell of apophatic theology, in that he repeatedly insists he cannot explain the numinous or its governing term, which he calls the *mysterium tremendens* (the awe-filled mystery). "Taken in a religious sense," he says, "that which is 'mysterious' is—to give it perhaps the most striking expression—the 'wholly other' (Θατερον, *anyad* [eva], *alienum*), that which is quite beyond the sphere of the usual, the intelligible, and the familiar, which therefore falls quite outside the limits of the 'canny,' and is contrasted with it, filling the mind with blank wonder and astonishment."[40] By "wholly other" (*ganz Andere*) and its Greek, Sanskrit, and Latin synonyms, Otto means to signal an experience that cannot be re-connected to ordinary understanding.

There are times when *The Idea of the Holy* runs up against secular concepts such as the sublime, the uncanny, and the incommensurate; in those cases, it is instructive to watch how the "secular" terms are put to religious uses. For Otto, the "truly mysterious object is beyond our apprehension and compre-hension, not only because our knowledge has certain irremovable limits"—Otto's nod to Kant, whom he wanted to supplement with a genuinely religious theory—"but because in it we come upon something inherently 'wholly other,' whose kinds and character are incommensurable with our own." The word *incommensurate* occurs frequently in Otto's writing; he uses it as he uses other Kantian terms, as a springboard to more important religious truths. Incom-mensurate is an incomplete or approximate name for the condition of the holy. The passage I have just quoted ends with an evocation of the feeling pro-duced by the "wholly other": "we therefore recoil," he says, "in a wonder that strikes us chill and numb."[41] Otto often traps himself in the mystic's dilemma: all that remains of the experience is its affective residue, which has to sit un-comfortably next to whatever philosophy is being summoned to explain it. That is the dead end that scholars, critics, and historians who use the sublime wish at once to conjure and avoid.

Let's articulate the problem in the form of two assertions. First, it is not a secret that much of modern and postmodern art criticism, theory, and history are infused with religious themes—like the ink in a blotter, as Walter Benjamin said. That might fairly be considered an open secret. But then—and this is the second assertion—the supposedly open secret really is a secret because it is so seldom analyzed, and when it is analyzed something in the writing is ruined.

From these two assertions follows a conundrum: what is the best way to analyze a secret that is so widely known that it is acknowledged, at the very start of any number of conversations, and just as quickly forgotten, in the tacit understanding that it might do damage? As in the case of Weiskel's text, an excavation of the religious meaning of putatively secular discourses would distort the authors' and readers' sense of their own work.

Let me conclude, and also bring this into art history, with a look at Michael Fried's "Art and Objecthood," possibly the most frequently cited example of religious tropes in late twentieth-century art history. A standard reading is that Fried's formalism in that essay is one of the few channels remaining for re-ligious discourse in the almost wholly secular domain of modernist criticism.

That reading is exemplified by an essay by the historian Randall Van Schepen. After a discussion of religious survivals in modernist discourse, Van Schepen concludes:

> According to the modernist principles under which Fried was operating, the only form of transcendence possible was through the tradition of modern epiphanic aesthetic experience. Therefore, the spiritual heritage of Western aesthetics enters in through the side door of formalist criticism as form, autonomy, manifestness, and other pseudo-religious notions in order to claim the only realm of experience that has (perhaps) not yet been subsumed by positivist materiality.[42]

In effect Van Schepen's move is to describe a wider historical context for "art and objecthood" in which religion is both explicit and crucial. I have no objection to that strategy if its purpose is to reveal a wider religious discourse and its unexpected remnants: but I am wary if it becomes a way to talk about "Art and Objecthood." In Van Schepen's essay, the description of the wider religious origins of Fried's text is almost a way to talk about Fried's text: it is as if he is implying that religion (or pseudoreligion, which seems to be Van Schepen's way of indicating that the religious discourse is inexplicit in "Art and Objecthood") is crucial for a full understanding of "Art and Objecthood," but at the same time leaving that understanding to the reader—apparently precisely because it is, after all, not explicit in Fried's text.

I hope this does not sound artificially elaborate: it is the on-again, off-again dynamics of the secret-that-is-not-a-secret. A project that disregards that dynamic, and seeks only to illuminate the religious within the nonreligious, is missing the pressure—historical pressure, Fried would say—to not speak directly of the religious in the context of modernism. To move forward, contemporary art criticism might begin by acknowledging that the sublime cannot be fully excavated from its crypto-religious contexts.

The sublime has been roundly critiqued by a number of writers for its direct appeal to pure presence and its obliviousness to poststructural doubts. It has also been criticized because it leads scholars to focus on images of things that are incomprehensibly vast, or unimaginably small, or frighteningly blank, dark, blurred, smeared, pixilated, or otherwise illegible. The sublime, so it is said, takes people away from the real world of politics and society, of meaning and narrative, of culture and value.

Poor anemic sublime. Poor elitist concept, born in the leisured classes of eighteenth-century Europe, lingering on into the twenty-first century as an academic hothouse plant. "One should see the quest for the sublime," according to the philosopher Richard Rorty, "as one of the prettier unforced blue flowers of bourgeois culture."[43] (He says that the sublime is "wildly irrelevant to the attempt at communicative consensus which is the vital force" of common culture.)

Poor sublime, in that case, which can only express the most atrophied and delicate emotions of distance and nostalgia, which requires a battery of arcane ideas to keep it afloat, which can only be found in the most hermetic postmodern art or the most recherché Romantic painting. Poor sublime, which can only sing a feeble plaintive song about longing, which has nothing to say about the things that count in visual culture—especially gender, identity, and politics. Poor irrelevant sublime, as Lacoue-Labarthe says, which "forms a minor tradition," following along after beauty is exhausted.[44]

Poor sublime, too, which seems like "a thoroughly ideological category" (as Terry Eagleton says), or a "discourse" with certain "effects" that need dispassionate Foucauldian study (as Peter De Bolla proposes).[45] Irresponsible sublime, which puts all kinds of things beyond the reach of critical thought, and so "becomes the luxury of the aesthete all over again," protecting postmodernists from having to make difficult judgments.[46] "Pallid" sublime, as I called it, which mingles with beauty and makes for easy pleasures.

Poor sublime: relic of other centuries, perennially misused as an attractive way to express the power of art, kept afloat by academics interested in other people's ideas, used—ineffectually, I have argued—as a covertly religious term, to permit academics to speak about religion while remaining appropriately secular. And finally, poor sublime, exiled from contemporary philosophy even as it suffuses so much of it.[47]

In the end, the sublime is damaged goods. It has been asked to do too much work for too many reasons, and it has become weak. I propose a moratorium on the word: let's say what we admire in art and science, but let's say it directly, using words that are fresh and exact.

Some Brief Conclusions

I have argued differently about iconoclasm and the sublime, and they are different concepts from different discourses. Yet I think it helps to think of them together, because they have both served recent art theory and art history as master tropes, driving and informing arguments about a wide range of artworks. I feel more strongly about the sublime, because I can see how it has been spread thin across contemporary art writing, and how transparently, and effectively, it stands in for religious interests. Iconoclasm and its related terms are a more difficult question, partly because their revival in art history is more recent. It is not yet clear what will happen to the interpretive power they have been given. The history of iconoclasm and its related terms is longer than the history of the sublime, because the tradition that was inaugurated by Longinus was discontinuous until Kant, while the tradition that began with the Byzantine iconoclasm has remained a central concern of Catholicism and Protestantism. It is the export of iconoclasm into the interpretation of modernism, and from there to the interpretation of pictures in general, that has a more recent vintage.

Whenever a new interpretive interest appears in art theory, it is prudent first to ask how long it has been in use, and what might have prompted its revival. Why is it that we, early in the twenty-first century, find these concepts so compelling?

WHAT WE SEE AND WHAT APPEARS

JEAN-LUC MARION

It would perhaps be useful first to attempt a quick sequencing of a certain number of concepts. I have become aware over time that, considering their conjectural appearance in the course of other lines of argument, these concepts are connected, more than I previously imagined, to other arguments taken up in books of diverse explicit subjects. I would thus like to try to lay out a general sketch: not of a doctrine of the image, of course, but of some concepts in regard to the visible that can match each other, be linked, be confirmed, at times maybe contradict each other.[1] By taking as title "What We See and What Appears," I want to suggest that the two verbs do not cover the same concept. We must maintain the difference between what appears and what we see—and this is a theoretical necessity that might even be an ethical need. We must deepen the distinction in order to uphold it. One of the results one could expect from this difference might also be to respond to an essential question for everyone whose work is focused on the visibility of the work of art. To simplify things I will call it "aesthetic visibility." This question is: what privileges and hence what boundaries allow us to distinguish within the vast field of the visible between these areas (are they areas or beings or objects?) that fall under what I will call simply "aesthetic visibility"? At stake is not only the determination of the boundary between what falls under art and what does not, but also a well-known sociological and theoretical problem. This is not what specifically interests me. Rather, I am interested in how, in our applications (in our theoretical practices), we somehow select the field that merits our attention and

our intervention. Why take into account the aesthetic visibility of certain re-
gions, certain areas that were not previously awarded the authority of aesthetic
visibility? What sorts of disagreements could we have (disagreements about
minimalism, photography, film, or concerning arts newly introduced into the
register of museology, tag, rap—why not?). Whatever might be the motives and
debates on this point, everyone agrees that it raises the question whether to
include or exclude certain areas from a particular excellence of phenomenality, namely the field of the aesthetic visible. By what right do we do this? That
we do not do so in the same fashion does not distinguish or pit us against each
other so much as the fact that precisely in order to make this distinction differently, we really must admit that a distinction can be made. Hence we share that
we admit this distinction between the visible that I will call the "common visible" and the visible that (to simplify again) I will call the "aesthetic visible." Can
we justify this distinction? Has it any rigor? And, even if one must abolish it (it
really seems to me that one must abolish it), one must deconstruct it, that is to
say, first think it. This is what I would like to attempt by giving some indications
on this point: what we see and what appears.

First, what we see. I would like to maintain the paradox that what we see,
often, does not appear. I understand appearing here in the sense of the short
and very celebrated phrase that Flaubert wrote in order to describe the first
vision of Madame Arnoux in *Sentimental Education*: "It was a sight."[2] While
climbing into the boat going down the Seine he sees her, and in a paragraph
of four words Flaubert says: "It was a sight." New paragraph. Well, this phrase
"It was a sight" is precisely not what we say when we see the majority of what
we see. When we see, we experience that it is not a "sight" (or vision). The
fact of seeing in no way entails a vision, that is to say, what we see most often
does not appear. Why does what we see not appear? By "does not appear" I
mean that it does not draw the gaze, does not focus it, does not captivate it.
The gaze passes, passes over what it sees and moves to the following visible,
as if the visible had given up its spatial determination to take on a temporal
determination. This means that the visible is not the visible in front of us, but
is the visible for a moment and we move on. In this sense, the visible does not
appear, the gaze does not even allow it the time to appear, we have already
moved on. The visible is what has no time to appear. Why does the visible
not have the time to appear? Why can we not give it the necessary time and
attention that would place it into full view for us? Why does the view remain
empty in a certain way and move on? I think that this absolutely fundamental

determination of seeing without appearing refers to a state of phenomenality that is the phenomenality of the object. I must, then, give some information about the object's phenomenality. I will not provide a theory of the object or an ontic determination of the object, but I will give some indications about the manner in which the object does not appear, that is to say, on the way in which we see the object.

Metaphysics has its virtues, among which is saying clearly what it thinks. The fact that the common phenomenon can refer to the object is absolutely basic. What we see first has the status of the object. I recall that, as everyone knows, the object is what is thrown in front of me [jeté face à moi].[3] What matters here is not the "throwing [jet]" but the "in front of [ob-]." It is what becomes an obstacle before me, what resists me, on what I set my sight [ce que je vise]. There is no object without an aim [une visée].[4] The object is what I see in front of me; beyond my reach it is an objective. The term *objective* is really essential here, because it is a contradictory term in a certain fashion: when one speaks of an objective, one speaks of what one has not yet reached. In this sense, then, the objective refers to an aim of which one does not know whether it has met its end. Hence the objective in this sense (in the sense of the artilleryman or the contractor who sets objectives) is perfectly subjective. The objective is what has not yet been realized. And yet, we use the same word, objective, to designate what is not subjective: objective information, objective givens, objective results, which no one can question. What does the objective—in the sense where it remains subjective, where it is the desire of the one who express it—have in common with the objectivity of the result? Is there a contradiction, the word trying to say both one and the other, or is there a common point? Of course they share a common point.

What is common to the subjectivity of the envisioned objective, and to the objectivity of the obtained result, is precisely the aim. The distinctive feature of the objective is that it may happen or not, but always at the end of my aim. What is subjective in it is the aim; what is objective in it is the fulfillment and the ratification of vision. In this sense even objectivity, as everyone knows, is a determination of subjectivity. When one speaks of objectivity, one does so in the style of subjectivity, and even of transcendental subjectivity. Hence the object is what I aim for. It is the objective that I have in my objective. What does aim mean? The aim naturally has a relation with phenomenality and with seeing. Yet the peculiar characteristic of the aim is that it often aims at the subjective aspect of the objective, it often takes aim at what is not yet there.

When one has an aim, the aim of an objective, one has precisely the aim for what one does not yet see, and thus for a future, a project, an intention, and so on—the object of desire. The object of desire, by definition, is not there, since that would be the object of possession or enjoyment. If it is the object of desire, it is not there. Hence, the peculiar feature of the object is that, in a certain fashion, it is not there.

First, the object is not there. That is to say, when there is an object, it will be at the second step of the ratification of the nonpresent object of the aim. The distinctive feature of the aim is that it anticipates on the actuality of the object. Hence the aim cannot see the object, since the object is not there, since it is precisely the aim which will make possible the conditions of the object's actualization, of the realization of desire, as one says. Thus what relation does the object maintain with phenomenality and visibility, since, in a certain fashion, by definition, the distinctive feature of the envisioned object is that the aim does without seeing it, since the aim envisions it? Is this a phenomenal contradiction? Absolutely not, since the phenomenality of the object means that it is not yet seen [vu] even though it is already foreseen [prévu]. The object is the foreseen. The object, as object of the aim, is always ahead of its actualization. Hence it is not visible in advance. Even so, it is seen in advance. Or rather it is seen in the mode of the advance, which exempts us from seeing it. It is seen in the mode of a realization not yet accomplished. Fundamentally, the object is the object of an expectation [une prévision], of an anticipation [une prévue]. The object is what I foresee, it is what I foresee before seeing it. That is to say, it is what I know and what I include in phenomenality in advance, that is to say, without having seen it. In a sense, what one calls objective knowledge is a knowledge that never deceives us.

What does that mean? It is a kind of knowledge where I have the full details.[5] Objective knowledge is a knowledge, in which, each time I make a mathematical or a physical calculation of preparation and execution, each time I try to see the object (that is to say, produce it), I know that the next time it will work as well as the previous. That means that the object is what I know without having any need to see it. And that is what objectivity is. If I know the conditions that make the production of the object intelligible (whatever that object might be, whether it is an actual, material or a purely rational object), I know it is enough that I know the object's conditions of possibility in order to see it without seeing it. I know that, if knowledge is objective, this is what is meant by knowledge being objective, namely, that I will be able to produce it (that is to say, actually reproduce it) each time identically. This means that it is unnecessary to produce it each time, it is enough that I know the conditions of its possibility. Thus, the distinctive feature of the object—this is crucial—is that I do not need to see it, it is enough to foresee it. It is what I see without seeing it. It is what I do not have to see and which suffices to foresee. The object has the status of unseen foreseen [prévu non vu]. It is in some way the result of an aim that is so certain of achieving its goal that it need not get down to work each time in order to see the object. Seeing it would only be, ultimately, a statistically useless verification of expectation, which is already established and always available. That is to say, in the case of the object, I can save myself its empirical verification precisely because I foresee it through the rationally known conditions of its possibility.

This point is crucial. It is the reason why, when we have to do with objects, they do not appear. Objects are simply the result (intuitively always possible, and hence finally largely optional) of expectation that gives access to an object without itself. The conditions of common phenomenality are inferred from the object, from this privilege of the object. The object, which in works such as *Being Given* I also call a "common phenomenon," has this characteristic— which is completely in keeping with the classical definition of the phenomenon in Husserl and before him in Kant—that it is a matter of a combination of intuition and concept.[6] (I remind you, as you know, that these two authors agree on the standard definition of the phenomenon in metaphysics. It is also the most positive definition one could give when one grants all reality of being to the phenomenon, when it is not an illusion.) The phenomenon is a concept or a signification that is validated by corresponding intuition. When there is as much intuition as concept, the philosophers say that there is adequation, that is to say the summit of truth, which means evidence, evidence as the subjective lived experience of consciousness corresponding to truth. What is interesting is that in effect the majority of the time we do not even require this adequation between concept and intuition. The concept is what we foresee and intuition is what we see. The majority of the time in the case of an object, in order to verify the concept, we only require a rate of weak intuitive overlap.

Allow me to use a banking comparison. Banks are assumed, I believe, to have a real capital 10 percent of what they can lend. Banks lend us money that they do not have and we repay with money that we do have. That is why it is a profitable business. The same is true for the visibility of objects. In a certain fashion, the object is first a draft drawn from the visible by the concept. This draft is honored, but it is not honored by the totality of intuition necessary to fill the concept. The more the phenomenon is a phenomenon of the technical type, the more the object is an object of the technical type, the less does the intuitive overlap matter. In fact, when we use a *Gerät* (as the Germans say), an electronic or electric device, we have a concept of this device, there is a blueprint of this device, its composition. This concept is exactly what we mean by saying: "This is an automobile, a computer, a portable telephone, a stereo . . ." Without exception, very few of us have a detailed idea of the concept. Besides, none is necessary. What we mean by "knowing" the technical object-phenomenon (that is to say the visible) is to be able to produce with certainty the minutest portion of intuition, of intuitive verification, which allows us not to confuse the handling of the telephone with the handling of the computer, the handling of the computer with the handling of the automobile. We actually ratify the totality of the concept with a very weak margin of intuitive verification. One says: "I know how to make it work," one turns a key, one pushes a button, and it works. We do not know why, we have absolutely not intuitively verified the total validity of the concept; what is more we do not even know the concept, which we reduce to the minimum. The technical object is what one does not see, but which always functions as foreseen. And the fact that it operates as foreseen in a way makes it disappear from visibility.

According to Heidegger's very beautiful analysis, the technical object only appears when it breaks down. If your computer functions, if you manage to make it function, you no longer look at it. When it does not work, you begin to eye it with a semivindictive, semipanicked and in any case murderous gaze. You ask yourself: "But what is going on in there? This is annoying. I want to know. I want to check." That's when you look at the manual, at which you have not glanced previously, you go talk to someone, and so on. You are very worried. And your anguish is an intuitive investment. In this very moment, possibly, the computer can appear. Yet when it functions, it does not appear. And the less it functions the more attention you give it, and vice versa. Hence the phenomenality of the technical object is that of not being seen. The less it is seen, the more it accords with its phenomenality. It is foreseen.

This definition of the object as "the foreseen that does not appear" is perhaps determined by taking account of two fundamental characteristics that Heidegger introduced in *Being and Time* and that I will review here, although they are rather well-known. There are two fundamental modalities of being in the world, of the inner-worldly [intra-mundane] being. It can be *vorhanden*, what I will translate as "the constant," what is present-to-hand, what stands and maintains itself before me, that is to say, the enduring. Being [l'étant], which can sometimes be called "object," designates first what remains identical to itself and which exists especially as it lasts in a renewed present, renewed and renewing its identity in itself. That is to say, this glass is essentially sand, carbon (more precisely, silicium), if I am not mistaken, with H_2O in it, plus a little drop of whiskey, that is, sugar. That's the *vorhanden*. In principle, the *vorhanden* can last a long time like that.

Yet Heidegger noticed that the *vorhanden* is in fact a reduction that places into parentheses the phenomenally anterior characteristics which are the characteristics of the *zuhanden*, that is to say of the being inasmuch as it is determined by its nature as a tool, what I will call "the useable," that is to say inasmuch as one puts it to use.[7] For—and this is a major discovery of Heidegger—the phenomenon is not first what is permanent, as the physicist, for example, would have a tendency to think. It is in the world in relation to me, who is the center of the world and who opens the world, inasmuch as it is capable of having ends (more or less arbitrarily), which are set by me or which I discover by accident on occasion, ends which are its mode of appearance. And to say that ends make being appear is exactly the example of the breakdown. This means that when you have a technical object that works, that is to say, one that is in accordance with its relations or determinations of use, it disappears precisely because it works. And it is to the extent that it no longer functions that you go look at it as such. Oddly, the automobile, for example, appears the day it has a breakdown, and then you will open the hood, you will maybe even crawl underneath, and that is the first time you see the motor or the wheels. A good car, the kind where one does not open the hood, which has a guarantee of three years or of a hundred thousand kilometers, that's a car one has no need to go see, a car where one need not check that everything works (as the saying goes), a car one has no need to see and which never appears.[8]

This is the paradox of the object: it is a common phenomenon whose visibility is more fully accomplished the less attention, of the sort one gives an appearance [apparition], is required. This detour, this introduction, is necessary in order to bring out, by contrast, what we might call the "phenomenality of what appears," and the fact that what appears, appears in a certain way without our seeing it. I turn the paradox upside down, I push the position a bit too far, but I do so to make more clearly visible what is at stake. What appears, that of which one says, "This is a sight," in a certain manner, appears without requiring that we see it.[9] What appears in this very moment precedes the act of seeing. The act of seeing is second in respect to the appearance. In order to describe this, let us ask an extremely simple question, one I asked at the beginning of *Being Given*, namely, whether Heidegger's distinctions between beings within the world, that is to say regarding phenomena, apply to the picture.[10] Can the framed picture, the classic painting, be said to appear as such, because it is constant, is *vorhanden*? Can it appear as useful, that is to say, as *zuhanden*? If we try to approach the picture as a reality of the world whose physical elements last and endure, it is very clear that we do not get to the picture as picture in this way. Besides, it is interesting to see how modern techniques of preservation and restoration have in a sense made the picture immaterial, that is to say, we can change not only the stand, the canvas, the mounting, but the pigments; we can in some way replace its entire subsisting materiality, and yet it is still the same picture. Here, incidentally, the problem of reproduction and of the status of reproduction is also raised. We see clearly that the picture is not attained as picture in its subsisting materiality. In the same fashion, we cannot reach the picture as picture, despite the fact that here one draws a bit closer to its determination. Obviously, first of all one would have to introduce questions of art history. Art history is an informative, formalistic approach to the picture as the remnant or concentration of all the information we have in its regard. That is a way of regarding it as a being subsisting in the world. It is very clear that all the information we can have about all pictures does not help us to get to the appropriate mode of appearing of a picture, which would in no way justify the almost sacred attention we give to it.

Let us move now to the picture as *zuhanden*, the picture understood as a set of purposes. This allows us to come close to the picture, but not as it appears with a phenomenal privilege. It is the picture inasmuch as it has a commercial value, inasmuch as it has an ideological meaning, inasmuch as it is a basis of identity or of recognition, or inasmuch as it has a function of social distinction—it doesn't really matter. All these are uses of the picture, meanings that we can give to the picture, but not the picture as such. How does the picture make us aware not only of its exceptional visibility but of its right to the special attention of those who experience this visibility? I will not provide a detailed analysis of this here, but I think that one would have to speak of the notion of "effect," not the effect of a cause, but effect in the sense in which one speaks of a painting "producing an effect." Kandinsky, Klee, and

Cézanne wrote some absolutely admirable passages about this. By what is a picture judged? By the effect it has.

Let us use another, equally admirable, expression: a picture is seen, is judged, by what it shows (its result), that is to say, by the effect it produces. Linguists would call it an "illocutionary" effect. I remind you that certain language acts are "illocutionary," in the sense that they are not language acts that are predicative or descriptive, not performative (that is, doing what they say), but language acts that produce an effect on the one who hears them, this effect often being different from what is being said.[11] For example, if someone says: "I could kill you," it does not necessarily mean that he or she wants to kill us. Luckily, it does not always mean that they will kill us; it can mean a whole lot of things. It produces an effect. It can mean: I love you, but you don't love me! It can mean: If I had the courage, I would kill you. It can mean many things; it can be a threat, a statement, a joke, it can be anything you want. There is an illocutionary effect. Thus, the picture has an illocutionary effect and it is on this illocutionary effect that its privilege of phenomenality is based. That is to say, in a certain fashion, the two fundamental determinations of being in the world do not apply to the picture. The picture is judged by the effect it produces. This is why it makes, oddly enough, an interconnection between aesthetics and ethics. This is because, by a Kantian and Levinassian choice, ethics is based on the effect that the moral demand has on me. What then is the type of phenomenality which corresponds to this third type of being which is neither constant, *vorhanden*, nor useful, *zuhanden*? It is the fact that, in contrast to the object, which is always foreseen, that is to say which is awaited as fulfillment of expectation [prévision] (the object is what will fulfill what has been foreseen, invalidating or confirming the concept already there, before the phenomenon is seen), the picture—that is, what is a matter of aesthetic visibility—plays on the impossibility of fore-seeing [pré-vision]. This means that one must always first see it, make the experience of its irruption into visibility. The picture, the aesthetic visible, not only escapes foreseeing, but annuls it. Before it, we are in a state of after-seeing [post-vision], if I can put it that way in order to say the opposite of foreseeing [prévision]. This after-seeing might equally well be described as taking seriously and as broadening or radicalizing its concept (common in art history) of "anamorphosis."

You all know what an anamorphosis is. Often an anamorphosis divides the picture in two. In a painting like Holbein's *Ambassadors*, for example, you stand before the picture and you have a picture.[12] It is perfectly organized or

at least it could be perfectly organized. You have a picture before you. There
is a task unlike any other in this picture. That is to say, the painting is constructed in an expectation, which actually often is the perspective, and if you
are at the center, you are supposed to see the picture organized around your
visual axis. In this sense, the picture is foreseen. You see it and you are the
center, your gaze is the center. In a sense, you can even move around the picture, you will still be the center. In an anamorphosis, by contrast, you cannot
see what there is to see until you put yourself in a certain place. This place
is not marked and it is not one you would choose spontaneously, that is, the
view facing the center. You must move around in front of the picture in order
to find yourself in the angle that the painter has imposed, but who all the
same has hidden it. Consequently, in a sole glance, if you place yourself where
the picture orders you to be, that is to say outside of the normal perspective,
you will see what should be seen appear—the skull in Holbein's painting. In
Rome, in the cloister of Trinità dei Monti, is the greatest anamorphosis ever
painted, by the Reverend Father Poisson, in praise of the order of the Pas-
sionists.[13] In art history, an anamorphic painting is a picture that optically
annuls perspective (anamorphosis, incidentally, appears at the moment in
which the perspective appears). This means that, on the one hand, there is the
picture seen from the point of view of perspective, where the one who sees
is the master, the one who sees is the transcendental subject who composes
the picture like the painter, and, on the other hand, there is another point
of view that forces me not to be master of the visible, but to go to the place
which the visible imposes on me in order to see it. This is anamorphosis and
anamorphosis is the opposite of intentionality. Intentionality is when my aim
precedes the visible. Here, the aim is the result of the visible, is the result of
the appearance of the visible. Thus appearance is an event here, that is to say,
here is this visible that to begin with precisely is not visible. One must move
about, get organized, yield to the requirements of the visible in order to see
it. And mark well that the celebrated phrase "It was a sight [apparition]" says
this, because Madame Arnoux was there and because there was a crowd of
people around in the boat. She was sitting alone on her bench, but it was necessary to be Frederic for there to be a vision, only for Frederic is there a vision.
Why? Because Frederic is in love. Frederic was the only one to be in a position
to see Madame Arnoux as a vision, something her husband had never seen.
Madame Arnoux's husband had never seen Madame Arnoux as a vision, one
had to be Frederic in order to see her as a vision, that is to say it is necessary

to be in the state of being preceded by visibility. Hence anamorphosis is not only this device of the history of painting, but it is a more general determination, a more general concept that takes account of visibility and aesthetic phenomenality.

It also makes us aware of the impossibility of foreseeing and the fact that all vision is the result of a summoning, of a summoning by and a submission to the appearance of the visible itself. It is a device not of foreseeing, but of after-seeing. And this helps us to understand the way we behave in regard to aesthetic visibility. The questions, "What is a work of art? What belongs in a museum? Should one even have museums?" and so forth, are questions raised because certain phenomena impose them. What phenomena force us to understand them as works of art, to become quasi-sacred or to be buried alive in museums? They are those visibles which cannot be foreseen, they are after-seen, and of which one can say that nobody has ever seen them. I insist on this point: What is a "work of art"? (I'm using this expression so dated and narrow that it is meaningful). What do the people, the middle class, call a "work of art"? Or the expert? It is that to which one returns [ce que l'on revoit]. The work of art is not something that one sees [voit], but it is to what one returns [revoit], what one goes to see again [va revoir]. The object is what one does not see as such, it is what one foresees and what one tries to see as little as possible as long as it works or functions. The work of art, in contrast, is that of which one can never say: I have seen it. If someone says: "I have seen a picture and thus I have no need to see it again," either it is not a picture or the speaker is a fool. The definition of the picture, of the work of art, is that it is always necessary to go see it again. And this is equally true for the ready-made. Once you have seen a bike, you have seen it. Yet when it is turned upside down, one must go see it again. And there is always a reason for it. What I call the "after-seeing" is empirically verified by the fact that the work of art is what has to be seen again, thus when one goes to a museum one goes there several times. Why? Because one knows it. The first time, certainly, it is because one does not know it, but once one "knows" it, as one says, that in itself is a good reason for going again. The quality of a museum depends on the number of things in it to which one returns. Thus this phenomenon of seeing again (a picture is what one must see again without cease) is not a reappraisal [révision], because when one revises [révise], one looks at [vise] the same thing several times and verifies that one has not been mistaken. In that case when one returns, one does go back to see something one had not seen.

What does "to see what one had not seen before" mean? It is not even to see a detail that one had not seen; that can be the case, as in Proust, where one drowns in too much detail. No, it is the effect that one goes to feel again. Why do we go to see and see again? Why must we return? Because here the intuition which should validate the concept is always in excess. The distinctive feature of the picture is that there is an excess of intuition. In my terminology it is what I call a "saturated phenomenon." In the case of a saturated phenomenon, unlike in the case of the technical object, there is no concept or a partial intuitive validation (I know how a car works, I get its concept, hence, regardless of the car, it will work). It is the fact that the better I know a picture, the more research I must undertake. That is why I want to undertake a hermeneutics that would have no reason to stop short. I lack concepts because intuition is constantly renewed for the picture. Hence in a way there is too much to see in the picture for any concepts to be able to organize the corresponding intuition. And that is why the picture requires being seen again. The picture and I share a life; that is to say, the picture will change to the extent that I will have seen it. The more I see it, the more it will give me to see, and the more my concepts will lag behind. That is why I might become very intelligent in explaining things in the picture, because in some way it is the picture that demands it of me, which imposes it on me. In this sense, the distinctive feature of the picture is that it forbids intentionality, which implies that the picture is not foreseen, not even by the painter. The picture unfurls according to its own logic, imposes itself on the painter, who does not always paint what he or she wants. And at times that is much better, and in some sense the painter improves by allowing the intentional project to pale increasingly.

There are rather exemplary cases of this. That of Cézanne is admirable. Cézanne is someone who at the end no longer knew how to paint a picture and who learned from the picture itself how to continue. At times, he did not continue the picture; he left it partially unfinished, saying that this is how it should be. Hence the picture, as an event, has initiative over who paints it and over who sees it. In this case, the picture is an appearance because it is what imposes on me that I see it, myself always in some way lacking the vision of the picture. The picture is what appears before the vision that I can have of it. From this derives the paradox that it is with a picture as with music, namely that the picture is right compared with me. If I say that I do not like the picture, the statement accuses me. The picture does not have to please me, it is up to me to adjust to it; the picture is in the right. The true picture is what is right over against me.

In this sense, one understands very well that the saturated phenomenon in the aesthetic mode is a process of the accumulation of the visible. The painter (and the photographer, etc.) has this Promethean privilege never to reproduce the world. He or she adds something visible so far unseen to the total of visible things in the world. Aristotle said that art either imitates nature or fulfills it, implying that it adds to nature. The painter increases the quantity, I might say the density, of the visible, that is to say of the world's phenomenality. And that is something we sense physically when we travel to countries without museums or without painting, for there are such places: there is a weakened density of visibility. I almost would dare say that in this sense museums are sanctuaries of intensity of appearance that enhance the visibility of the world in some way. Museums do not contain a different visible, but the same visible, quantitatively and qualitatively stronger, so much so that we see the common visible that is outside the picture in some way on the model of the visible of the picture, because the visible of the picture is more visible than the common visible.

This is so much so that the landscape I see in Aix (I live in the region of Ornans, home to Gustave Courbet), I see according to the pictures. Paintings are not reproductions of landscape, but exactly the reverse. In fact, I believe I see the visibility of the landscape and what I see is what Courbet has produced (I do not say: "has put there"), has added to it. We see inside of pictures. Pictures are the paradigm of shared visibility. In this sense, as in novels, the great novels of Proust and Célan, the novel has the truth, the absolute truth of experience. We are before an instance of a saturated phenomenon.

The saturated phenomenon is the excess of intuition over the concept and, in this case, of the intuition in the mode of what Kant calls "quality." Among Kant's categories there is quantity, quality, relation and modality. What is interesting when he determines quality is that Kant says that any concept allows an anticipation of perception. Why an anticipation of perception? He claims it is because I know that any phenomenon will have an intensive size, that is to say, a degree of stimulation of sensible intuition. And the problem is to measure this degree of intensity of any perception. Yet what is strange in Kant is that he speaks of a grade of degrees, like a thermometer, rising from zero. He says that starting from zero, we can determine the degrees of intensity of perception—of intuition, as it happens. What is very strange is that he does not consider the question of the maximum, which is the essential question for me. This means that phenomenality has degrees of intensity, but this degree of intensity reaches subjectively, and according to individuals, a maximum beyond which we cannot tolerate what we nevertheless perceive. The real question, in fact, is the determination of the maximum. Why does the work of art shock? It is a question of the tolerable maximum of intensity of intuition. And the evolution of taste is an evolution of variations of tolerable maximum of intensity of intuition. This is characteristic of the saturated phenomenon. When the aesthetic performance shocks or scandalizes it is not a question of morality; it has nothing to do with morality, it is an illusion, the wrong sort of conventionality. It is neither a moral nor a political problem. It is a problem of the degree of intensity that we can bear, which itself varies. There are glories that we cannot bear—which incidentally is the biblical definition of glory. It is such a perfect presence that anyone who is imperfect cannot bear it. It is precisely this that we face when we are in front of a picture. Moreover, that is why we can get used to it, because we can make progress. It is quite funny to see how at times a painter sets off a scandal and why, eventually, some no longer are considered scandalous, why, for example, the whole world has assimilated lyrical abstraction without any difficulty. For we are capable of enduring a stronger intensity than our ancestors, than what we have learned. In this way the aesthetic phenomenon, aesthetic visibility, should be conceived as a privileged and particular case of visibility, in opposition to the visibility of the object for instance, but also as one of the places from which the whole question of phenomenality is raised. This means that aesthetic questions are too serious to be left to people who specialize in questions of aesthetics. It is fundamental for philosophers, because it is here that the possibilities, not at the extreme but as the standard for phenomenality, are defined in part (I think that theology also has a word to say on this very subject and so do other areas). The phenomenality of the object is a derived and not a normative case, because it is impoverished. The fact that the poor phenomenality of phenomena like objects is quantitatively dominant does not give it a normative status in any way. On the contrary, aesthetic phenomenality is not a marginal indication, despite the fact that it is in the minority; hence it points to the possibilities of phenomenality. In its freedom and strength phenomenality extends from saturated phenomena of the aesthetic type in a way absolutely normative for poor phenomena.

From this we understand, I conclude, how the brilliant (to say it directly) phenomenological definition, which Heidegger gave to the phenomenon, hinges on the question of the image, of the icon, of aesthetic visibility. Philosophers (who were not the majority) before Heidegger gave the phenomenon not the status of an illusion with regard to reality but of reality itself, that is to say they gave the phenomenon the status of an object, which in their language is one of the highest determinations they can give. I mean Husserl and Kant; for Husserl and Kant the phenomenon is an object. In this sense, it is real, it exists, it is a being, it has nothing to do with illusion, it is the world. Yet the object, by definition, is always submitted to and produced by the subject. The subject, possibly called transcendental, synthesizes the object in Kant's language; in Husserl's it constitutes it—we say: produces it, introduces it into phenomenality and into visibility. Hence, the phenomenon as object only appears when it is seen.

The question remains open as to what extent Heidegger himself accomplished what he implies as a watchword and thus also as a program. Heidegger introduces for the first time the definition of the phenomenon in which the phenomenon is not synthesized, not constituted by an instance depending on it; that is to say, the phenomenon is not an object because it does not depend on any subject, whatever one might call it, not even on *Dasein*. The phenomenon appears starting from itself, which means that it shows itself. I repeat the celebrated phrase from *Being and Time* (§7): ". . . to make visible from itself what shows itself as it shows itself from itself" means allowing what shows itself as it shows itself from itself and by starting from itself, allowing it to show itself as such. The phenomenon is what shows itself starting from itself, and the distinctive feature of phenomenology is to allow what shows itself from itself to show itself from itself. This is a radical change. The phenomenon is seen because it appears, because it shows itself starting from itself, because it manifests itself. It is not that it would appear, because we produce it or because we see it. The phenomenon manifests itself. And it manifests itself from itself, because when one manifests, one always starts from oneself. Is it then possible to admit that phenomena manifest themselves starting from themselves rather than being constituted or produced? In order to say that, it is at the very least necessary that the phenomena would not be straightaway understood as objects. Yet the question is: where can we experience phenomena that would not have the status of objects, phenomena which show themselves starting from themselves? The answer, or one of the answers, is maybe the most obvious. It is: in aesthetic visibility. I am not taking a stand on the limits of aesthetic visibility, but I am saying that the stake of the work of aesthetics, of aesthetic visibility, is to make autonomous, independent phenomena accessible. These phenomena manifest themselves as free citizens within the horizon of phenomenality. They manifest themselves unconditionally as they see fit. This is what adds seriousness to the aesthetic enterprise, which, if I may say so, often goes well beyond the stakes that the specialists in the field of aesthetics assign to it. Only by beginning there, and only there, can questions be broached that I mention for the record, questions that I have tackled but which now appear to me as particular specifications: the question of the distinction between idol and icon; the idol is the first visible and hence the invisible mirror of the gaze; the question of the icon, which is the visibility of the invisible, because it is the visibility of the gaze aimed at us (the gaze, by definition, is invisible); the question of the abstract and of the figurative.

And in this sense, I take up the principle that Michel Henry has underlined, but which belongs to Kandinsky, namely, that all painting is abstract. The greatness of a painting is judged by the effect it produces, hence any painting is abstract, even figurative painting. A painting that is not abstract would certainly not be a painting. In that case, can photography be abstract? I will not reply to this question, but it is one of the questions that should be raised. Of course, the fundamental question is, if the phenomenon produces itself starting from itself, what is the status of the one who is its witness and who sees it? In the statement "It was a sight," the one who sees is the one who is in love. That is to say, if one is not in love, one does not see the sight [apparition], there is no appearance [apparition]. This can be transposed into different areas—theology has much to teach us on this point—but the aesthetic question is finding out who is the subject of the aesthetic experience. Can one do without the category of aesthetic experience? Some think so, others do not. Can one be the actor of an aesthetic experience? What does a "performance" really mean? Is there not a contradiction in these terms? Perhaps not, but then one must explain this: what is the function of the one who sees when one's visibility is second in relation to the event of what gives itself to be seen, of what appears? For, of course, one must say that, contrary to what the discourse of the painter as king, as creator, as prince has long allowed us to assume, in painting, the one who sees it is precisely not the one who produced it. That is to say, the experience of seeing the aesthetic visible is an experience in which the one who sees is not the master of his or her vision, is stripped of vision, in contrast to ordinary vision. What sort of subjectivity is implied here? What are the sorts of subjectivities implied here? These are questions that interest me. And also the fundamental problem of the density of stimulation, the intensity of intuition one can bear. Who sets its standards? A theory of genius is possible here, in the sense of the Romantics: the genius is the one who settles the laws of nature. Here, it is the one who sets the limits of that for which we can become witnesses. These are more technical and, in a sense, secondary questions. I end on this point. Once again, what is decisive, and without doubt why phenomenology pays such almost obsessive attention to questions of painting and of aesthetics in general, is that what is at stake there is an exceptional realm of visibility. Phenomenology in particular realizes that, far from being marginal, it is one of the access roads to the original situation of the manifestation of phenomena.

Translated by Christina M. Gschwandtner

ON HEIDDEGER, THE IDOL,
AND THE WORK OF THE WORK OF ART

DANIEL DONESON

Energeia means the presence—*to huparchein*—of the thing but
not only in the sense which we mean by potentiality. We say that
a thing is present potentially as Hermes is present in the wood.

Aristotle, *Metaphysics*, 1048a32–33

Hegel saw it coming. In the first part of his *Lectures on Aesthetics* he famously announced: "It is certainly the case that art no longer affords that satisfaction of spiritual needs which earlier ages and nations sought in it, and found in it alone. . . . In all these respects art, considered in its highest vocation, is and remains for us a thing of the past. . . . For us art counts no longer as the highest mode in which truth fashions as existence in itself." In the twentieth century, no less a thinker than Heidegger took Hegel's lectures as his cue when he asked whether "art is still an essential and necessary way in which that truth happens which is decisive for our historical existence." I want to approach the question of the idol by means of a reading of Heidegger's notoriously difficult reflections, "The Origin of the Work of Art."[1]

First, I will discuss the critique of what Heidegger calls "the metaphysical interpretation" of art. Since the traditional discussion of the cult-statue is bound up with the metaphysical interpretation of art, it can only be approached by thinking through that interpretation and its inadequacies. According to Heidegger, the tradition of aesthetics simultaneously fails to make sense of both the species (cult-statue) and the genus (the work of art). It is precisely the misunderstanding of the artwork by the metaphysical approach of aesthetics that renders the cult-statue an "idol"—mistakenly interpreting it as a "representation" and simultaneously declaring it a failure according to this criterion. To understand Heidegger's critique of traditional aesthetics and what he proposes in its place—to understand "the origin of the work of art"—is to understand the core of the problematic of "idolatry" and its failure to account properly for works that mediate between a people and "the holy," that commence and sustain a relationship between them.

Second, I will discuss Heidegger's alternative attempt to think about the meaning of artworks, free from the metaphysical interpretation of aesthetics. According to Heidegger, artworks must be thought in relation to the truth, now understood as an activity, or "the setting into work of truth," its inauguration or commencement. It is this claim about the artwork's relation to truth that is so difficult to grasp, not to say controversial. Through a careful consideration of his central example, the Greek temple, I hope to make clear what Heidegger is after. Works like the Greek temple allow us to think about made objects that "plug" mortal life into divinity or "the holy" by "opening up the world" and "setting forth the earth." Aesthetics, founded on metaphysics (according to Heidegger's sweeping claim, all aesthetics hitherto has been metaphysical), dubs such works "idols." In so doing it profoundly misunderstands them: both what they are, and how they work, seeing only a failure of some sort of representation or manifestation.[2]

Finally, I want to explore Heidegger's elusive reflections on whether works of art can still function—open up a world—and serve as a genuine new opening or foundation for us. If they can continue to do so, how is it possible? The great works of art of the past, the temple, the cathedral, like the cult-statue, were intimately tied to "the holy." But even freed from metaphysical interpretation, there remains for us "the withdrawal of the holy." We cannot simply return. After "the death of God," what does Heidegger think the place of art can be in our lives? Can art function as a kind of "anti-idol"?

The Metaphysical Interpretation of the Artwork and "the Idol"

Most attempts to think about the made cult-object, the so-called "idol," merely bring out in an especially perspicuous fashion what is implicit in aesthetics: that the man-made object brings together the suprasensible (or "holy") and the sensible (the material object). In effect, by critiquing this aesthetic approach, Heidegger accuses the tradition of aesthetics of "idolatry." In both cases—cult-object and aesthetically approached art object—Heidegger argues, the thing and its peculiar power are not properly understood. Why, exactly, does Heidegger refuse aesthetics?

Heidegger declares that the meditation on art, or aesthetics, began with Plato and Aristotle, and that since then all theory of art has been subjected to a remarkable fate (1935:52).[3] Because the work of art has been understood right from the start of this tradition as a fabricated thing, the conception of art has always been allegorical or symbolical, the sense that in the work of art there is something else than the mere product: "The artwork is indeed a thing that is made, but it says something other than what the mere thing itself is, *allo agoreuei*. The work makes publicly known something other than itself, it manifests something other: it is an allegory. In the artwork something other is brought into conjunction with the thing that is made. The Greek for 'to bring into conjunction with' is *symballein*. The work is a symbol" (1935:52). Understanding the work of art as an allegorical or symbolical product means understanding the work as consisting of two different parts: matter plus something else—the form—or material content plus spiritual meaning. As far as art is understood as the process of bringing together of matter and spirit, it is defined as a representation of the suprasensible in the sensible (1935:53). The metaphysical logic at work here is that of addition. In the metaphysical tradition the human being and language are understood in the same manner: animal body plus soul, mind, or spirit; phonetical material plus meaning.[4]

Now, the metaphysical interpretation at work in the history of aesthetics and the conceptualization of the cult-statue conceives our encounter with the work, typically, as representationalism or formalism. Both of these approaches are traceable to the way in which metaphysical thought fails properly to state the question of truth, the happening of truth. In other words, if the cult-object or any artwork's relationship to truth is emphasized but still conceived metaphysically, the value and meaning of it will be seen to consist in *manifestation*, that it makes visible, on the plane of sensibility, a propositional truth that somehow expresses "the given fact of the matter," be it the emotional state of a human being (the artist), or the social configuration of such and such a time and place (sociological representationalism), or the very structure of the highest form of being, the divine.

The basic difficulty of every representational position is that it renders art merely provisional and inessential. Hegel's *Aesthetics* itself, where art is justified precisely because it is *aufgehoben*, overcome and sublated by philosophy, provides a particularly famous case. According to such representationalism, there are a number of elements that imply the inessentiality of the work. If the work is the bearer of a message of truth, then it will address itself principally to the intellect; all the interest drawn from the sensible and physical presence of the work is not essential, but only a provisional covering for a truth that remains to be abstracted. To argue that the work in its concrete physical nature is inessential proves fatal to any theory of aesthetic judgment. What matters in the work is the truth of which it is a mere sign or the mythical representation. Nothing else counts.

On the other hand, apart from this representational approach, we have the approach of formalism. Here, art objects do have an original function that is not simply another form of knowledge: they may be viewed as a pure formal construct, objects that "impose" themselves and their validity. But this approach is still bad metaphysics, as we see from the way in which the formalist returns willy-nilly to representational positions. For example, the pleasure taken in a beautiful structure can be tied to the way in which our intellect or sensibility works, or to the perceptual or evaluative habits that are rooted in our belonging to this or that social group. In all these cases, the work is viewed as a more or less provisional incarnation of forms, which are otherwise given, and which only find in the work the occasion for recognizing and explicating themselves.

So in formalism, just as in representationalism, we confront the insufficiencies of the metaphysical interpretation: after every *Aufhebung* and every analysis, once the truth of which it is the bearer is recognized, the work presents itself as something that allows itself to be simply bracketed. Since the truth is given prior to and outside the work, the work itself is only a contingent manifestation of a representation. There is the godhead, or the "the holy," and there is the statue. The relationship between truth and the work's contingency, or that of every event, is tied, ultimately, to an interpretation that continues to take truth to be correspondence with the given.

By contrast, for Heidegger the statue of the god is not a picture made after him, not some made representation, but rather the god himself, that is to say, his coming into presence and not the reproduction of an absent or remote being. Nothing is represented, there is no addition of something suprasensuous to the material form. Likewise, tragedy is not the telling of a story and does not speak *about* the battle of the gods, but in it the battle *is* being fought. In other words, the work of art initiates and founds, and does not represent or exhibit something absent. The cult-statue, like the temple or any great work of art, portrays nothing; rather, it simply stands there, and opens a space which "gives place" to everything. There are no two worlds there, a human world and a world beyond, making contact; there is no beyond; rather, there is the artwork at work. Heidegger defines this work of the artwork as *das Ins-Werke-setzen der Wahrheit*, the setting-into-work of truth. But what does it mean for the artwork to be the setting-into-work of truth?

The Origin of the Work of Art Beyond Metaphysics

The title of the essay "The Origin of the Work of Art" may seem to imply a research into a cause, and thus the origin of the work of art would seem to be the artist. But the artist, Heidegger reminds us, is only the artist in relation to the works that he or she creates. If the artist is the origin of the artwork, the artwork is no less the origin of the artist. And so we are compelled to recognize that the "artist and work *are* each, in themselves and in their reciprocal relation, on account of a third thing, which is prior to both; on account, that is, of that from which both artist and artwork take their names," that is, art (1956:1). Art is both the origin of the artist and the artwork. Art is that which determines particular beings—work and artist—in their being. But this is ambiguous. In one sense of the genitive, the question of the origin *of* the work of art is a question of art as an origin, of *how* art is, and can be the origin of work and artist. In another sense of the genitive, the question of the origin of the work of art is a question about *what* the artwork can originate, *what* is its work, the capacity or power of the work of art itself.

Since Heidegger is asking about the *essence* of the work of art, any question about the causal sense of origin takes for granted that we have selected out works of art, as if one only needs simply to document their production. But it is precisely the initial designation of something as art that is at issue. Don't we have some sense of art as a distinctive category? Heidegger thinks that by moving in this circle between works of art and the concept of art we can find a clue to the question of origins—in his distinctive sense of origins—that is not merely empty. Indeed, that we tend to identify some *things* as works of art provides Heidegger with the initial clue: all works of art have a "thingly" character. It is by trying to clarify the thingliness of things that Heidegger invites us to think about the work of art. He begins by articulating three traditional metaphysical conceptions of "things."

In the first conception, the thing is understood as a bearer of properties. According to this way of thinking, the thing serves as a kind of logical unity, that x in which various properties inhere. But Heidegger finds this conception inadequate because it holds the thing at too far a distance; we never apprehend the core, that which bears the properties; we get only the properties and the thing disappears.

In the second conception, the thing is understood as the unity of a sensible manifold. In other words, the second conception draws a conclusion from the first: since we never apprehend the x underlying the properties, but only the properties themselves, then the thing is really nothing more than the properties; the thing is just the perceived qualities taken together. Heidegger objects for two reasons. First, the conception seems to do injustice to our experience: our perceptual experience is not directed toward perceptible properties, or "a throng of perceptions," but rather our perceptions are more thingly from the beginning: we hear the sonata, not a collection of sounds that we interpret as the sonata. Second, the thing disappears here as well. Thinking that the thing is nothing more than the perceptions we have of it fails to think the way that the thing is self-contained, as something out there.

In the third conception the immediate problem of the first two conceptions is surmounted: the thing is understood as formed matter, or form and matter. As material, the thing has a certain bodily density and the reference to form captures the sense in which the thing is individual, self-contained, set off from its surroundings. For example, take a stone lying on the beach. Such a stone is a mere thing, an individual, material entity, naturally occurring without any purpose or intended use. It is just a stone and nothing more. Its form would seem to be nothing more than its accidental shape—the distribution of matter. But this idea of form is not what is at work in more complicated kinds of things, such as equipment or works of art. Here the idea of form is not accidental. The form is what determines the distribution of the matter. In this sense, the form is prior to the matter. In the case of equipment, unlike the stone, the determinative character of form is bound up with use. The case of artworks is markedly different. For one thing, they are not useful in the same, obvious sense. According to Heidegger, the traditional form-matter distinction fails to capture these differences in what *form* means in regard to things, equipment, and artworks.

According to Heidegger, all three of the above conceptions of thing are distortions. They all compel one to force things into categories that obscure the thing by falsifying our experience of it, usually by assimilating things, equipment, and artworks. They are incapable of properly grasping the difference in differences.

Still, the thingly character of equipment may furnish a clue. Equipment is something *for* something; since it is for something, equipment serves some purpose within the context of ongoing activity and has a place within that activity. Every piece of equipment is embedded in the referential totality constitutive of worldliness; it "refers," as Heidegger says, to that world, although not in any explicit sense. A principle characteristic of equipment is that it is not noticed when it is working properly as the equipment it is meant to be; we only notice it when something has gone wrong, when the item of equipment is missing or broken, or when it is in the way, or when it has completed the activity.[5]

The tendency of items of equipment to "withdrawal" implies that they are not useful for revealing themselves, for revealing the kind of things they are. For example, Heidegger says, consider a peasant's shoes. The shoes play a very specific role in the life of the peasant. Shoes protect the feet, allow one to persevere in toil; their material may bear the mark of a particular time and place; moreover, they possess traces of one's work, little by little conforming to one's feet, soiled by the ground upon which one walks, wearing out with time. While the shoes, as equipment, are constituted by their role in the activity of the life of the peasant, and bear the marks of that life over time, the shoes themselves do not call attention to that role, nor to that life in which they play that role. As mere equipment, they are used up, so to speak, in the life of the peasant.

But consider a painting of a peasant's shoes. Unlike an actual pair of shoes that withdraw as they are put to use, the shoes in Van Gogh's painting are there, on the contrary, precisely to be noticed. One cannot take these shoes and put them on, there is no question of putting them to use in the manner of an actually existing pair of shoes. Moreover, the whole point of the shoes in the painting is to be looked at, to be taken in visually and not withdraw.[6] The painting, we may say, holds forth the shoes, and therewith announces something about the shoes: we take notice of the shoes and their place in the life of one who wears them. According to Heidegger, the painting lets "us know what the shoes, in truth, are" (1956:15). The painting makes manifest precisely the very aspects of the shoes—and the life of the one who wears them—that the actual shoes possessed but withdrew. Thus, according to Heidegger, "the essential nature of art would be this: the setting-itself-to-work of the truth of beings" (1956:16).

What Heidegger is after becomes less obscure, perhaps, with his central example, the Greek temple: "A building, a Greek Temple, portrays nothing. It simply stands there in the middle of the rocky, fissured valley. The building encloses the figure of a god and within this concealment, allows it to stand forth through the columned hall within the holy precinct. Through the temple, the god is present in the temple. The presence of the god is, it itself, the extension and delimitation of the precinct as something holy." The Greek temple is bound to its place; "standing there, the building rests on the rocky ground" (1956:21). It thus belongs to a region. It doesn't just happen to be in some spot or other, it is *of* the region in some way, by being "installed" there, and not somewhere else; and it is of the region in that it is crafted out of material rooted in that place.

But that is not all. The site-specific character of the temple is also bound up with the particular people for whom the temple is significant. It is not so much that the temple belongs to the region and a people. On the contrary, according to Heidegger, "men and animals, plants and things, are never present and familiar as unalterable things fortuitously constituting a suitable environment for the temple that, one day, is added to what is already present" (1956:21). The claim is that the temple is what first even allows there to be a region and a people: "It is the temple work that first structures and simultaneously gathers around itself the unity of those paths and relations in which birth and death, disaster and blessing, victory and disgrace, endurance and decline acquire for the human being the shape of destiny" (1956:20–21). Heidegger is suggesting that it is only by means of the temple that it makes sense to speak of a people at all. "Standing there the temple first gives to things their look, and to men their outlook on themselves" (1956:21). The temple "fits together" and "gathers around itself" the "paths and relations" of a group of people so that they might be more than a simple throng, and so that the events in their lives may be more than a series of events that befall them. Heidegger's choice of examples—"birth and death, disaster and blessing, victory and disgrace, endurance and decline"—suggests that the temple gathers together and sets up the meaningful distinctions in terms of which things matter or constitute a form of life for a people.

The temple gives things their "look," opens up a "view" that "remains open as long as the work is a work, as long as the god has not fled from it"

(1956:21). The implication for thinking about made objects that plug determinate human communities into "the holy" is not hard to discern. Heidegger calls this "opening" established by the work the founding of a world: "As a work, the work holds open the open of a world" (1956:23). In other words, were it not for the work of the work of art, there would be no such world, no such historical people who understand themselves and their surroundings in such-and-such ways: "World is not a mere collection of things—countable and uncountable, known and unknown—that are present at hand. Neither is world a merely imaginary framework added by our representation to the sum of things that are present. *World worlds*, and is more fully in being than all those tangible and perceptible things in the midst of which we take ourselves to be at home" (1956:23). Heidegger is trying to capture the way in which what exists is understood, as long as there are people who stay "in the openness of beings" (1956:23). World, here, is like a form of life, wherein possibilities interlock, and activities and things are manifest or show up in distinctive and variegated ways, ones that hang together.

So works of art do something, in that they can be at-work. In this way, their form is no mere distribution of matter, nor is their form, as with equipment, *simply* bound to their function. That is to say, works of art do not work like equipment; they do not withdraw or become transparent in their functioning. The work of the work of art opens the world, rather than accomplishes this or that end within an already formed world of interlocking activities.

Now what about the materiality of artworks? The thingliness or materiality of artworks is not some mere accident, but essential to how artworks reveal and make manifest. The matter matters. The gold of the calf, the marble of the statue, the brick of the pyramid, the stone of the temple, all matter. The work of art brings out something we would not notice otherwise: not just the place of the shoes in the life of the peasant, but also that they are grounded, that they belong to a materially specific setting. Heidegger even says that the temple itself first "makes visible" the natural and material setting: it "lights up that on which and in which man bases his dwelling" (1956:21). The Greek temple or the cathedral at Bamberg, like the temple in Jerusalem or the Kaaba in Mecca, is grounded, opens up a particular human world, precisely because it is grounded in a particular natural setting that is also the ground of the world it opens up. According to Heidegger, the materiality of works of art reveals something about the concept of world, of how a world is opened up or sustained, and what it means for a world, or form of life, to close off, or even die.

Heidegger speaks of the earth to capture the materiality of a work of art in its complex interplay with the world it opens up. Just as the work of art "sets up a world," it also "sets forth the earth." These are two essential features of the work of the work of art: "The setting up of a world and the setting forth of earth are two essential traits belonging to the work-being of the work. Within the unity of that work-being, however, they belong together" (1956:26). It is not that the work accomplishes two separate tasks. Rather, the "unity" of the "work-being" means they are both "essential features." By "setting up a world, the work sets forth the earth" (1956:24).

The setting up of a world and the setting forth of earth are two essential traits belonging to the work-being of the work. Within the unity of that work-being, however, they belong together. The earth is "undisclosable." That it is stubbornly opaque and elusive implies that the various historically "sent" understandings of being are themselves finite. Crucial to Heidegger's thinking of earth is that it is precisely what resists natural science and any attempts to grasp it theoretically.

Earth "rises up through world" in the sense that every space of intelligibility is inherently finite, mortal, an opening onto the things that are, that will eventually close. World and earth are thus in opposition to one another, in the sense that every world, as clearing, clears away some part of the earth. Any clearing requires effort. Moreover, whatever has been cleared remains vulnerable to its environment. Metal rusts, wood decays, and so on. A world imposes itself on earth, and while the earth accommodates this imposition, it resists it as well. Things, after all, get dirty.

What is it about a work of art that "sets forth the earth"? What is the role of the work of art in this interplay between world and earth? Heidegger says, "The work moves the earth into the open of a world and holds it there. The work lets the earth be an earth" (1956:24). The emergence of the Greek temple delineates, as if for the first time, its surrounding environment as *that* particular environment. This work of delineation is not just the accidental articulation of what surrounds the work. A work of art is something material, matter has been worked over, formed; a work of art, like items of equipment, uses raw materials. However, in contrast to the work of art, equipment uses up the raw materials such that they disappear. In the manufacture of equipment—for example, a sword—the metal is used and used up. Equipment does not "let the earth be an earth" in any meaningful sense, because nothing conspicuously earthy remains in the finished item of equipment.

In contrast to equipment, the work of art uses raw materials without using them up, in a manner consistent with its essentially conspicuous character. The materiality of the raw materials used in the work is itself made manifest: "On the one hand, the temple work, in setting up a world, does not let the material disappear; rather, it allows it to come forth for the very first time, to come forth, that is, into the open of the world of the work" (1956:24). Unlike equipment, the work of art displays the materiality of its composition: the colors, paint, and textures of the painted canvas; the mass and density of the carved rock; the sonority of the voice or musical notes; the rhythm and linguistic feel and field of the poet's words. This coming forth of the earth is not a separate moment of the work of art, but part and parcel of the work's "setting up a world." As Blanchot observes, "The statue glorifies the marble."[7] The vein and luster of the marble shines through within the limits of the configuration of the statue.

Heidegger speaks of "the strife" between earth and world to capture the intricate relation of the imposition of world and the resistance of earth. Moreover, the strife is not some general property of works of art; rather, great works of art, like the temple and the cathedral, instigate this strife in very particular ways. The strife instigated by the founding work of art is particular to the world set up by the work. Since every world embodies a particular understanding of being, a particular "truth of beings," so both the way the earth is set forth and the way the earth resists that way of understanding pertain uniquely to that world. For example, the strife in the temple is different than that in the cathedral: each uses matter differently, so each makes manifest a different opposition between world and earth. What resists the world of the temple is the inarticulate surge of the sea that surrounds it: "The steadfastness of the work stands out against the surge of the tide, and, in its own repose, brings out the raging of the surf" (1956:21). In the case of the cathedral, however, the vaults and the archways that gather together the understanding of things, heavenly and divine, are resisted by the ground's earthy pull, which is emphasized all the more by the angularity and loftiness of the imposing edifice.

The opposition between earth and world founded by a great work of art may cease. A work, and with it a form of life, may go dead. This is not the same as saying the work has ceased to exist, or that it is no longer admirable; rather, the work ceases to be *at work*, it no longer stands in the middle of the world founded by it. A work of art may create and sustain an "opening" onto beings, but it may just as well close up, like the ancient Greek understanding of being founded by the temple, or the specific Christianity of the medieval cathedral.

Whether by means of neglect, abandonment, disuse, or repudiation, a work of art may cease to gather in any active sense.

In thinking about the world opened up and the earth set-forth by the artwork, Heidegger is inquiring into how artworks work. Artworks are created, so there is need for a creator, an artist. But given the work the artworks do, and their vulnerability, there is just as much need for preservers: "Just as a work cannot be without being created, just as it stands in essential need of creators, so what is created cannot come into being without preservers" (1956:40). By "preservers" Heidegger does not mean the various specialists who dedicate themselves to the physical preservation and restoration of works of art, but rather those who "respond to the truth happening in the work" (1956:41). A great work of art, one that founds a historical people in its understanding of being, releases things from their concealment, renders them unconcealed, open to becoming part and parcel of our activities. But such unconcealment means little if there is no one to whom and for whom things are so revealed. If nobody abides by the way of understanding of what there is, opened up by the work, the artwork is no longer working. Heidegger's preservers—like sages of the Torah or Talmud, or the priests of pharaoh—preserve the truth of that world and keep the work alive. Without preservers, a great work of art becomes merely a ruin or a relic, the way the Talmud without its sages becomes just another book, or the pyramids get sealed with their secrets.

The Anti-"Idol"

Both the Freiberg and the Frankfurt versions of Heidegger's lecture pose the question of how far, and to what extent, art can still exist.[8] Heidegger narrates the history of art and aesthetics within a framework taken over from Hegel. Art is not defined on the basis of aesthetic judgments concerning the relative merits of artistic styles, but following Hegel's phrase, according to an "absolute need."[9] Its task, in a paraphrase of Hegel, is to be "the definite fashioner and preserver of the absolute."[10] Hegel had understood art as belonging together with religion and philosophy, in "bringing to consciousness and expressing the Divine."[11] Art, like religion and philosophy, attempts to express "the highest," *das Höchste*. In Heidegger's own terms, art is the definite formulation and preservation of beings as a whole.[12] But as Hegel famously declared, the work performed by art passed to religion and finally to philosophy: "Art is and remains for us, on the side of its highest vocation, something past."[13]

What remains to be decided, according to Heidegger, is whether art is to be something secondary, as happens when it is conceived in terms of representationalism or formalism and the metaphysical interpretation that underlies them, looking to an expression and elucidated further in terms of such concepts as embellishment, entertainment, recreation, and edification; or whether art is to be "an instigator of our history" (1935:22). The conclusion of the Freiberg version no longer asks whether and how art is an origin, but whether it can be an origin again, and not simply an ornament, supplement, or excitation.

Is art dead? If Hegel were right it would remain to understand why art had died and what the consequences were of this failure.[14] Heidegger cannot accept the Hegelian verdict of the death of art. This would also be the end of history and peoples. This is the dilemma Heidegger confronted: either modern art is an art entirely set apart from the people and thus undermines any national notion which grounds his attempt to determine both art and politics; or modern art is not an art at all, in which case the problem is truly serious: Hegel would be right.

But if art in modernity is an art, certain decisive, enigmatic questions remain: Where does it come from? What are its origins? What is this epoch? To this question Heidegger responded only with hesitation. Already in "The Principle of Reason," Heidegger makes a brief but striking allusion to abstract art as he delineates its provenance. It is to a new world, dominated by scientific technology, that abstract art corresponds. More precisely, it is the *axiomatic* character of modern scientific thought, a character that divests such thought of any specific object, that commands a "construction of the world" in which "nonobjective" or "abstract" art finds its legitimate function.

Later, in Athens in 1967, in one of his last lectures, "The Origin of Art and the Determination of Thinking," Heidegger poses the question:

> Is there today, after two and a half millennia, an art which commands the same exigency as did the art of ancient Greece? And if not, from what region comes the exigency to which modern art, in all its domains, responds? Its works no longer emerge marked by the seal of the limits of a world defined by the people or the nation. They belong to the universality of global civilization. Their composition and their organization are part of that which scientific technology projects and produces. This science has determined the mode and the possibilities of man's stay in the world.[15]

This is remarkable. Modern art is no longer produced as the expression of a people or a nation. It is transitional and accords with the universal homogenizing tendencies of techno-science. But it seems that Heidegger here accedes to a positive notion of modern art. Heidegger acknowledges the legitimate historical presence of modern art in the current civilization, and its necessary correspondence with the decisive role played by techno-science. But, then, for Heidegger it is this science and technology, and no longer art, which now define human existence.

Nevertheless, this interpretation is not fully satisfying for Heidegger. He continues: "The modes by which we determine reality in a scientific world, and by the name 'science,' we understand natural science, mathematical physics, emphasize something that is only too well known. By this means one is easily prompted to explain that the region from which the requirement to which modern art responds is none other than the scientific world. We hesitate to give our assent. We remain in indecision."[16] Must we now assign to modern technology what was formerly merited by the work of art? How are we to understand the relation or role of art in the coming technological, global civilization?

For Heidegger, art has become simply a nihilistic placeholder, an "anti-idol": a place in which we behold something that is not an object for productive use, mere equipment or craft, nor an object to be properly represented by the methods of mathematical physics for purposes of prediction and control. On the contrary, art assumes the place once occupied by the cult-statue, ritual, prayer, the temple or cathedral service, the Sabbath, or classical contemplation—human activities understood as the completion of action, or as a telos in which we fully realize our essence as more than mere animal, simple nature, or energy for manipulation. In that sense, art is still world-determinative—except that now the activity is without recourse to eternity, a metaphysical beyond, "the holy," or something secure outside life. In this sense, it is what Heidegger calls "nihilistic." For example, the Greek temple, or Mecca, or the temple in Jerusalem completely articulate the truth of their worlds for their respective peoples (the unity, look, direction and organization, given to a series of interlocking activities and events, the first things and the last, a sense of direction to life, and "the final why"). They determine what is god, what is man, our difference from the animal, the sacred and profane, what is the center of the world (or spatiality), and so on. As we have seen, they gather together and set up the meaningful distinctions in terms of which things matter, and matter in highly determinate ways, constitute a form of life for a people. Clearly, art has not done that for some time.

By contrast, the artwork understood as a nihilistic placeholder is a place in the midst of life that is neither simply production (equipment or craft) nor representation (science or reflection); and nor is it ordered teleologically toward completion in an act in which we participate in eternity (*nous*, divine rest, sacrifice, cultic worship, etc.). Rather, it is an activity that holds open the possibility for something else. Our activity, and ultimately our humanity, is not understood with the Romantics on the model of biological organism or vitalism. Nor is it understood with Cartesianism (mechanically), or with German Idealism, as freedom understood as a different order of causality. Rather than the site in which we "plug in" to Being or the eternal via traditional relations to the sacred, art now, in the age of technology, becomes on the contrary the site in which we "unplug." That is, it is the site in which we exhibit or reveal our uncanny strangeness, the fact we are not at home in the world, not just another piece of energy for manipulation, to be ordered for ever greater efficiency.

Heidegger tries to think this uncanniness in our mysterious relation to creation, the fact we initiate new forms not causally explainable by, or reducible to, prior conditions, objects, or cause. He does so in a way that is of course distinct from German Idealism's notion of freedom. In Heidegger's prose, truth arises "out of nothing." In determining the ex nihilo character of the historical openings that the work of art can originate, Heidegger wants to understand us as being shorn of any residues from the theological and metaphysical traditions at work in "the idol," and still at work in Romantic and Idealist aesthetics (i.e., the suprasensuous, metaphysical designations of freedom, spontaneity, genius, etc.). In this way, Heidegger is asking: can artwork—now this empty placeholder—operate in some way analogous to the way an ancient cult-statue operated in its sacred dispensation? In artwork thus understood, we reveal that we unplug from absorption and captivation in the rest of life (goal-directed, choosing means toward ends of production, consumption, representation, etc.), but not so as to "plug-in," via prayer, or sacrifice, or rituals involving made objects, or the divine rest of the Sabbath, or classical contemplation (*nous*). Beyond activities of "right worship" or "idolatry," the community formed around the artwork to come is the site internal to human life that reveals its ex nihilo character to itself from out of itself.

BEYOND INSTRUMENTALISM

AND VOLUNTARISM

Idol Anxiety and the Awakening

of a Philosophical Mood

DANIEL SILVER

This essay seeks to understand a particular kind of response to the felt collapse of a cultural practice that purports to link humans, things, and the divine. The cultural practice I am referring to is philosophy; the feeling of collapse occurred in early twentieth-century Europe; the response is that of Martin Heidegger in his 1929–30 lecture course, *The Fundamental Concepts of Metaphysics: World, Finitude, Solitude.*[1]

Understanding the philosophical consequences of the possibility of cultural collapse was arguably one of the great concerns of Heidegger's *Being and Time* investigations of anxiety and death.[2] In *FCM*, Heidegger continues similar lines of thought. But he also engages directly with contemporary authors writing about a crisis in culture whereby cultural objects—poems, paintings, music, philosophy books—which hitherto had ostensibly provided vital manifestations of something divine were experienced as having been emptied out of meaning. The pages of the lectures are suffused with such anxiety. Heidegger assumes and in many ways seeks to heighten that anxiety in his audience, before taking them through a pedagogical process of phenomenological inquiry designed to "awaken a fundamental philosophizing mood." That mood is boredom, the "awakening" of which will, Heidegger hopes, tune his students into authentic questioning that raises the fundamental concepts of metaphysics—world, finitude, and solitude—in the right way, in the right mood.

In what follows, I want to suggest that understanding Heidegger's attempt to restore philosophical practice to its proper mood and tone can help us to better understand at least one way a culture can respond to what the editors of this volume call "idol anxiety"—not by managing or minimizing their anxiety but by finding spiritual resources in it. If "idolatry" is a charge typically levied against the sacred objects of an alien or rival culture, "idol anxiety" turns inward, expressing worries about a group's own techniques and objects for engaging with the divine. These worries in turn may prompt related practices, such as the *mīs pî*, or "mouth-washing" ritual, apparently designed to ward off the potential collapse of those objects and practices into idolatry. This would secure a stable cultural bond between humans, their things, and their gods.

Heidegger's "mood awakening" may be read as a kind of latter-day *mīs pî*, one designed not to infuse cult-objects with divine presence but to infuse philosophical practice and settings with "the mystery" and "inner terror" necessary to live up to their promise (*FCM* 164). Understanding this attempt is highly instructive. For one thing, it shows us a response to idol anxiety close to home, one that speaks a language we understand and which still resonates. For another, it offers what may be a novel and distinctively modern response to the feeling of cultural collapse. Through creating new cultural objects or forms, Heidegger aims to get behind, investigate, and give positive meaning to the phenomenological sources of this anxiety itself. For even a collapsed form of life is still a form of life, one with its own distinctive mood and tone. Though few would desire to put themselves in such a mood, facing its possibility may in fact be a revealing way, in certain circumstances, for certain people, to enter into and raise fundamental questions about how things come to count as significant or insignificant—and therewith sacred or idolatrous—in the first place. That is, rather than combating what he took to be the trivialization of philosophy through a frontal assault, Heidegger seeks to find resources for its renewed vitality in attending to what is manifest in the very sense that it has become trivial, boring, formless, incapable of inspiring full-blooded commitment.[3] And finally, attending to the passive intentionality implicit in Heidegger's practice of "mood-awakening" and in the *mīs pî* may help us to develop a richer and deeper conceptualization of human action capable of doing justice to this nonvoluntaristic dimension of action.

School Metaphysics as Idolatry

Heidegger begins his lectures with a discussion of the contemporary situation in philosophy. Philosophy is typically presented as "absolute science" or "the proclamation of a world-view" (*FCM* 1). Both miscast the "innermost essence of philosophy," since both fail to treat and enter into philosophy as a practice. Philosophy as absolute science sets up external and fixed standards; philosophy as proclamation of a worldview parades a series of personal convictions and normative commitments before the viewer. Both treat philosophy as something that can be watched from the outside.

But philosophy for Heidegger is a practice—"philosophy is philosophizing" (*FCM* 4). As such, philosophy can only be understood by and in doing it. Becoming familiar with what various people called philosophers said about various topics is a way of avoiding philosophy (*FCM* 3).

Philosophy is a practice, Heidegger explains, that gives primacy to "metaphysical thinking" (*FCM* 24). Heidegger articulates what he means by "metaphysical thinking" through an elucidation of the word *physis*. *Physis*, Heidegger emphasizes, is not the same as the modern term *nature* that contrasts with *history*. Rather, *physis* refers to the "general prevailing of beings, which comprehends within itself human fate and its history," what Hubert Dreyfus sometimes refers to as a "whooshing up," in which a space is cleared for a world to unfold. *Physis* even "in a certain way includes divine beings" (*FCM* 26). Whatever this ultimately means, philosophy for Heidegger constitutes a practice that, in seeking to illuminate the character of *physis*, brings humans into some sort of relation to the divine.

Like any living practice at the human-thing-divine nexus, philosophy has its materials and techniques. The techniques, among other things, include questioning and conversation. The materials include such things as Aristotle's lecture notes (*FCM* 35). By engaging with these in the right way, Heidegger suggests, the philosophical manifestation of the divine can happen: Aristotle's First Philosophy records and enables "philosophizing proper," which, as it presses after "beings themselves and after being" understood as "movement . . . goes back to the first mover . . . which is simultaneously designated the *theon*, the divine" (*FCM* 34).

And like any other living practice, philosophy can go dead. This is what happens, Heidegger says, with "the formation of schools." When schools form, "living questioning dies out. The proper grip that held philosophical questioning is absent" (*FCM* 35). This "rootlessness" (*FCM* 35) is evident in the application of the label *metaphysics* to Aristotle's First Philosophy. First Philosophy was Aristotle's invitation into philosophizing proper. But the schoolmen could not fit that philosophizing into the disciplinary schema of logic, physics, and ethics. So the core of philosophizing was pushed into the periphery, into the *meta-* of metaphysics (*FCM* 36). This, says Heidegger, is a "technical title for an embarrassment in the face of *prote philosophie*" (*FCM* 37). It is an embarrassment that for Heidegger persists to this day.

One way to interpret Heidegger's point about the schoolmen's embarrassment is to say that Western and contemporary philosophers can succumb to their own form of idolatry. The techniques and practices and materials of philosophy can grip practitioners in such a way that manifests the divine. But that grip can loosen, and the materials—the books, Aristotle's lectures on First Philosophy—can seem empty husks, an afterthought incapable of captivating.

For Heidegger, much of philosophy since then has been an exercise of covering up and managing this void at the center of core philosophical practices and materials. Medieval philosophy sought to secure itself against this concern by reinterpreting Aristotle's metaphysics substantively, as the science of the suprasensuous being, God. Yet this "trivialized" philosophy (*FCM* 43), by making it into an inquiry like any other, one about a specific entity, albeit the highest one.

The Philosophy of Culture as an Expression of Idol Anxiety

For Heidegger, this trivialized scholastic philosophizing was in large measure trivial to the extent that it suppressed anxiety about the fact that philosophical practice had lost its distinctive revelatory power. Heidegger views the cultural discourse of his day, however, as an expression of deep anxiety about this philosophical idolatry, singling out the writings of Oswald Spengler, Ludwig Klages, Max Scheler, and Leopold Ziegler. These all begin with a broad, world-historical assessment of the current human predicament and argue that the modern utilitarian, rationalistic spirit is suppressing "life" (Spengler); what is needed is a return to "simmering drives" and the "mythical" (Klages); a new balance between life and spirit (Scheler); or an overcoming of the opposition itself (Ziegler). In each case, the call for a reenergizing of philosophy through new cultural objects (like books and paintings) and a new mythology expresses a background worry that some measures be taken to resuscitate practices taken to have gone dead, to create new vibrant, resonating, captivating techniques for authentic engagement with matters of the deepest concern.

The reader may fill in the relevant contemporary examples of similar diagnoses of cultural decline, calls for a return to the primitive, efforts to attain renewed balance, and drives to wipe out dichotomies. For Heidegger, these sorts of reports on the human condition are just as trivializing as school metaphysics. They express idol anxiety without enabling us to engage it and understand its significance as an occasion for authentic philosophizing. For in reporting on ourselves as if from the outside, as if we were not the ones doing the reporting, they "untie us from ourselves" (*FCM* 77). They present sensational accounts of the world-historical situation and encourage stories about how things stand with "us." But diagnosis and prognosis "leads a literary existence" (*FCM* 77); that existence does not relate itself to its own practices but at best seeks to imagine what they would look like from the outside, as if talking about a living philosophical engagement could make progress toward living it.[4]

Boredom: The Mood of the Moodless

Another way to describe Heidegger's view of his contemporary situation in philosophy is to say that philosophy was not proceeding in the right mood. The cries of the likes of Spengler and company register attempts to activate the mood again, to get turned on again by philosophizing, to recover its materials from the threat of idolatry. This, for Heidegger, is a fool's quest. Moods do not arise by thinking or deciding or forcing them into existence, as the host of any good party knows. They "assail" us. We can prepare for them, take steps to arrange the situation so that a mood may arise. Still, captivation by a mood always involves some passive moment, something carrying us away. Moods indicate a dimension of human action beyond voluntary effort.

Anxiety about how to get into a philosophizing mood does, however, suggest a background mood that gives the various programs for cultural renewal their vitality. By seeking a new, spirited, gripping role for "man," calls for cultural renewal implicitly promise to "make ourselves interesting to ourselves again" (*FCM* 77). This suggests to Heidegger that the mood that gives this cultural practice of cultural diagnosis and prognostication its grip is: "deep boredom." In calling for a renewal of human creativity and vitality in the future, and diagnosing the sources of its loss in the past, modern cultural critics in fact register that they are already passionately drawn into a mood—without effort or anxiety—that defines their present. That mood is boredom.[5]

This is Heidegger's rhetorical reversal of typical discourse about cultural decline. Rather than participating in debates that seek to confront philosophical idol anxiety by sterile means, Heidegger situates those very anxieties in the practical and emotional contexts in which they could matter to the agents involved. They can matter if they covertly express another, captivating mood, in which those agents are already gripped. Awakening philosophizing proper, for Heidegger, can happen by allowing what is implicit in this mood to speak out more clearly and forcefully.

Awakening a Mood

Heidegger, like many other writers of his and our generation, sees a pervasive sense of emptiness in the materials and practices of philosophical questioning, and with it, a loss of the distinctive way in which that questioning could bring people into a certain connection with the divine. This sense that something has gone awry in that philosophy no longer connects us with the divine, I have argued, should be understood as a form of idol anxiety.

But Heidegger, in contrast to most others in the tradition, suggests not managing and controlling that anxiety to assuage fears but awakening a fundamental philosophizing mood of boredom. What does this mean? What is at stake in this puzzling approach?

First, let us reflect on the notion of *awakening* a mood. We can contrast "awakening" boredom to "inducing" boredom (*FCM* 82). To induce boredom would be to create it actively in people who are not already subject to the mood. This is what Andy Warhol seems to have been up to in some of his film projects.[6] By contrast, to awaken boredom is to let the mood resonate for those already in its grip, to articulate the significance of an experience that is somehow already there.[7] Like the Mesopotamian artisans chanting "I did not make it" as they generated cult-objects, Heidegger's phenomenological practice aims to heighten a mood in which its characteristic activities—"authentic philosophical questioning" that brings the meaning of being itself into question—can be experienced as the result of opening oneself to a captivating power beyond the self. What is manifest in the process is articulated in, but not willfully determined by, human action.

Smashing philosophical idols and creating new ones does not therefore constitute for Heidegger a successful response to philosophical idol anxiety. Instead, successfully awakening a philosophizing mood means finding a way to get his audience of aspiring philosophers to feel philosophical practice as something which, without choosing, is demanded by their own being in the world. No renewal or rearguard action is needed—just listening more attentively to what is already there, and releasing the philosophizing and reflective potential in that orientation. The renewal has already happened, he is urging them to understand, since we are the sorts of beings who always, even (and in particular) in our boredom, are manifesting a stance on the meaning of being, a stance on how things are to show up as significant. Heidegger's rhetorical program of "mood awakening" aims to set a mood in which philosophical questioning and materials appear for his students as already having grabbed them and demanded a response from their deepest core. His aim is to clear a space where judgments about what that response means can occur.

Awakening Boredom

The phenomenology of boredom is meant to accomplish this task. Like the *mīs pî*, if "awakening a fundamental philosophizing mood of boredom" works, those who go through the process are to experience what results as a gift rather than as a result of their willful making. How is it supposed to work?

To begin with, Heidegger discourages his students from thinking about boredom as an inner psychological quality to be ascertained and dissected. To do so would disconnect the mood from the everyday world. Whatever insights that result would therefore be impotent, simply a "matter of concocting a region of lived experiences in the soul and suchlike . . . of working our way into a stratum of interrelations of consciousness" (*FCM* 91). Ascertaining a mood as a piece of psychology, however interesting or detailed, amounts to observing it from the outside, without allowing its dynamics to show up as constitutive of the shape of a world.

Boredom, by contrast, is a fundamental mood or *attunement*. And moods are more than fleeting inner states caused by or transferred to objects. Moods, Heidegger stresses, even if they are not objective properties of things, are not psychological projections of subjective attitudes (*FCM* 66). When we fall in love with somebody, we are not experiencing a psychological state that we transfer to a blank object; rather, the beloved *is* in a certain way, a way that resonates in an erotic key, as it were, that we, as lovers, can tune into. When we find a book boring, Heidegger insists, we are not transferring psychological states onto an object, nor are we experiencing a psychological condition caused by an object. We are, instead, registering that "the book itself—in it-self—is boring, not only for us to read and while reading it, but it itself, is boring" (*FCM* 84).

The book resonates, one might say, in a key of boredom; entering into the mood is to become tuned into that key. A boring movie gives our world a boring configuration. If we are drawn into its spell, the world lights up to us in a way that is imbued with boredom, as a place without energy or excitement.[8] Moods can be shared; they are public.[9] Moods are infectious. They draw us in and define the shared feeling of a common space.

To awaken a philosophizing mood in a fundamental attunement of boredom, then, would mean articulating how that mood is implicitly manifest in the ways in which boredom is already resonating in certain everyday situations. Heidegger's students are to slow down and allow the philosophical potential of those situations to speak. In so doing, they are to relate to themselves as already having been drawn into philosophical questioning as a challenge that has called them, even if they have not registered it as such.

Boredom Number 1:
Boredom as Suspension of the Instrumental

Heidegger starts this exercise in awakening by describing an everyday situation full of boring objects. Since our typical reaction to boredom is to drive it away (as evidenced, for example, in the philosophy of culture attempt to flee boredom for the drama of "life"), Heidegger begins with an everyday situation defined by that very effort to keep boredom down by passing the time.[10] In analyzing the phenomenology of passing the time, he wants to invite his students to press deeper toward the philosophizing mood contained in situations structured through an attunement of boredom, an attunement, again, in which, he insists, they already find themselves.

Heidegger's awakening process takes his audience through three increasingly "deep" ways in which time becomes something we seek to make pass. He begins with a carefully chosen example—being delayed in a train station—and describes the boredom of pacing around the station, going outside for a smoke, shuffling through schedules. It might help if we update the example and think of an airport instead—the uncomfortable fake leather seats, the walks up and down the terminal, the endless magazines to be picked up and put down, and so on.

The example is chosen to provide a setting familiar to his students. It is one infused with meaning through a scientific-instrumental comportment. The train station or airport provides a field in which it is fitting to "have no time" (*FCM* 94). In the airport, we encounter things and others as impediments to be overcome on our way to our given goals; they are instrumentalities, means to and conditions of ends by means of which we seek to move on to where we need to go. When it runs smoothly, the airport allows us to achieve those ends with maximal efficiency. The various conditions—distance, time, weather, traffic, people, and so forth—that separate us from our ends are to be made as minimally relevant to action as possible. Time is precisely what one cannot "have" in such a setting, as the whole situation conspires to move one on to the next place or purpose.[11]

Being moderns, Heidegger's students are quite likely to feel the compelling force of this utilitarian way of being in the world. Heidegger wants their authentic philosophizing to grow out of the demands implicit in, but masked by, this comportment. He asks them to attend to the odd type of temporality contained in being bored.

For despite "having no time," boredom number 1 does manifest a relation to the temporality of things that cannot be made intelligible under an instrumental conception of action. Now, in general, Heidegger believes that time is always "time-when" and things always have "their time" (*FCM* 105).[12] What it is to be, say, a desk is not exhausted by its properties (brown, wooden, hard, etc.) or its spatio-temporal location (in my office at eleven o'clock). The desk is also there to make time for work and writing; it is a proper desk at the time when work and writing are occurring. A similarly shaped object that came into its own at the time when people sacrifice and worship would not be a desk, but an altar.

The things in a train station or airport also have their specific "times when" they can come into their own: when they carry travelers along smoothly to their goals. They succeed in this when they do not obtrude, when they do not "force us to wait" (*FCM* 103). When this happens, each object shows up "in its specific time, which in a certain way is the ideal time of a railway station" (*FCM* 105). Time is not a simple passing on from one moment to the next. Things are timely; they show at the right or wrong time—beings and time are intimately linked.[13]

If things are timely, they can also be *untimely*.[14] Untimeliness constitutes the temporal structure manifest in boredom number 1: being stuck waiting in a place devoted to not waiting. Nothing shows up in its time. Magazines, books, music, people, do not fully appear as copresent with us. Dragging time means that each thing is distanced, forced out of what it could be.[15] "Passing the time" is not speeding up slow time. It is dealing with "untimely" things in anticipation of their return to "their" times (when the train arrives and they can be useful again). Things are there for preoccupation, without interest in the object or the results. This is boredom as a way of existing within a sphere where the instrumental relation to given ends through the most efficient means has been suspended.[16]

Boredom Number 2: Boredom as Suspension of the Normative

The means-end schema out of which boredom number 1 arises cannot make sense of the nonteleological actions it inspires. For in boredom number 1, actors are not efficiently pursuing given ends. If Heidegger's students want to tune into the philosophical potential in boredom, analysis of a deeper form is required.[17]

Heidegger finds this deeper form in a type of boredom that occurs not in reference to the efficient pursuit of goals but in reference to the committed realization of normative worldviews. Actors' *relations* to their goals are made central (*FCM* 128). Airports and train station lobbies are more than places to achieve goals; they are also dedicated to the normative value of efficiently moving people and bringing them together. Passing the time in boredom may not seek particular goals. Yet it may well reflect a normative commitment to perseverance and friendship, as actors express their commitments to these values in the face of obstacles.

The second form of boredom that Heidegger analyzes arises from out of this deeper, normative stance. He describes a cocktail party in which the time flies. Afterward, returning home, one looks at one's desk and feels overcome by a sense that the party was an expression of boredom with oneself and one's commitment to more important pursuits. Even though it was fun, it was time wasted, time we let ourselves waste of our own volition.

This is a form of boredom that happens when a normative commitment lapses. In Heidegger's example, the work left on the desk expresses such a commitment. The party's boredom marks a departure from that commitment. Being moderns, Heidegger's students are likely to be familiar with the attraction of this voluntarist, self-determining attitude, as well as with its recurrent lapse into guilty pleasures.

Heidegger's students are now to find that boredom number 2 reveals the philosophizing potential contained in, but covered up by, this voluntarist attitude. The temporal structure of boredom is again the key. In this case, Heidegger stresses not that things have "their time" but that, as evaluating, active participants in the world, we too have our "times-when."[18] What it is to be, say, committed to the value of social justice is not exhausted by my demographic characteristics (race, class, gender, education, income, etc.) or by my position in a social role (lawyer, writer, journalist, organizer, democrat, etc.). My commitment is there in my readiness to intervene at the right time and in the right way on behalf of those denied their appropriate social rights and respect.

The person returning to his writing desk also has his "time-when" he comes into his own: when a thought finally blossoms to maturity, focusing past ideas while framing future ones. We succeed at this when our "entire activity [is] fulfilled," when we can "rest our existence" on this occasion "in such a way that our being and non-being would depend on it" (*FCM* 119). "Every thing, and more fundamentally every Dasein as such, has its time" (*FCM* 127).[19] My time is not an empty vessel which I fill with events until I die or an entropic force slowly degrading my capacities; being timely, showing up ready at the right time, is part of what makes me who I am—my being and my time are intimately linked. "Our Dasein itself is temporal" (*FCM* 127).

In the first type of boredom, Heidegger was especially concerned to analyze the ways in which *things* can be untimely. Here he is concerned with how *actors* can be untimely. We too can be "untimely": "We take time from that time which is apportioned to us; from the time to which our whole Dasein is given over (*FCM* 123)." Taking time out characterizes the temporal structure of this form of boredom. Everything becomes filled with a kind of carefree lassitude—making small talk, steering the conversation away from work, laughing at bad jokes to avoid conflict. Party time is time that empties out the tension and seriousness characteristic of timely action. It is "passing the time" as pastime paradise, creating a space freed from value-charged striving.[20] This is boredom as a way of existing within a sphere where normative effort has been suspended.

Heidegger wants to move his students to understand that this sort of familiar situation can give rise to a philosophical mood that is not intelligible as the expression of given and preconstituted normative worldviews. For to actively suspend oneself in boredom is precisely *not* to be ordering one's life as an expression of a given value. To be there, at the party, is to have turned away actively from what one cares about, the work on the writing desk. One's relation to oneself and one's deeds has come into question. A voluntaristic schema cannot address and in fact represses this inquiry, as it has no positive way to describe the activity of actively setting aside effort to conform with norms. Boredom number 2 reveals but cannot address the experience of falling away from the desire to be serious. If Heidegger's students can comprehend this kind of boredom, then they are now in a position to interpret themselves as tuned into a kind of nonvoluntaristic mood defined by concern for what it would mean to possibly become "full" (or empty), voluntary committed or uncommitted, in the first place. This is an entrée to a philosophizing mood.

Boredom Number 3:
Philosophizing Boredom

The third form of boredom directly manifests this more philosophical way of being in the world. It does not occur in reference to an initially fixed goal that is blocked (as in the train station) or by an initially fixed worldview that is avoided (as at the party). It is characterized by an (often unbearable) openness to the question of how goals and values become gripping at all. Heidegger's formula for this changed stance is, "It is boring for one."[21] The impersonal form is here meant to convey the sense that one's personality, life course, ambitions, and so on, have been placed in question and suspension. A sense of having lost one's distinct identity becomes decisive.[22]

At this point, we might expect Heidegger to provide his students an illuminating phenomenological description of this deepest boredom, one that could be placed alongside the train station and the cocktail party. But, for essential reasons, Heidegger does not provide one (at least directly). Because this third boredom does not rest on a fixed set of ends (my destination at the airport) or a fixed worldview (my work as a writer), Heidegger cannot allow his students to identify it with any fixed, determinate situation. This form of boredom "explodes the situation" (*FCM* 143), places the space within which we could pursue goals or express values into suspension and question.[23]

In the third form of boredom the world shows up as a field of open possibilities that emerge and dissolve. In contrast to the train station (where we "shout down" boredom by passing the time since we "have no time"), and the party (where we "do not want to listen" to boredom by avoiding ourselves through pastimes), in this case we are "compelled to listen" to the "overpowering essence" of boredom that "no longer permits" any passing of the time (*FCM* 136). In Heidegger's language, this means that "boredom bores": deep boredom is not about something else; deep boredom is about the very processes of becoming timely and untimely that the other types of boredom implicitly manifest. This demand to "listen to" rather than control boredom is possible because this boredom marks a moment when our sense of what is under our control is lost or being reformulated. To be ready for this sort of possibility means, in Heidegger's terms, to allow oneself to be "transposed into a realm of power over which the individual person, the public individual subject, no longer has any power" (*FCM* 136).

Deep boredom provides a paradigmatic case of what has been called a "meaningful loss of control."[24] In it, Heidegger aims to bring home to his students how they already are acquainted with moods in which their given ends and values can cease to matter in a flash without being subject to reason or will. They are to find therein a phenomenological "demonstration" of the fragility and contingency of that mattering succeeding when it does. A meaningful world—one in which things and people connect to manifest an understanding of being—is not simply made. Rather, in that such a connection could collapse in boredom without our being able to think or decide ourselves into it, they are prepared to encounter the world as a wondrous gift rather than the result of planning and ordering.

Awakening Boredom as Spiritual Technique

This step brings the awakening process to its peak. For deep boredom manifests a way of being in which Heidegger's great philosophical question—why is there something rather than nothing?—presents itself in an authentically lived way and can be posed in its true form. Elijah Millgram, a philosopher of action, discerns a similar significance in boredom: "Boredom helps us to understand the place of ends in human life."[25] It can do so, because "the more you're bored, the less you're there."[26] This sort of experience marks a phase of action that raises, for the actor, questions about "the necessary conditions of our existence" as agents, what it is "to be there" with the lights on at all.[27] Literary authors such as Joseph Brodsky and David Foster Wallace have come to similar conclusions. Writes Wallace, "Bliss—a-second-by-second joy and gratitude at the gift of being alive, conscious—lies on the other side of crushing, crushing boredom. Pay close attention to the most tedious thing you can find (Tax Returns, Televised Golf) and, in waves, a boredom like you've never known will wash over you and just about kill you. Ride these out, and it's like stepping from black and white into color. Like water after days in the desert. Instant bliss in every atom."[28] For Heidegger as well, the significance of articulating the dynamics of being overcome by deep boredom is that doing so presents philosophical activity to his students as thrust upon them as a matter of utmost concern. There is no guarantee that they will respond in the right way or even at all. But whatever emerges, the aim of the process is to move the students to a mode of revelatory philosophical engagement that will not be experienced as a willful effort to vitalize lost symbols. It will be a response to a mood that already—without choosing it—has them in its grips.

The Place of Captivating Moods in Human Action

Like the *mīs pî*, this exercise is meant to yield and make intelligible a kind of nonwillful doing—in the one, sanctifying cult-objects, in the other, releasing the power of philosophical questioning. Both seem related to the worry that core cultural practices might arise from the arbitrary will of an individual and seek to institute techniques through which those practices can be legitimately experienced as having arisen through tuning into powers beyond the self.

Later in his career, Heidegger would try to capture this kind of passive intentionality with the term *releasement*. This term refers to activities that cannot happen by decision but only when we release ourselves to them, like falling asleep (though one can of course design the atmospherics of a bedroom to be more or less conducive to such release). What the *mīs pî*, "releasement," and "awakening a mood" all point to is the large and meaningful but nonvoluntary, nonutilitarian aspects of human action, as well as the persistent, but not very well understood, cross-cultural attempt to develop techniques for articulating and enabling these dimensions. Heidegger insists that "the awakening of attunement, and the attempt to broach this strange task, in the end coincide with the demand for a complete transformation of our conception of man" (*FCM* 62). But we have barely begun to work out what it would mean to do justice to this dimension of attunement—to *homo affectus*, man the moody.

One way to start is to briefly reconsider the *mīs pî*. The editors of this volume suggest that the *mīs pî* involves a kind of cover up. In having their arms ceremonially chopped off by priests, chanting, "I did not make it," and throwing their tools to the craftsmen gods in the river, the Mesopotamian artisans and priests were "assuaging fears" about their agency, working to "forget" their own voluntary effort in the genesis of the cult-object. Interpreted as a form of "anxiety" about the relation between human manufacture and divine power, the *mīs pî* registers a false consciousness in the priests and artisans. They know they are really making these objects, they are worried about that, and the ceremony aims, however strange and implausible it might sound to us, to wipe away this knowledge.

From Heidegger's perspective, the *mīs pî* will indeed look like a cover-up if we approach it exclusively within a utilitarian or voluntaristic understanding of human action. Treated in a utilitarian way, the priests are out to efficiently pursue goals, such as power or status or wealth. The *mīs pî* is a useful (though perhaps unconscious) means to these ends, designed to secure such goals more effectively through granting them divine authorization. Treated in a voluntaristic way, the priests are out to assert and sustain commitment to basic cultural values. The *mīs pî* is an effective way to maintain and control individuals' determination to conform with these ideals, one that is likely to be more powerful if attributed to Something Else. Either way, what is "really" going on is the utilitarian pursuit of goals or the voluntaristic effort to produce conformity with social norms, coupled with anxiety that the attribution of these actions to a higher power will be discerned and the true actions will come out.

Certainly, there may be some instrumental and normative dimensions to the *mīs pî*. But if Heidegger has awakened us to the role of attunement to moods in human action, then we can at least imagine the possibility of the *mīs pî* being something more than conspiracy or reassurance. Viewed in this light, the ceremony would be designed to tune priests and artisans into the power of a certain mood to open up a way of engaging with their situation. This is the artisanal mood that draws the craftsman into the flow of making resonating things—like cult-objects—dedicated to releasing other moods, much like Hephaestus makes jewelry to enhance the erotic appeal of Aphrodite. Ceremoniously cutting off their hands acknowledges the grip this mood has had over the craftsmen, the way their crafting attunement is neither voluntary nor utilitarian but something that overwhelms them. They did not will the mood, it took them over; captivated by it, the situation has been activated for them as one of shared flow in their craft. Throwing their tools into the river after the production is complete acknowledges that the mood that allows the artisanal aspects of their situation to shine must not be noticed during the process lest the flow be disrupted. Afterward, the power and character of the mood may be noticed and gratitude for its arrival affirmed by showing that the tools' creative powers come from having been activated in the context of the right artisanal attunement, which the craft gods, thankfully, have opened. Seen in this way, the priests and artisans are not only pursuing goals; they are not only willfully asserting their cultural ideals. They are enacting practices that enable them to release themselves into a mood.

As an act of mood-awakening, the *mīs pî* is thus intelligible from the perspective of both the agent and the observer. The agents are putting themselves in a situation in which they can be subject to moods that open up a particular way of tuning into their world, namely, in the artisanal way that clears a space to bring into existence mood-awakening things like cult-objects. The crafts gods are for them that which awakens and draws them in to this kind of mood.[29] For observers, not subject to this mood but to others, the craftsman's activity is intelligible as a way of providing stimulants to other moods—the craftsman's products (the cult-objects) will presumably be taken into temples or households, where those gods will work to make those places resonate in the moods over which each particular god holds influence, tuning people into the erotic, friendly, warlike, intellectual, and so on, dimensions of their situations. And, perhaps most importantly, we can see the *mīs pî* not as an anxiety-ridden cover-up for something else, like preexisting goals or norms, but as the appropriate and intelligent way to tune into the mood that enables the craftsman to do his work.

▪ ▪ ▪

Clearly, drawing the full implication of the type of action indicated in Heidegger's mood awakening and in the *mīs pî* requires much slower and fuller elaboration, as well as more detailed comparative analysis of a number of different phenomena, from art to religion and beyond.[30] For the moment, having somewhat breathlessly reviewed Heidegger's technique for awakening a fundamental philosophizing mood and elaborated its (and the *mīs pî*'s) significance for our understanding of the moody dimension of human action, let us take stock of what we have found.

Heidegger begins by trying to seize his students where they are, in the grips of a worry about how and whether they can be interesting to themselves. He then articulates everyday situations that express this boredom, situations that would be familiar to his students. Though these types of boredom may seem trivial, they in fact manifest a living philosophizing mood. Staring at the clock shows that we can be "entranced" by the ways in which things emerge and dissolve; seeking pastimes shows that we are already involved with questions about how our commitments come into and out of their times. Deep boredom makes these concerns explicit, tuning Heidegger's audience into a mood about the very process of being timely, about having something show up as significant.

We may find in Heidegger's lectures a provocative call to include a "moody dimension" to our conceptualization of human action and its environments, as I have suggested above. We may also find resources for understanding how living philosophical questioning can emerge where it seems to have faded. Whether or not it has succeeded, the attempt shows a powerful engagement with the question of how to respond to the feeling of collapsed culture, one that does not aim to minimize this anxiety but to unlock the philosophizing potential in those situations where it seems to be most absent.

REFERENCE MATTER

NOTES

INTRODUCTION

1. Michael B. Dick and Christopher Walker have recently brought together and translated the texts that document this ritual in an excellent volume, *The Induction of the Cult Image in Ancient Mesopotamia: The Mesopotamian "Mīs Pî" Ritual* (Helsinki, 2001), with bibliography. For a particularly insightful essay, see Dick's contribution "The Mesopotamian Cult Statue: A Sacramental Encounter with Divinity," in *Cult Image and Divine Representation in the Ancient Near East*, ed. Neal H. Walls (Boston, 2005), 43–67. Cf. Angelika Berlejung, "Washing the Mouth: The Consecration of Divine Images in Mesopotamia," in *The Image and the Book: Iconic Cults, Aniconism, and the Rise of Book Religion in Israel and the Ancient Near East*, ed. Karel van der Toorn (Leuven, 1997), 45–72.

2. For a more extensive treatment of the *mīs pî* ritual in relation to the prophetic critique of idolatry in the Bible (especially "Second Isaiah"), see Mark S. Smith, *The Origins of Biblical Monotheism: Israel's Polytheistic Background and the Ugaritic Texts* (Oxford, 2001), 179–88. For an interrogation of how Israelite religious practice may or may not have fit in among the broader array of Near Eastern image-use, see Jack M. Sasson, "On the Use of Images in Israel and the Ancient Near East: A Response to Karel van der Toorn," in *Sacred Time, Sacred Place: Archaeology and the Religion of Israel*, ed. B. M. Gittlen (Winona Lake, Ind., 2002), 63–70.

3. Second Isaiah's indictment of the Mesopotamian ritual, of course, serves equally to bring into being the opposing category "Israelite." For a treatment that focuses on how the term *idolatry* has traditionally been aimed polemically against an "other," as a means toward the self-definition of the accuser, see Moshe Halbertal and Avishai Margalit, *Idolatry*, trans. N. Goldblum (Cambridge, Mass., 1992), discussed below.

4. Quoted in Berlejung, "Washing the Mouth," 47.

5. Halbertal and Margalit, *Idolatry*, 8.

6. Ibid., 237.

7. Ibid., 236.

8. This is the case even for Maimonides' antagonism toward the vulgar anthropomorphic conception of God, for he thereby establishes a division within the Jewish community between those who have an enlightened understanding and *hoi polloi*. For this reading of Maimonides, see ibid., 108–36.

9. One should note how, as a matter of simple fact, worries over idols have generally been worries about images. A rich literature has developed in recent years that uses this state of affairs as a way to illuminate, by the question of the idol, the wider history of the image in the West. A classic example would be David Freedberg's *The Power of Images: Studies in the History and Theory of Response* (Chicago, 1989). Cf. Moshe Barasch, *Icon: Studies in the History of an Idea* (New York, 1992); Alain Besançon, *L'image interdite: Une histoire intellectuelle de l'iconoclasme* (Paris, 1994; Eng. trans., *The Forbidden Image: An Intellectual History of Iconoclasm*, trans. Jane Marie Todd, Chicago, 2000); Marie-José Mondzain, *Image, icone, economie: Les sources byzantines de l'imaginaire contemporain* (Paris, 1996; Eng. trans., *Image, Icon, Economy: The Byzantine Origins of the Contemporary Imaginary*, trans. Rico Franses, Stanford, Calif., 2004). The present anthology aims specifically to contribute to this discussion.

10. Jean-Luc Marion has underscored the difficulty of treating the idol as an essential identity, a thing with a character that one can define and fix. As Marion puts it, "The idol does not indicate, any more than the icon, a particular being or even class of beings. Icon and idol indicate a manner of being for beings, or at least for some of them" (Jean-Luc Marion, *God Without Being* [Chicago, 1991], 7–8). W. J. T. Mitchell, for his part, similarly insists that the idol cannot be understood as one among many "discrete, essential categories of objects," but rather must be treated under the larger rubric of "object relations." That is, the idol is not a thing, but a particular way of establishing "*relations* to things" (W. J. T. Mitchell, *What Do Pictures Want? The Lives and Loves of Images* [Chicago, 2005], 188; italics in original).

11. Though he does not present his work as a "grammar of the idol," Charles Barber's work on Byzantine iconoclasm has great value in this connection. The chapters of his book *Figure and Likeness: On the Limits of Representation in Byzantine Iconoclasm* (Princeton, N.J., 2002) provide astute treatments of dichotomies (such as "figure and sign," "form and likeness," "word and image") that correspond to certain of the structural variables that this introduction treats.

12. As such, the problematic of idolatry surpasses specifically religious concerns. In his contribution to this volume, James Elkins discusses how contemporary scholars in art history, as well as neighboring fields, often take analytic issues and lines of interrogation originally rooted in religious discussions and use them to address nonreligious objects. Many of the contributions to the impressive exhibition catalog *Iconoclash: Beyond the Image Wars in Science, Religion, and Art* (ed. Bruno Latour and Peter Weibel [Cambridge, Mass., 2002]) are particularly valuable in this way.

13. This broadened meaning, in turn, has found its way back into biblical contexts originally free of it, such as when the recently produced New English Translation has Jehu say to Jehoram, at 2 Kings 9:22, "How can everything be all right as long as your mother Jezebel promotes idolatry and pagan practices?" The Hebrew text has the word *keshef* and the Greek uses the word *pharmakon*—each meaning something closer to the English "sorcery." These distinct notions are subsumed into the category "idolatry" by the modern translator-commentators.

14. As already indicated, *idol* does not have to refer to a material thing in every case.

Francis Bacon's "four idols" of the marketplace, the theater, the cave, and the tribe come to mind here.

15. For an intriguing example from West Africa, see Warren L. d'Azevedo, "Mask Makers and Myth in Western Liberia," in *Arts of Africa, Oceania, and the Americas: Selected Readings*, ed. Janet Catherine Berlo and Lee Anne Wilson (Upper Saddle River, N.J., 1993), 111–32.

16. Gilbert Dagron, *L'image de culte et le portrait* (Paris, 1984), 124.

17. In addition to the texts treated here, the issue of a cult-statue's required likeness to a previous original comes vividly to the fore in a ritual text from Kizzuwatna in southeastern Anatolia. See Jared L. Miller, *Studies in the Origins, Development and Interpretation of the Kizzuwatna Rituals* (Wiesbaden, 2004), esp. 273–74, 290.

18. Walker and Dick provide the translation of this text from the Sippar cult-relief, *Induction*, 22–24.

19. Although it is valid to say that the Mesopotamian cult-object functioned in certain senses as an original, it is also the case that it was an original that needed a model if it was to be a worthy presentation of the god. Furthermore, the fact that a sun-disk, owing to its symbolic status in Mesopotamian theology, had been used before the creation of the new statue also illuminates the resources that could serve as constraints on the production of originals. It presumably would not have been proper, in the context of Mesopotamian religion, to treat any random object as Shamash.

20. El Amarna letter 55. The foreignness of this way of thinking is highlighted by the fact that in his authoritative translation of the Amarna Letters, William Moran inserts the phrase "the statue of" in parentheses preceding each mention of Akizzi's god (*The Amarna Letters*, trans. William L. Moran [Baltimore, 1992], 127–28).

21. A rich literature treats these questions. H. Schützinger argues for equality of essence in "Bild und Wesen der Gottheit im alten Mesopotamien," in *Götterbild, in Kunst und Schrift*, ed. Hans-Joachim Klimkeit (Bonn, 1984), 61–80; Karel van der Toorn uses a language of manifestation or "extension of the divine personality," in *Sin and Sanction in Israel and Mesopotamia* (Assen, 1985); Irene Winter takes a similar approach in "'Idols of the King': Royal Images as Recipients of Ritual Action in Ancient Mesopotamia," *Journal of Ritual Studies* 6 (1992): 13–42; A. Leo Oppenheim, in *Ancient Mesopotamia: Portrait of a Dead Civilization* (Chicago, 1964), 183–98, emphasizes the idea of real presence.

22. Walker and Dick, *Induction*, 23.

23. See St. John of Damascus, *Three Treatises on the Divine Images*, trans. Andrew Louth (Crestwood, N.Y., 2003).

24. Ibid., 29.

25. For a brilliant treatment of a later chapter in this story, see Joseph Leo Koerner, *The Reformation of the Image* (Chicago, 2008).

26. Marion, *God Without Being*, 7. Marion reiterates this point on the next page: "In short, the icon and the idol are not all determined as beings against other beings, since the same beings (statues, names, etc.) can pass from one rank to the other. The icon and the idol determine two manners of being for beings, not two classes of beings."

27. See Martin Heidegger's thinking of unreadiness-to-hand and breakdown in *Being and Time*, 1.3, §16; cf. Robert Pippin, "Necessary Conditions for the Possibility of What Isn't: Heidegger on Failed Meaning," in *The Persistence of Subjectivity: On the Kantian Aftermath* (Cambridge, 2005), 57–78.

28. On the idol as "first visible," see Marion, *God Without Being*, 9–11. With respect to the issue of failure, Marion states: "The idol pays the price of its limitation: it is an experience of the divine in the measure of a state of *Dasein*. What renders the idol problematic does not stem from a failure (e.g., that it offers only an 'illusion') but, on the contrary, from the conditions of its validity—its radical immanence to the one who experiences it, and experiences it, rightly so, as impassable" (ibid., 28).

29. Mitchell, *What Do Pictures Want?* 188.

30. Mitchell considers above all the work of Richard Neer in this context.

31. Mitchell, *What Do Pictures Want?* xv; italics in original.

32. Summers's important endeavor has received systematic exposition in his massive *Real Spaces: World Art History and the Rise of Western Modernism* (London, 2003), which develops an idea of space rooted in Heidegger. A shorter essay that prefigures certain of the concerns of *Real Spaces* is his essay "Form and Gender," in *Visual Culture*, ed. Norman Bryson, Michael Ann Holly, and Keith Moxey (Hanover, N.H., 1994), 384–412.

33. See Halbertal and Margalit, *Idolatry*; and W. J. T. Mitchell, "Holy Landscape," in *Landscape and Power*, ed. W. J. T. Mitchell (Chicago, 2002).

34. Above all, he thinks of scholarly works such as those gathered in *Iconoclash*, many of which considered nonreligious practices in art, as well as in science, from the vantage point of theological questions.

35. See, especially, *God Without Being*; and *The Idol and Distance*, trans. Thomas Carlson (New York, 2001).

36. Marion, *God Without Being*, 10.

37. Jean-Luc Marion, *Being Given: Toward a Phenomenology of Givenness*, trans. J. L. Kosky (Stanford, Calif., 2002), 229. Cf. Marion's essay "The Idol or the Radiance of the Painting," in *In Excess: Studies of Saturated Phenomena*, trans. Robyn Horner and Vincent Berraud (New York, 2002), 54–81.

This essay develops ideas first broached in my German piece "Was ist so schlimm an den Bildern?" in *Die Zehn Gobote: Ein widersprüchliches Erbe?* ed. Hans Joas (Cologne, 2006), 17–32. All translations are my own unless otherwise noted.

1. For a treatment of the different traditions of numbering the commandments, see Bernard M. Levinson's notes to Deuteronomy 5 in *The Jewish Study Bible*, ed. Adele Berlin and Marc Zvi Brettler (Oxford, 2004), 374–77.

2. The pertinent texts are collected and commented on by Horst Dietrich Preuss, *Verspottung fremder Religionen im Alten Testament*, Beiträge zur Wissenschaft vom Alten und Neuen Testament 92 (Stuttgart, 1971). For a convincing criticism of Preuss's theological approach, see Othmar Keel, *Kanaan—Israel—Christentum: Plädoyer für eine "vertikale" Ökumene* (Münster, 2002), 7 ff.

3. Peter Seibert, in his magisterial study of the ancient Egyptian examples of satire, has admirably analyzed the specific devices of satirical distortion, defamiliarization or "estrangement" in "Die Charakteristik: Untersuchungen zu einer ägyptischen Sprechsitte und ihren Ausprägungen," in *Folklore und Literatur*, Ägyptologische Abhandlungen 17 (Wiesbaden, 1967).

4. *Asclepius* 24, Brian P. Copenhaver, *Hermetica: The Greek Corpus Hermeticum and the Latin Asclepius in a New English Translation*, with notes and introduction (Cambridge, 1992), 81.

5. *Asclepius* 24–26. Cf. Garth Fowden, *The Egyptian Hermes: A Historical Approach to the Late Pagan Mind* (Princeton, N.J., 1993), 39–43; Jean-Pierre Mahé, *Hermès en Haute-Égypte: Les textes hermétiques de Nag Hammadi et leurs paralleles grec et latins*, vol. 2 (Quebec, 1982), 69–97; David Frankfurter, *Elijah in Upper Egypt: The Apocalypse of Elijah and Early Egyptian Christianity* (Minneapolis, 1993), 188 ff.

6. Stefan George, "Entrückung," in Stefan George, *Der siebente Ring* (Berlin, 1927), 122.

7. Carl E. Schorske, *Thinking with History* (Princeton, N.J., 1998), 125–40.

8. Heinrich Heine, *Werke in vier Bänden*, ed. Hans Mayer (Frankfurt, 1994), 4: 350.

9. Sigmund Freud, *Moses and Monotheism*, trans. Katherine Jones (New York, 1939), 144.

10. Immanuel Kant, *Critique of Judgment*, trans. W. S. Pluhar (Indianapolis, 1987), 135.

11. Goethe, *Sämtliche Werke*, 18 vols. (Zurich, 1977), 1: 617.

CHAPTER 2: THE CHRISTIAN CRITIQUE OF IDOLATRY

1. See Paul Corby Finney, *The Invisible God: The Earliest Christian Art* (New York, 1994).

2. See T. N. D. Mettinger, *No Graven Image? Israelite Aniconism in its Ancient Near Eastern Context* (Stockholm, 1995).

3. See Louis Ginzberg, *The Legends of the Jews*, 7 vols. (Philadelphia, 1968), 3: 334–36.

4. See Giovanni Garbini, "Le serpent d'airain et Moïse," *Zeitschrift für die altetestamentliche Wissenschaft* 100 (1998): 264–67; J. Assurmendi, "Le serpent d'airain," *Estudios biblicos* 46 (1988): 283–94; and Jean Pierre Mahé, translator of the Georgian version of *La caverne des trésors* (Lovuain, 1992), 70, and of its Syriac translation (*La caverne*, 116). These authors and texts take it as evident that Hezekiah destroyed the Brazen Serpent, Garbini going so far as to make the model of Moses' "sculpture" go back to the Egyptian Uraeus and to the cult the pharaonic religion devoted to him. The fact is that the canonical Christian Bible says nothing about the Brazen Serpent among the acts of reform of the cult of the temple by Hezekiah, related in 2 Chronicles 30:14.

5. See Hugo Odeberg, *The Fourth Gospel* (Uppsala, 1929), 106–9.

6. Roberto Calasso, *Il rosa Tiepolo* (Milano, 2006).

7. Although the theme of Moses and the Brazen Serpent was not treated by Nicolas Poussin, one of his imitators, the Frenchman Nicolas Chaperon (1612–55), took it for his subject in a painting preserved under this title in the Musée des beaux-arts in Nimes, and painted in 1652. The same museum also preserves a *tableau d'histoire* by

Pierre Subleyras treating the same subject, but dating from 1727. The Royal Academy of Painting and Sculpture took this theme for the subject of its competition at Rome that year, and Subleyras won the contest.

8. This interdiction recalls, to some degree, the one in Plato's *Republic*, which, beyond the ban on reading Homer, forbids the deceptive enjoyment of the visual arts of imitation.

9. Susan Sontag, *Regarding the Pain of Others* (New York, 2003).

10. Tertullian, *De idolatria*, critical text, translation, and commentary by J. H. Waszink and J. C. M. Van Winden (Leiden, 1987), 23.

CHAPTER 3: CONCEPTS OF IDOL ANXIETY IN ISLAMIC ART

I would like to thank Patricia Crone and Virginia Raguin for commenting on an earlier draft of this chapter.

1. The Quran discusses in great length the idea of *tawḥid*, that is, the oneness and uniqueness of God with no partners and no idols. For the study of art and architecture in the Quran see Oleg Grabar, "Art and Architecture and the Quran," in *Encyclopedia of the Quran*, 6 vols. (Leiden, 2001), 1: 161–74. Much has been written about the idea of aniconism and iconoclasm in Islamic art, and therefore I shall not include it in my discussion. See, for example, Oleg Grabar, "Islam and Iconoclasm," in *Iconoclasm: Papers Given at the Ninth Spring Symposium of Byzantine Studies*, University of Birmingham, March 1975, ed. Anthony Bryer and Judith Herrin (Birmingham, Eng., 1977), 45–52; Terry Allen, "Aniconism and Figural Representation in Islamic Art," in *Five Essays on Islamic Art* (Manchester, Mich., 1988), 17–37; Finbarr Barry Flood, "Between Cult and Culture: Bamiyan, Islamic Iconoclasm, and the Museum," *Art Bulletin* 84, no. 4 (2002): 641–59.

2. However, there are a few examples that stand in contrast to this statement. See Flood, "Between Cult and Culture," 644 and nn. 26–27.

3. This type of coin was rapidly abandoned. For the identification of the image on the Umayyad coins see the article by C. Foss, "The Coinage of the First Century of Islam," *Journal of Roman Archaeology* 16 (2003): 748–60. These have been published by Stephen Album and Tony Goodwin in *Sylloge of Islamic Coins in the Ashmolean Museum 1: The Pre-reform Coinage of the Early Islamic Period* (Oxford, 2002), nos. 730, 731. The parallel between the Muhammad coin and the representation of Christ on state coins during the reign of Justinian is fascinating. For a discussion regarding the Christ coins, see James D. Breckenridge, *The Numismatic Iconography of Justinian II* (New York, 1959).

4. See Nomi Heger, "The Status and the Image of the Persianate Artist," Ph.D. diss., Princeton University, 1997, 29–33. The story of Jesus and the bird of clay appears in surat al-'Imrān (3:49) and al-Māʾidah (5:110); the episode of the *djinn*s building statues for King Solomon occurs in surat Sabāʾ (34:13). All Quranic passages in English in this essay are from Ahmed Ali's translation, *Al-Qurʾān* (Princeton, N.J., 1984).

5. Heger, "Status and the Image of the Persianate Artist," 33.

6. Al-Azraḳī, *Akhbar Makkah al-Musharrafah*, ed. Ferdinand Wüstenfeld (Leipzig, 1858), 77. According to Muslim tradition the Kaaba was rebuilt by Abraham and Ish-

mael. After taking care of all the unwanted objects in the shrine, Muhammad went to consecrate and "Islamicize" it. Rudi Paret, s.v. "Ibrāhīm," in *Encyclopaedia of Islam*, 2nd ed., 6 vols. (Leiden, 1960–2004), 3: 980.

7. There is an ongoing discussion regarding the nature of the Kaaba, and some scholars have suggested that it was a monotheistic shrine because of the pictures of Mary and Jesus, as well as Abraham, that were found in it. See G. R. Hawting, *The Idea of Idolatry and the Emergence of Islam: From Polemic to History* (Cambridge, 1999), 14–15 and nn. 28 and 29.

8. The persistence of idols and images in Muslim life is further demonstrated by the following story. According to unverified oral sources, in 1979 a rebel group caused an explosion in the Kaaba which exposed "a pile of statues buried below ground," to the great dismay of the Saudi authorities, who got rid of them quickly. Toufic Fahd, s.v. "ṣanam," in *Encyclopaedia of Islam*, 9: 5.

9. There is a clear stance in the Quran regarding idols, which are considered to be *shirk*: Abraham smashes them, one should avoid the impurity of idols, etc. See G. R. Hawting, "Idolatry and Idolaters," *Encyclopedia of the Quran*, 2: 475–80.

10. For a discussion on the Sunni and the Shi'ite traditions regarding images see Heger, "Status and the Image of the Persianate Artist," 36–41.

11. Sahih Bukhari, *The Translation of the Meanings of Sahih al-Bukhari*, trans. Muhammad Muhsin Khan (Lahore, 1983, 1979), vol. 9, bk. 93, 647.

12. Patricia Crone, in her article "Islam, Judeo-Christianity and Byzantine Iconoclasm," mentions a parallel Talmudic passage dated from ca. 250 by Joshua b. Levi. The Talmudic section deals with the shortcoming of painters to put souls into their pictures, as God breathes life into whatever he creates or shapes (Berachot, f.10a). Crone, "Islam, Judeo-Christianity and Byzantine Iconoclasm," *Jerusalem Studies in Arabic and Islam* 2 (1980): 67, n. 33.

13. David Freedberg, *The Power of Images: Studies in the History and Theory of Response* (Chicago, 1989), 60.

14. Hawting, *Idea of Idolatry*, 1–3, 5. Ignaz Goldziher argued much earlier that the hadith sources are reflecting their own time rather than the period of Muhammad, and thus are close to the spirit of the Talmud. *Vorlesungen über den Islam* (*Hartzaot al ha-Islam*), ed. Martin Plesner, trans. J. J. Rivlin (Jerusalem, 1951), 41 and n. 16.

15. This political tension may also be linked to the *Mu'tazila*.

16. P. Crone and M. Hinds, *God's Caliph: Religious Authority in the First Centuries of Islam* (Cambridge, 1986), esp. 97–110.

17. Ibid., 5–6.

18. Hans Belting, *Likeness and Presence: A History of the Image Before the Era of Art*, trans. Edmund Jephcott (Chicago, 1994), 14–16.

19. See Oleg Grabar and Mika Natif, "The Story of Portraits of the Prophet Muhammad," *Studia Islamica* 96 (2003): 19–38.

20. By the sixteenth century, the same core story is used to justify figural painting at the Safavid court rather than discuss the preknowledge of the coming of Islam by Jews and Christians. Wheeler M. Thackston, *Album Prefaces and Other Documents*

on the History of Calligraphers and Painters (Leiden, 2001), 12 (Persian text); See David Roxburgh's analysis in "Prefacing the Image: The Writing of Art History in Sixteenth-Century Iran," *Studies and Sources in Islamic Art and Architecture* 9 (2001): esp. 170–74.

21. Belting, *Likeness and Presence*, 47–49.

22. See, for example, the discussion about divine made images in: Barber, *Figure and Likeness*, 24–27; Belting, *Likeness and Presence*, esp. 62–69; M. J. Mondzain, "The Holy Shroud: How Invisible Hands Weave the Undecidable," in *Iconoclash: Beyond the Image Wars in Science, Religion, and Art*, ed. Bruno Latour and Peter Weibel (Cambridge, Mass., 2002), 324–35; Bruno Latour "What Is Iconoclash? or, Is There a World Beyond the Image War?" in *Iconoclash*, 16.

23. Latour, "What Is Iconoclash?" 16.

24. Ibid.

25. Mani lived in the second half of the third century C.E. in Central Asia, Iran, and mostly in Iraq. The story of Mani and his magical pictures appears in several texts of different type, the most important ones for our discussion are the *Shahnama* of Firdausi, the *Khamsa* of Nizami, Sa'di's *Gulistan*, and Mirkhwand's *Rawżāt al-safā*. Dust Muhammad also brings these stories in his preface to the album of Bahram Mirza. See the thorough discussion by Roxburgh in his "Prefacing the Image," 174–78.

26. See for example, Mirkhwand, *Tarikh rawżāt al-safā*, 10 vols. (Tehran, 1959–60), 2: 138.

27. Latour, "What Is Iconoclash?" 18.

28. Mirkhwand, *Tarikh rawżāt al-safā*, 2: 138–39.

29. Priscilla Soucek, "Nizami on Painters and Painting," in *Islamic Art at the Metropolitan Museum of Art*, ed. R. Ettinghausen (New York, 1972), 10.

30. Bukhari, *Translation of the Meanings*, vol. 5, bk. 58, no. 235.

31. Ibid., vol. 7, bk. 72, no. 842.

32. Ibid., vol. 3, bk. 43, no. 659; *Muslim*: bk. 024, no. 5262 and 5264.

33. Priscilla Soucek, "The Theory and Practice of Portraiture in the Persian Tradition," *Muqarnas* 17 (2000): 98–101; Michael Brand, "The City as an Artistic Center," in *Fetehpur-Sikri*, ed. Michael Brand and G. D. Lowry (Bombay, 1987), 112. The change in concepts of visuality that occurred in Mughal India in the late sixteenth century deserves a separate study, which I hope to embark on in the near future.

34. Heger, "Status and the Image of the Persianate Artist," 71–74.

35. Thomas W. Arnold, *Painting in Islam* (New York, 1965), 3–4 and n. 1. He further states that figurative painting "was condemned by religious authority," *Painting in Islam*, 3.

36. Gülru Necipoğlu, "The Life of an Imperial Monument: Hagia Sophia after Byzantium," in *Hagia Sophia from the Age of Justinian to the Present*, ed. Robert Mark and Ahmet S. Çakmak (Cambridge, 1992), 197, 204; Cyril Mango, *Materials for the Study of the Mosaics of St. Sophia at Istanbul* (Washington, D.C., 1962).

37. This page is from the *Muraqqa-i Gulshan*.

38. See *Manṭik al-Ṭayr*, ca. 1600, Safavid Iran, Metropolitan Museum of Art (63.210.11).

39. Yves Porter, "From the 'Theory of the Two Qalams' to the 'Seven Principles of

Painting': Theory, Terminology, and Practice in Persian Classical Painting," *Muqarnas* 17 (2000): 113.

40. Yves Porter, *Painters, Paintings, and Books: An Essay on Indo-Persian Technical Literature, 12–19th Centuries*, trans. S. Butani (New Delhi, 1994), 105.

41. Porter, "'Theory of the Two Qalams,'" 112.

42. See, for example, Ibn Rushd's commentary on Aristotle's *Metaphysics*, Porter, "'Theory of the Two Qalams,'" 113.

43. Porter, "'Theory of the Two Qalams,'" 113 and note 43.

44. Oleg Grabar, "Islamic Art and Byzantium," *Dumbarton Oaks Papers* 18 (1964): 69–88.

45. W. J. T. Mitchell, *What Do Pictures Want? The Lives and Loves of Images* (Chicago, 2005), 7.

46. Grabar, "Islamic Art and Byzantium," 71–72.

47. Such connections can be seen in early Islamic buildings. Several of the most prestigious Islamic monuments built by the Umayyads in the seventh and the eighth centuries owe much of their artistic concepts to Byzantine architecture and artisans. The mosaics at the Great Mosque of Damascus are stylistically and, to a certain extent, iconographically based on Byzantine mosaics, similar to the ones at the Church of St. George in Thessalonica. Furthermore, the shape of the Dome of the Rock, with its octagon structure and some of the vegetal motifs in its mosaic decoration, present strong links to late antique Hellenistic traditions, such as the Church of the Kathisma near Jerusalem. Grabar also recognizes the contradiction between the text and archeological and art historical evidence which point to flourishing artistic connections between Islam and Byzantium as early as the seventh century. He does not, however, provide an explanation to this problem in the text ("Islamic Art and Byzantium," 72). For a fascinating interpretation of the mosaics at the Great Mosque of Damascus see the article of Nasser Rabbat, "The Dialogic Dimension in Umayyad Art," *Res: Anthropology and Aesthetics* 43 (Spring 2003): 78–94.

48. Zamakhsharī, *Al-Kashshaf*, 4: 509–10, as it appears in Heger, "Status and the Image of the Persianate Artist," 62 and n. 162.

49. Mitchell, *What Do Pictures Want?* 7.

50. Ibid., 10.

51. Belting, *Likeness and Presence*, 6–7.

52. I am following Moshe Halbertal and Avishai Margalit's definitions of a fetish as "an object to which people attribute powers that it does not have," in *Idolatry*, trans. Naomi Goldblum (Cambridge, Mass., 1992), 42.

53. Ibid.

54. At the same time, opposite opinions were also expressed by such legalists as al-Shahīd al-Thānī (d. 1558), who objected to any representations of animated images. His contemporary, the Safavi jurist al-Karakī (d. 1534), who opposed the making of idols, permitted their selling because no intention of idolatry was committed. Heger argues that his judicial innovation was the introduction of the notion intent (*ḳaṣd*) with respect to the usage of images. See Heger, "Status and the Image of the Persianate Artist," 68–69.

55. This passage appears in the love story between Humāy and Humāyūn. Teresa Fitzherbert noticed it in her article "Khwaju Kirmani (689–733/1290–1352): An Émi-nence Grise of Fourteenth-Century Persian Painting," *Iran* 29 (1999): 149 and nn. 8 and 138. On the inner meaning of portraiture and painting see Yves Porter's article "'Theory of the Two Qalams,'" as well as Porter's *Painters, Paintings, and Books*, 104–6 and 138–44.

56. These ideas were adopted by important scholars such as al-Ghazzali, al-Makdisi, Ibn al-ʿArabi and many others. See Doris Behrens-Abouseif, *Beauty in Arabic Culture* (Princeton, N.J., 1999), 25–31; James William Wafer, "The Development of Male Love in Islamic Mystical Literature," in *Islamic Homosexualities: Culture, History, and Literature*, ed. Stephen Murray and Will Roscoe (New York, 1997), 107–31.

57. Tj. de Boer [H. Daiber], s.v. "naẓar," *Encyclopaedia of Islam*, 7: 1050.

58. See the discussion by Khaled El-Rouayheb in his book *Before Homosexuality in the Arab-Islamic World, 1500–1800* (Chicago, 2005), 111–18.

59. Wafer, "Development of Male Love," 111.

60. See the work of Hellmut Ritter, *The Ocean of the Soul: Man, the World and God in the Stories of Farīd al-Dīn Aṭṭār*, trans. John O'Kane, with editorial assistance of Bernd Radtke (Leiden, 2003), esp. 484–517.

61. This would be what James Wafer calls the "vision complex" of some Muslim mystic practitioners ("Development of Male Love," 107). The subject of homoeroticism in Persian painting is complex and requires further discussion that goes beyond the scope of this chapter.

62. Bibliothèque nationale, Paris, MS suppl. Turc 190, fol. 36v. Published in Marie-Rose Séguy, *The Miraculous Journey of Mahomet* (New York, 1977), pl. 34.

63. In the illustration to al-Biruni's "The Day of Cursing" from *Kitab al-athar al-baqiya* (Chronology of Ancient Nations), fol. 16r, 1307–8, there are clouds above the heads of the Prophet Muhammad and his descendants that may be interpret as "em-blems of sanctity," as suggested by Priscilla Soucek. See her "The Life of the Prophet: Illustrated Versions," in *Content and Context of Visual Arts in the Islamic World*, ed. Priscilla Soucek (University Park, Pa., 1988), 198. The painting was published in Linda Komaroff and Stefano Carboni, eds., *The legacy of Genghis Khan: Courtly Art and Cul-ture in Western Asia, 1256–1353* (New York, 2002), fig. 136. In the *Jami al-Tawarikh* of Rashid al-Din there are several illustrations with clouds that may also be representing a divine presence, as in the illustration of "Moses hearing God's voice," or "Muhammad leading his army against Banu Qaynuqa." These pictures have been published in D. T. Rice, *The World History of Rashid al-Din* (Edinburgh, 1976), 58; and Sheila S. Blair, *A Compendium of Chronicles: Rashid al-Din's Illustrated History of the World* (London, 1995), fig. 35.

64. Halbertal and Margalit, *Idolatry*, 2, 37, 239.

65. The best work on the mystical aspect of the Arabic script is still Annemarie Schimmel's *Calligraphy and Islamic Culture* (New York, 1990).

66. Anthony Welch considers the use of some calligraphy as icons. See his "Epi-graphs as Icons: the Role of the Written Word in Islamic Art," in *The Image and the*

Word: Confrontations in Judaism, Christianity, and Islam, ed. Joseph Gutmann (Missoula, Mont., 1977), 63–74.

67. According to some Muslim scholars *ḥulūl* means "the appropriation of one thing by another, or the 'infusion' of one thing into another, such that when one is described the other is also described." See Louis Massignon, s.v. "ḥulūl", *Encyclopaedia of Islam*, 3: 570. The idea of revering words or books but not images is suggested by Belting, who argues that "Torah scrolls are venerated like cult images by the Jews" (*Likeness and Presence*, 7).

68. Belting, *Likeness and Presence*, 47.

69. Freedberg, *Power of Images*, 60.

70. Ibid., 59.

71. A. Grohmann, "Anthropomorphic and Zoomorphic Letters in the History of Arabic Writing," *Bulletin de l'Institut d'Égypte* 38 (1955–56): 117–22.

72. See for example the Bobrinski bucket and Richard Ettinghausen's article "The Bobrinski 'Kettle,'" in *Islamic Art and Archaeology: Collected Papers*, ed. M. Rosen-Ayalon (Berlin, 1984), 315–30.

73. This idea is treated by Ibn al-ʿArabi or the Ikhwān al-Ṣafa, for example. See Schimmel, *Calligraphy and Islamic Culture*, 79–80; Seyyed Hossein Nasr, *Islamic Art and Spirituality* (Albany, N.Y., 1987), 17.

74. Soucek, "Nizami on Painters and Painting," 19.

CHAPTER 4: NIETZSCHE, BLAKE, AND POUSSIN

1. Denounced, of course, as idols by the Taliban. It is important to note, however, that a Taliban spokesman who toured the United States prior to the destruction of the Buddhas, claimed that the statues would be destroyed, not because there was any danger of their being used as religious idols, but (on the contrary) because they had become secular idols for the West, which was expressing interest in pouring millions of dollars into Afghanistan for their preservation. The Taliban blew up the "idols," in other words, precisely because the West cared so much about them.

2. See the remarks by General William Boykin, undersecretary of defense during Donald Rumsfeld's tenure as secretary of defense. For a discussion of the response to Bush's declaration of a "crusade" of "good against evil," see (among numerous commentaries) Peter Ford's piece in the *Christian Science Monitor*, September 19, 2001: "Europe Cringes at Bush 'Crusade' Against Terrorists."

3. Richard Neer, "Poussin and the Ethics of Imitation," in *Memoirs of the American Academy in Rome*, ed. Vernon Hyde Minor, vols. 51–52 (2006–7): 297–344.

4. Revised Standard Version.

5. Walter Benjamin, "Critique of Violence," in *Reflections*, ed. Peter Demetz (New York, 1978), 298.

6. The best study of this sort is Avishai Margalit and Moshe Halbertal, *Idolatry*, trans. N. Goldblum (Cambridge, Mass., 1992), which surveys the major themes of idolatry and iconoclasm from the rabbinical commentators through the history of Western philosophy.

7. For a fuller discussion of the concept of "secondary belief," see "The Surplus

Value of Images," chapter 4 of my *What Do Pictures Want? The Lives and Loves of Images* (Chicago, 2005).

8. *Idolatry*, 5.

9. See my "Holy Landscape: Israel, Palestine, and the American Wilderness," in *Landscape and Power*, 2nd ed. (Chicago, 2002), 261–90.

10. As Halbertal and Margalit note, "the prophets speak of protective treaties with Egypt and Assyria as the worship of other gods" (*Idolatry*, 5).

11. The second commandment makes explicit the mandate of collective punishment: "You shall not bow down to them or serve them; for I The Lord your God am a jealous God, visiting the iniquity of the fathers upon the children to the third and the fourth generation" (Revised Standard Version).

12. See my "The Rhetoric of Iconoclasm: Marxism, Ideology, and Fetishism," in *Iconology: Image, Text, Ideology* (Chicago, 1986), chap. 6. For a survey of the sublimated, immaterialist concepts of idolatry, see Halbertal and Margalit, *Idolatry*.

13. Friedrich Nietzsche, *Thus Spake Zarathustra*, in *The Portable Nietzsche*, ed. Walter Kaufmann (New York, 1954), 317.

14. Ibid., 315.

15. Ibid., 324–25.

16. Ibid., 325.

17. *Twilight of the Idols*, in *Portable Nietzsche*, 466.

18. Giorgio Vasari, *The Lives of the Artists* (New York, 1991), preface.

19. *The Marriage of Heaven and Hell*, pl. 11, in *The Poetry and Prose of William Blake*, ed. David V. Erdman (Garden City, N.Y., 1970), 37.

20. See W. Robertson Smith, *The Religion of the Semites: The Fundamental Institutions* (1889; repr., New York, 1972), 93: "In semitic religion the relation of the gods to particular places . . . is usually expressed by the title Baal."

21. Burke is of course speaking here of the idols of *Native* Americans in this passage. Edmund Burke, *A Philosophical Enquiry into the Origin of Our Ideas of the Sublime and Beautiful* (1757), ed. James T. Boulton (South Bend, Ind., 1968), 59. See my discussion in "Eye and Ear: Edmund Burke and the Politics of Sensibility," in *Iconology*, chap. 5, 130.

22. Immanuel Kant, *Critique of Judgment*, trans. J. H. Bernard (New York, 1951), 115.

23. Neer, "Poussin and the Ethics of Imitation," 297.

24. Ibid., 298.

25. Ibid., 299.

26. Ibid., 312.

27. Ibid.

28. Ibid.

29. Ibid., 309.

30. Ibid., 313.

31. Ibid., 318.

32. This shift of the question from the meaning of the painting to "what it wants" is of course the procedure for which I have advocated in *What Do Pictures Want?*

33. It is hard to ignore the fact that Ashdod is located in the short space of land

(about twenty miles) between Tel Aviv and Gaza. During the invasion of Gaza in January 2009, it suffered rocket attacks from the Palestinians in Gaza.

34. See Nadav Shragal, "An Amalek in Our Times?" *Haaretz*, January 21, 2009.

35. Alan Cowell, "Gaza Children Found with Mothers' Corpses," *New York Times*, January 8, 2009.

36. In a fuller exposition, I would explore the relation between the dogmatic historicism of art history, its assumption of a proper "horizon of meaning," and the closely related problems of anachronism and intentionalism. Richard Wollheim is among the most prominent supporters of a strict historical psychologizing of pictorial meaning, which in his view "always rests upon a state of mind of the artist, and the way this leads him to work, and the experience that the product of this work brings about in the mind of a suitably informed and sensitive spectator," *Painting as an Art* (Princeton, N.J., 1987), 188. See my forthcoming essay, "The Future of the Image," for a discussion of the inevitability of anachronism and unintentional meaning in pictures; also Georges Didi-Huberman, "The History of Art Within the Limits of Its Simple Practice," in *Confronting Images: Questioning the Limits of a Certain History of Art*, trans. John Goodman (University Park, Pa., 2005), 12–52: "Anachronism is not, in history, something that must be absolutely banished—in the end, this is no more than a fantasy or an ideal of equivalence—but rather something that must be negotiated, debated, and perhaps even turned to advantage" (41). We should note as well that when Wollheim asks himself, "Where have I seen this face before?" in Poussin's *Rinaldo and Armida*, his answer is—of all things—Courbet! See *Painting as an Art*, 195.

37. See Michel Foucault, *The Order of Things* (New York, 1994), 10, and my discussion in *Picture Theory: Essays on Verbal and Visual Representation* (Chicago, 1994).

38. The Israelites dancing around the Golden Calf, like the Palestinians in terror at the plague, are both depicted as classical figures—as Greeks, in other words. As it happens, contemporary archeology research suggests that the Philistines were, in fact, Myceneans who migrated from Greece down to Palestine. This fact gives the historical dimension of Poussin's painting an uncanny accuracy in relation to modern historical knowledge that he could not have known. Thanks to Richard Neer for this factoid.

39. Émile Durkheim, *The Elementary Forms of Religious Life*, trans. Karen Fields (New York, 1995). The totem "expresses and symbolizes two different kinds of things. From one point of view, it is the outward and visible form of what I have called the totemic principle or god; and from another, it is also the symbol of a particular society that is called the clan. . . . God and society are one and the same" (208).

CHAPTER 5: DREADFUL BEAUTY

I wish to extend my thanks to my student and research assistant, Nika Elder; to Laura Giles, curator of Prints and Drawings at the Princeton University Art Museum; and to those students who have taken my History of African American Art and Race and Representation in American Art courses.

1. For further discussion of the meaning and power of images in *Bamboozled*, see Rachael Z. DeLue, "Envisioning Race in Spike Lee's *Bamboozled*," in *Fight the Power!*

The Spike Lee Reader, ed. Janice D. Hamlet and Robin R. Means Coleman (New York, 2009), 61–88; and W. J. T. Mitchell, *What Do Pictures Want? The Lives and Loves of Images* (Chicago, 2005), chap. 14.

2. See Bill Brown, ed., *Things*, special issue of *Critical Inquiry* 28, no. 1 (Autumn 2001); Brown, *A Sense of Things: The Object Matter of American Literature* (Chicago, 2003); Lorraine Daston, ed., *Things That Talk: Object Lessons from Art and Science* (New York, 2004); Mitchell, *What Do Pictures Want?* and Barbara Maria Stafford, *Echo Objects: The Cognitive Work of Images* (Chicago, 2007). Although I am aware of the need for historical and conceptual differentiation, I use the terms *thing* and *object* interchangeably here and throughout, not least because the work under discussion itself blurs the distinction.

3. Mitchell, *What Do Pictures Want?* 189–90.

4. See for example Hilton Als, "The Shadow Act: Kara Walker's Vision," *New Yorker*, October 8, 2007; Franklin Cason, "Look Away! Political Vision," *New Art Examiner* 27, no. 3 (November 1999): 28–31; Thelma Golden, "Oral Mores: A Postbellum Shadow Play," *Artforum* 35, no. 1 (September 1996): 92–93; Eleanor Heartney, "The Long Shadows of Slavery," *Art in America* 95, no. 9 (October 2007): 170–77, 226; and Mark Reinhardt, "The Art of Racial Profiling," in *Kara Walker: Narratives of a Negress*, ed. Ian Berry, Darby English, Vivian Patterson, and Mark Reinhardt (New York, 2007), 118.

5. Hilarie M. Sheets, "Cut It Out!" *ArtNews* 101, no. 4 (April 2002): 129. In "Circum-Atlantic Superabundance: Milk as World-Making in Alice Randall and Kara Walker," *American Literature* 78, no. 4 (December 2006): 769–98, Patricia Yaeger provides a compelling analysis of what she calls Walker's "aesthetics of excess," namely the superabundance and "pleasurable overdoing" of her art, particularly her representations of milk and nursing, which Yaeger describes as a way to think about the role of lactation in a slave-based economy.

6. Nancy Bless, "Michael Ray Charles," *New Art Examiner* 25 (September 1997): 67. See also Steven Heller, "Black on Black," *Print* 52, no. 3 (May–June 1998): 69; Calvin Reid, "Air Sambo," in *Michael Ray Charles* (New York, 1998), 5, where Reid refers to Charles's "almost inappropriate physical facility"; and Roberta Smith, "Art in Review: Michael Ray Charles," *New York Times*, October 3, 1997. Charles comments on what he calls the "truths of beauty and ugliness" in his art, in Steven Heller, "Painted Black: Interview with Michael Ray Charles," *Trace* 1, no. 3 (2001): 85.

7. Tony Shafrazi and Michael Ray Charles, "A Conversation," in *Michael Ray Charles* (1998), 9–10; Don Bacigalupi and Marilyn Kern-Foxworth, "An Interview with Michael Ray Charles," *Michael Ray Charles: An American Artist's Work, 1989–1997* (Houston, 1997), 27.

8. Shafrazi and Charles, "A Conversation," 10. For Lorraine Daston, it is precisely the quality of being a chimera that renders things, as she puts it, "talkative," able to "instantiate novel, previously unthinkable combinations" and generate "new constellations of experience." (Daston, *Things That Talk*, 21, 24.)

9. Mitchell, *What Do Pictures Want?*, xiii, xv.

10. See, for example, Golden, "Oral Mores"; Reinhardt, "The Art of Racial Pro-

filing"; Darby English, "This Is Not About the Past: Silhouettes in the Work of Kara Walker," in *Kara Walker: Narratives of a Negress*, 141–67; and Gwendolyn DuBois Shaw, *Seeing the Unspeakable: The Art of Kara Walker* (Durham, N.C., 2004), chap. 2.

11. Mitchell discusses the potential dubiousness of the idea of a desiring picture in *What Do Pictures Want?* 28–29. For a detailed and useful summary of the controversy and its central characters see Shaw, *Seeing the Unspeakable*, chap. 4. For additional coverage see Jerry Cullum, "Stereotype This," *Art Papers* 22, no. 6 (November–December 1998): 16–21; Karen C. C. Dalton, "The Past Is Prologue but Is Parody and Pastiche Progress? A Conversation," *International Review of African American Art* 14, no. 3 (1997): 17–29; "Extreme Times Call for Extreme Heroes," *International Review of African American Art* 14, no. 3 (1997): 2–16; Jane Farber, "Change the Joke and Slip the Yoke: A Series of Conversations on the Use of Black Stereotypes in Contemporary Visual Practice," *New Art Examiner* 26, no. 2 (October 1998): 14–15; Sander L. Gilman, "Confessions of an Academic Pornographer," and Thomas McEvilley, "Primitivism in the Works of an Emancipated Negress," in *Kara Walker: My Complement, My Enemy, My Oppressor, My Love*, ed. Phillipe Vergne et al. (Minneapolis, 2007), 26–35, 52–61; Troy Gooden, "An Evening with Michael Ray Charles," *International Review of African American Art* 14, no. 3 (1997): 62; Pamela Newkirk, "Controversial Silhouette," *ArtNews* 98, no. 8 (September 1999): 45; and Kelefa Sanneh, "Stereotypes Subverted? The Debate Continues: Much Ado," *International Review of African American Art* 15, no. 2 (1998): 44–47.

12. Mitchell, *What Do Pictures Want?* 49.

13. David Freedberg discusses the Lucas van Leyden triptych (ca. 1530, Rijksmuseum, Amsterdam) within a larger discussion of idolatry and iconoclasm in *The Power of Images: Studies in the History and Theory of Response* (Chicago, 1989), chap. 14. The full title of the Nolde work is *Dance Around the Golden Calf* (1910, Bayerische Staatsgemäldesammlungen, Munich).

14. See Carol Duncan, "The Art Museum as Ritual," in *The Art of Art History: A Critical Anthology*, ed. Donald Preziosi (Oxford, 1998), 473–85, for discussion of the museum as sacred space. See Arjun Appadurai, *The Social Life of Things: Commodities in Cultural Perspective* (New York, 1988), for discussion of objects as part of a social fabric or network and as mediums within human social practice. For Charles and commerce, see Katy Siegel, "Consuming Art," in *Art21: Art in the Twenty-First Century* (New York, 2001), 177–78.

15. Hans-Ulrich Obrist, "Interview with Kara Walker," in *Safety Curtain: Kara Walker* (Vienna, 2000); "Thelma Golden/Kara Walker: A Dialogue," in *Kara Walker: Pictures from Another Time*, ed. Annette Dixon (Ann Arbor, Mich., 2002), 45; Sheets, "Cut It Out!" 129. As Anne M. Wagner has written, Walker's work "generates effects in wild disproportion to the elegant spareness of its technical means"; similarly, Robert Storr attributes the power of her imagery in part to its mismatching of "decorative elegance" and "taboo-breaking vulgarity." Walker, again: "I wanted accessibility, something that was easily read and could operate on some sort of innocuous level to engage people—then I could pull the rug out from under them." Wagner, "Kara Walker: The Black-White Relation,'" in *Kara Walker: Narratives of a Negress*, 91; Storr, "Spooked,'" in *Kara Walker: My Complement, My Enemy*, 69; David Colman, "Pretty on the Out-

side," *George* (June–July 1996): 118. See also Marion Ackerman, "Kara Walker: Snared by Form," *Kara Walker* (Frankfurt, 2002), 71–72; and Carroll Dunham, "Film Noir: The Films of Kara Walker," *Artforum* 45, no. 8 (April 2007): 241–42.

16. Elaine Scarry, *On Beauty and Being Just* (Princeton, N.J., 1999). For the matter of definition see also Susan Sontag, "An Argument About Beauty," *Daedalus* 134, no. 4 (Fall 2005): 208–13. There exists a substantial, recent literature about the place and/or resurgence of beauty and pleasure in art. See, for example, *Uncontrollable Beauty: Toward a New Aesthetics*, ed. Bill Beckley (New York, 1998); *Beauty*, ed. Dave Beech (Cambridge, Mass., 2009); Jeremy Gilbert-Rolfe, *Beauty and the Contemporary Sublime* (New York, 1999); Alexander Nehamas, *Only a Promise of Happiness: The Place of Beauty in a World of Art* (Princeton, N.J., 2007); and Wendy Steiner, *Venus in Exile: The Rejection of Beauty in 20th-Century Art* (Chicago, 2001).

17. Sontag, "Argument About Beauty," 212. The philosophical questions to which I refer are, at base, aesthetic ones—concerned with visual affect, sensory response, and critical judgment—and a longer version of this essay would of course trace their roots to Plato, Thomas Aquinas, Burke, Hume, and Kant; it would thus also, and necessarily, contend with the sublime, a concept very much at issue for the work under discussion.

18. Scarry, *On Beauty*, 3, 4, 9.

19. Ibid., 6.

20. "I've made pictures that I thought were hilarious. I just couldn't stop laughing as I made them—a very disturbing, kind of cackling, giddy kind of picture. . . . But you really ought not laugh." Kara Walker, quoted in Sidney Jenkins, *Slice of Hand: The Silhouette Art of Kara Walker* (Annandale-on-Hudson, N.Y., 1995), in Alexi Worth, "Black and White and Kara Walker," *Art New England* 17 (December 1995–January 1996): 26. It is worth noting that Walker has likened racist symbols to contagion: "Still, racist icons, like resistant new strains of bacteria inhabiting the body, linger in our collective American minds. The shadow of the racist icon is the dormant form of the virus." Kara Walker, "The Debate Continues: Kara Walker's Response," *International Review of African American Art* 15, no. 2 (1998): 48–49.

21. Anne M. Wagner writes of Walker: "These black and white tableaux declare that the artist's own imagination has drunk deeply at a tainted well" ("Kara Walker: 'The Black-White Relation,'" 98). In Walker's words: "It seems like I had to actually reinvent or make up my own racist situations so I would know how to deal with them as black people in the past did. In order to have a real connection with my history I had to be somebody's slave. But I was in control. That's the difference" (James Hannaham, "Pea, Ball, Bounce: Interview with Kara Walker," *Interview* [November 1998]: 119). For discussion of the "acheiropoietic" image, see Hans Belting, *Likeness and Presence: A History of the Image Before the Era of Art*, trans. Edmund Jephcott (Chicago, 1994), 63–73; Alain Besançon, *The Forbidden Image: An Intellectual History of Iconoclasm* (Chicago, 2000), 111–13; Joseph Leo Koerner, *The Moment of Self-Portraiture in German Renaissance Art* (Chicago, 1993), chap. 5; and Bruno Latour, "What Is Iconoclash? or, Is There a World Beyond the Image Wars?" in *Iconoclash: Beyond the Image Wars in Science, Religion, and Art*, ed. Bruno Latour and Peter Weibel (Cambridge, Mass., 2002), 16–18.

22. Koerner, *Moment of Self-Portraiture*, 80. For the Walker works, see *Kara Walker: Narratives of a Negress*. For further discussion of the complicated issue of self-portraiture in Walker, see English, "This Is Not About the Past"; and Reinhardt, "Art of Racial Profiling," 124–29. English offers a particularly compelling analysis of Walker's intricate and multifaceted exploration of the possibility of representing subjectivity and self to and within history, including the historical present.

23. Katherine Brimberry, Michael Ray Charles, Ken Hale, "Michael Ray Charles," *Contemporary Impressions* 3, no. 1 (1995): 14.

24. "Thelma Golden/Kara Walker: A Dialogue," 44.

25. Jerry Saltz, "Kara Walker: Ill-Will and Desire," *Flash Art* 29, no. 191 (November–December 1996): 82.

26. English, "This Is Not About the Past," 142, 156. A photograph of the Carnegie International installation of *The Emancipation Approximation* captures the unruliness of Walker's silhouettes: sections of the net held aloft by a winged woman and out of which a male figure falls peel away from the wall (*Narratives of a Negress*, 64).

27. Lisa Saltzman, "Negative Images: How a History of Shadows Might Illuminate the Shadows of History," in *Making Memory Matter: Strategies of Remembrance in Contemporary Art* (Chicago, 2006), 48–74. I borrow the concept of the renunciatory from Saltzman's analysis of Ligon's work (50) and my reading of Walker owes much to Saltzman's understanding of Walker's use of the silhouette. For a related discussion of the silhouette form, see David Joselit, "Notes on Surface: Toward a Genealogy of Flatness," *Art History* 23, no. 1 (March 2000): 19–34; and Wagner, "Kara Walker: 'The Black-White Relation.'"

28. Freedberg, *Power of Images*, 392–405. See also Belting, *Likeness and Presence*.

29. "Thelma Golden/Kara Walker: A Dialogue," 44.

30. Elaine Scarry, *On Beauty*, 13.

31. Kara Elizabeth Walker, *Kara Walker: After the Deluge* (New York, 2007), 7, 9.

32. English, "This Is Not About the Past," 156, cites Walker's pinning technique.

33. Reinhardt, "Art of Racial Profiling," 122; Saltz, "Kara Walker," 84; Walker, "Debate Continues: Kara Walker Responds," 48. Some critics suspect that the art world's enthusiasm for Walker's work may well derive from titillation rather than edification. See, for example, Dan Cameron, "Kara Walker: Rubbing History the Wrong Way," *On Paper* 2, no. 1 (September–October 1997): 14.

34. Saltz, "Kara Walker," 86; Elizabeth Armstrong, "Kara Walker Interviewed by Liz Armstrong 7/23/96," in *No Place (Like Home)*, ed. Elizabeth Armstrong et al. (Minneapolis, 1997), 107. For discussion of Walker and romanticization of the past, see "Kara Walker at the São Paulo Biennial: A Conversation with Robert Hobbs," *Art Papers* 26, no. 2 (March–April 2002): 13; "Reading Black Through White in the Work of Kara Walker: A Discussion Between Michael Corris and Robert Hobbs," *Art History* 26, no. 3 (June 2003): 430–32; Robert F. Reid-Pharr, "Black Girl Lost," in *Kara Walker: Pictures from Another Time*, 27–41; and Saltzman, *Making Memory Matter*, 64–65.

35. Scarry, *On Beauty*, 57; "Thelma Golden/Kara Walker: A Dialogue," 45. For further discussion of the value of the aesthetic and the potential productiveness of beauty

or elegance within contemporary art, see Carol Armstrong, "Identity Aesthetics," *Artforum* 46, no. 1 (September 2007): 131–32; and Christopher Bedford, "Glenn Ligon: Regen Projects II," *Artforum* 46, no. 5 (January 2008): 289. For a counterargument to Scarry's, see Denis Donoghue, *Speaking of Beauty* (New Haven, Conn., 2003). In *Unwanted Beauty: Aesthetic Pleasure in Holocaust Representation* (Urbana, Ill., 2007), Brett A. Kaplan offers a related discussion of representations of the Holocaust including examples from contemporary art, positing beauty as enticement to reflect and question, a means to deeper historical understanding.

36. For discussion of art and the unrepresentable see Saul Friedlander, *Probing the Limits of Representation: Nazism and the "Final Solution"* (Cambridge, Mass., 1992); *Impossible Images: Contemporary Art After the Holocaust*, ed. Shelly Hornstein, Laura Levitt, and Laurence Silberstein (New York, 2003); Kaplan, *Unwanted Beauty*; and Michael Rothberg, *Traumatic Realism: The Demands of Holocaust Representation* (Minneapolis, 2000).

CHAPTER 6: ICONOCLASM AND REAL SPACE

1. I have used, more extensively than these notes indicate, Bruno Latour and Peter Weibel, eds., *Iconoclash: Beyond the Image Wars in Science, Religion, and Art* (Cambridge, Mass., 2002).

2. Revised Standard Version.

3. St. John of Damascus, *Three Treatises on the Divine Images*, trans. Andrew Louth (Crestwood, N.Y., 2003), 119, 132.

4. Z. S. Strother, "Iconoclasm by Proxy," in *Iconoclash*, 458–59.

5. David Freedberg, *The Power of Images: Studies in the History and Theory of Response* (Chicago, 1989), 42.

6. In *Real Spaces: World Art History and the Rise of Western Modernism* (London, 2003), 685, I defined an icon as "any image understood primarily as a gathering of powers, of materials, resemblant forms, characteristics or attributes." In the present discussion, the possibility of mediation provided by an icon is central. See Hans Belting, *Likeness and Presence: A History of the Image Before the Era of Art*, trans. Edmund Jephcott (Chicago, 1994).

7. *Webster's* gives "statue" as a synonym for the first definition of *image*.

8. Freedberg, *Power of Images*, 393. The theological definition of the divine image is very similar to the definition of allegory. See E. H. Gombrich, "*Icones Symbolicae*: Philosophies of Symbolism and Their Bearing on Art," in *Symbolic Images: Studies in the Art of the Renaissance*, vol. 2 of *Gombrich on the Renaissance*, 4 vols. (Chicago, 1972), 2: 123–91.

9. Plato, *Sophist*, 234b.

10. St. John of Damascus, *On the Divine Images*, 158.

11. Ibid., 147.

12. Ibid., 150, 158.

13. Ibid., 79–80.

14. Brigitte Derlon, "From New Zealand to a Museum: Opposing Views of the Malanggan," in *Iconoclash*, 139–42.

15. Homer, *Iliad*, bk. 18, ll. 417–21; and David Summers, "Pandora's Crown: On Wonder, Imitation, and Mechanism in Western Art," in *Wonders, Marvels, and Monsters in Early Modern Culture*, ed. Peter G. Platt (Newark, Del., 1999), 45–75.

16. Aristotle, *Politics*, 1253b.

17. Pliny the Elder, *Natural History*, 35.36.66 and 35.36.94; and Ovid, *Metamorphoses*, 10.243–97.

18. David Summers, "Cogito Embodied: Force and Counterforce in Rene Descartes's *Les Passions de l'Ame*," in *Representing the Passions: Histories, Bodies, Visions*, ed. Richard Meyer (Los Angeles, 2003), 13–36.

19. Xenophon, *Memorabilia*, 3.10.1–8.

20. Plato, *Sophist*, 234b.

21. Rensselaer W. Lee, "Ut Pictura Poesis: The Humanistic Theory of Painting," *Art Bulletin* 22 (1940): 197–269; also Rensselaer W. Lee, *Ut Pictura Poesis: The Humanistic Theory of Painting* (New York, 1967).

22. See Philostratus, *Imagines*; and Callistratus, *Descriptions*, with a translation by Arthur Fairbanks (Cambridge, Mass., 1969).

23. See, for example, Aristotle, *Rhetoric*, 1404a 5–6; style addresses *phantasia* and makes things clearer, but "no one teaches geometry in this way"; also 1405b: it makes a difference when we speak of the "rosy-fingered dawn" rather than the "purple-fingered" or "red-fingered."

24. In its turn, the word *convince* is related to words like *victory*, as if one might be vanquished by rational argument, or as if one might really "win" an argument. We are convinced by proof, and we are convicted by evidence.

25. Aristotle, *On the Soul*, 431a 16–17.

26. Aristotle, *On Memory and Recollection*, 450b–451a.

27. Aristotle, *On the Soul*, 433b 29–30.

28. David C. Lindberg, *Theories of Vision from Al-Kindi to Kepler* (Chicago, 1976); Martin Kemp, *The Science of Art: Optical Themes in Western Art from Brunelleschi to Seurat* (New Haven, Conn. 1990); and David Summers, *Vision, Reflection and Desire in Western Painting* (Chapel Hill, N.C., 2007).

29. Hans Belting, "Beyond Iconoclasm: Nam June Paik: The Zen Gaze and the Escape from Representation," in *Iconoclash*, 390–411. According to the argument I am making here, the axis-line of sight along which *TV Buddha* is arranged might be seen as comparable to the stripe in Paik's *Zen for TV* (1975).

30. Quoted in Edward A. Burtt, ed., *The English Philosophers from Bacon to Mill* (New York, 1939), 11.

CHAPTER 7: HOW MANY WAYS CAN YOU IDOLIZE A SONG?

I wish to thank two former Brown students, Jonathan Greenberg and Benjamin Ewing, for pointing me in directions that I never would have taken myself.

1. Walter Benjamin, "The Work of Art in the Age of Its Technological Reproducibility," 3rd version, *Selected Writings, Volume 4: 1938–1940*, trans. Edmund Jephcott et al., ed. Howard Eiland and Michael W. Jennings (Cambridge, 2003), 251–83.

2. On distance see ibid., 255 and 272, n. 11. The archetype for this phenomenon is found in nature (255).

3. Ibid., 253. See also his claim: "It was more important for [such] figures to be present than to be seen" (257).

4. See ibid., especially on how a "ritualistic basis . . . is still recognizable as secularized ritual in even the most profane forms of the cult of beauty" (255). See also p. 272, n. 12 (attached to this same text), and 261 and 267, on painting, beauty, and contemplation.

5. On collecting see ibid., 272, n. 12.

6. Ibid., 257.

7. Theodor W. Adorno, "On the Fetish-Character in Music and the Regression of Listening" (1938), in *Theodor W. Adorno, Essays on Music*, ed. Richard Leppert (Berkeley, Calif., 2002), 288–317.

8. For the typology, see ibid., 308–10.

9. Ibid., 293–94.

10. Ibid., 295–98.

11. See ibid., 295–97.

12. Ibid., 296.

13. On "distraction" see Benjamin, "Work of Art," 267–69.

14. Ibid., 267 and 281, n. 40. Benjamin situates this assessment in what he sees as the degeneration of the bourgeoisie.

15. Adorno, "Fetish-Character," 297.

16. Wilfrid Sheed, *The House That George Built (With a Little Help from Irving, Cole, and a Crew of About Fifty)* (New York, 2007).

17. See, e.g., ibid., 28–32 and especially 131 (on Astaire); 108 (swinging), 187, 190 (irreverence), 191, 238 (on Crosby); 262–63 (on Crosby and Johnny Mercer); 110, 181, 225, 227, 248, 251, 309, and esp. 238 (on Sinatra); 229 and 233 (on Crosby and Sinatra); and 230 (on the hypnotic power of singers).

18. On "culinary" in Adorno, see "Fetish-Character," 290; cf. Sheed, *House That George Built*, xxvi and xvii. For *addict* and *connoisseur*, see ibid., xi and xxvi, respectively.

19. Theodor W. Adorno, *Philosophy of New Music*, trans. and ed. Robert Hullot-Kentor (Minneapolis, 2006), 79; Sheed, *The House That George Built*, xxii.

20. Adorno, "Fetish-Character," 305; Sheed, *The House That George Built*, 109.

21. Adorno, "Fetish-Character," 293; Sheed, *House That George Built*, 218 (and also 109).

22. Sheed, *House That George Built*, 167. The "list" here is of songs by Rodgers and Hart.

23. Adorno, "Fetish-Character," 310; also, "On Popular Music," in *Theodor W. Adorno, Essays on Music*, ed. Leppert, 456.

24. Sheed, *House That George Built*, 7.

25. Benjamin, "Work of Art," 264–65 and esp. 279, n. 33; Adorno, "Fetish-Character," 297.

26. Sheed, *House That George Built*, xi.

27. Ibid., 28–29 (Mailer) and 300 (Carmichael).

28. Adorno, "Fetish-Character," 304, and esp. 305.

29. Sheed, *House That George Built*, xvii.

30. Maryanne Wolf, *Proust and the Squid: The Story and Science of the Reading Brain* (New York, 2007), 7, quoting from Proust's book *On Reading*. See also Israel Rosenfield and Edward Ziff, "How the Mind Works: Revelations," *New York Review of Books*, June 26, 2008, 64.

31. Sheed, *House That George Built*, xvii.

32. Ibid., xviii.

33. Sam Wong and Sandra Aamodt, "Your Brain Lies to You," *New York Times*, June 27, 2008.

34. Sheed, *House That George Built*, xvii.

35. Joseph Bottum, "The Soundtracking of America," *Atlantic Monthly*, March 2000, 66 and 68.

36. See Wolf, *Proust and the Squid*, 74–76.

37. See Nadezhda Mandelstam, *Hope Against Hope: A Memoir* (New York, 1970), 228. Nadezhda doubted that her husband held onto his Dante the second time.

38. Quoted by Wolf, *Proust and the Squid*, 76.

39. Sheed, *House that George Built*, xiv.

40. Ibid., xviii and also 74.

41. Ibid., 31; italics in original.

42. Ibid., 226. The words are Sheed's not Schwartz's.

43. Ibid., 10 and 33.

44. Ibid., 250–51.

45. Ibid., 300. The image conjures up notions of Benjamin's aura.

46. For Sheed on the 1930s see ibid., 160–61 and 250. On Adorno and childhood songs see "Fetish-Character," 303–4; on Lawrence see the discussion in Bottum, "Soundtracking of America," 70.

47. Sheed, *Frank and Maisie: A Memoir with Parents* (New York, 1985).

48. Sheed, *House That George Built*, 303.

49. Ibid., 34.

50. Ibid., 244.

51. Ibid.

52. Ibid., 167.

53. Ibid., 250.

54. Ibid., 237.

55. Ibid., 236–37.

56. Ibid., 238.

57. Ibid., 255. Adorno had particular scorn for the illusion of the song that was "just for you." See, e.g., Theodor W. Adorno, *Introduction to the Sociology of Music*, trans. E. B. Ashton (New York, 1976), "Popular Music," 31; also "On Popular Music," 457; and especially the section "Especially for You," in "Commodity Music Analyzed," *Quasi una Fantasia: Essays on Modern Music*, trans. Rodney Livingstone (London, 1994), 43–45.

58. Sheed, *House That George Built*, 229.

59. Ibid., 191 ("whines") and 264 (Mercer).

60. Benjamin, "Work of Art," 256.

61. Sheed, *House That George Built*, 19.

62. Ibid., 19.

63. Ibid., 228.

64. Rogan P. Taylor, *The Death and Resurrection Show: From Shaman to Superstar* (London, 1985).

65. Ibid., 208.

66. See, for example, ibid., 18, 23–25, 26–28, 42–43.

67. Ibid., 40–43, 103, 207; italics in original.

68. Ibid., 188–92 and 203–4.

69. Ibid., 188 and 192.

70. Ibid., 19, 82–83 and 200.

71. Ibid., 186. On Adorno's actual reaction to the youth culture of the 1960s, see, e.g., Carlin Romano [Critic at Large], "Legacies of the 60s: The Agitation of Adorno," *Chronicle of Higher Education*, June 20, 2008.

72. Taylor, *Death and Resurrection Show*, 174; italics in original.

73. Ibid., 195.

74. Ibid., 189 and 203.

75. Ibid., 174–75.

76. Ibid., 198–99; italics in original.

77. Ibid., 195.

78. Ibid., 188.

79. Ibid., 192.

80. Ibid.; italics in original.

81. Ibid., 190.

82. Ibid.

83. Ibid., 187, 189–90, and 193.

84. Ibid., 189; italics in original.

85. Sheed, *House That George Built*, 83 and 243.

86. Taylor, *Death and Resurrection Show*, 191–92; italics in original.

87. Ibid., 200.

88. Carl Wilson, *Let's Talk About Love: A Journey to the End of Taste*, series 33 1/3 (New York, 2007).

89. Adorno, "Fetish-Character," 294.

90. Wilson, *Let's Talk About Love*, 64.

91. Ibid., 67 and 72; italics in original.

92. Ibid., 66 ("Schmaltz"), 70–71 and 161 (*Idol*).

93. Ibid., 1.

94. Ibid., 88.

95. Ibid., 89 (capital), 84, 125–26 (new), and 98 (taste).

96. Ibid., 96–97 and 150.

97. Ibid., 116 (quote from a fan), 84–85 (eclecticism), and 15, 97 (exclusion).

98. Adorno, "Fetish-Character," 302.

99. Wilson, *Let's Talk About Love*, 122.

100. Ibid., 125.

101. Ibid.

102. Ibid., 126–27.

103. Richard Taruskin, "Shall We Change the Subject? A Music Historian Reflects," unpublished manuscript, University of California, Berkeley, 2008.

104. Wilson, *Let's Talk About Love*, 69.

105. Ibid., 124.

106. Ibid., 69; italics in original.

107. Ibid., 129.

108. Ibid.

109. Ibid., 55.

110. Ibid., 147.

111. Ibid., 112.

112. Ibid., 123.

113. Ibid., 132.

114. See, for example, ibid., 72 and especially 140.

115. Ibid., 131.

116. Adorno, *Introduction to the Sociology of Music*, "Musical Life," 129.

117. Bottum, "Soundtracking of America," 59.

118. Joan Anderman, "Ever Lower Fidelity: Many Listeners Are Trading Quality for Convenience," *Boston Globe*, March 14, 2007.

119. David Lowenthal, *The Past Is a Foreign Country* (Cambridge, 1985), 399.

120. Ibid., 196–97.

121. Sarah Rodman, "The 1 Site for Nostalgic Mixmasters," *Boston Globe*, June 16, 2008.

122. Maura J. Casey, "Nuala O'Faolain," *New York Times*, May 13, 2008.

123. Sheed, *The House That George Built*, 100–101.

CHAPTER 8: ICONOCLASM AND THE SUBLIME

1. James Elkins, *Our Beautiful, Dry, and Distant Texts: Art History as Writing* (University Park, Pa., 1997).

2. Holly, "Interventions: The Melancholy Art," *Art Bulletin* 89, no. 1 (2007): 7–18.

3. There are summaries of my own and other people's theories about these concepts in my *Six Stories from the End of Representation: Images in Painting, Photography, Microscopy, Astronomy, Particle Physics, and Quantum Mechanics, 1980–2000* (Stanford, Calif., 2007).

4. For example, Rosalind Krauss and Yve-Alain Bois, *Formless: A User's Guide* (New

York, 1997); Georges Didi-Huberman, *The Invention of Hysteria: Charcot and the Photography of the Salpêtrière* [Hospital], trans. Alisa Hartz (Cambridge, Mass., 2003).

5. James Elkins, *On the Strange Place of Religion in Contemporary Art* (New York, 2004).

6. There were no religious people at that conference, in the sense that none represented their religions. The speakers were artists, historians, and theorists of themes related to religion. Rirkrit Tiravanija from the group The Land talked as a religionist, proposing or proselytizing spiritual ideas; when I was present, his interventions went largely unanswered.

7. The book that is projected is Joseph Koerner, *Last Experiences of Painting*, with an introduction by Elena Calvillo, vol. 5 in *Theories of Modernism and Postmodernism in the Visual Arts*, ed. James Elkins (Cork, Ireland, 2005–11).

8. *What Is an Image?*, ed. Maja Naef and James Elkins, vol. 2 of the *Stone Theory Institute* (College Park, forthcoming).

9. *Iconoclash: Beyond the Image Wars in Science, Religion, and Art*, ed. Bruno Latour and Peter Weibel (Cambridge, Mass., 2002).

10. See the Iconology Research Group Web site, at www.iconologyresearchgroup .org. The book, coedited by Barbara Baert and Hilde Van Gelder, is on the subject of the body and religion in art. It will be published by Peeters, in their series Art and Religion. This paragraph is adopted from my introduction to that book.

11. The following is from my review of *Iconoclash*, "Visual Culture: First Draft," in *Art Journal* 62, no. 3 (2003): 104–7. This passage continues until the callout for note 20, below.

12. Bruno Latour, "What Is Iconoclash?," in *Iconoclash*, 17.

13. Pierre Centlivres, "Life, Death, and Eternity of the Buddhas in Afghanistan," in *Iconoclash*, 77.

14. Dario Gamboni, "Image to Destroy, Indestructible Image," in *Iconoclash*, 88–135.

15. Bruno Latour, "What Is Iconoclash?" in *Iconoclash*, 16–17.

16. Joseph Koerner, "The Icon as Iconoclash," in *Iconoclash*, 167.

17. Ibid., 179, 182.

18. Ibid., 183.

19. *Iconoclash*, 213.

20. Note I am not saying Koerner's statement is bold because he connects a Reformation fear of images to a wider fear that religion might be representation. It is bold because it acknowledges that scholarship itself turns away from the ostensible object of its attention.

21. This is the end of the abbreviated excerpt of my review; the full text continues with questions about how art history is developing *away* from these themes, and how they might figure in visual studies.

22. Information on the faculty is available on the Stone Summer Theory Institute Web site, at www.stonesummertheoryinstitute.org.

23. See Marie-José Mondzain, *Image, Icon, Economy: The Byzantine Origins of the Contemporary Economy*, trans. Rico Frances (Stanford, Calif., 2005).

24. This is one of two epigraphs in Elkins, *Strange Place of Religion*.

25. Marie-José Mondzain, *L'image peut-elle tuer?* (Paris, 2002), trans. Sally Shafto, *Can Images Kill?* (unpublished in English), 7, 14. "Art broke with the Church in order to remain faithful to the incarnation of the invisible image," she writes, and among the consequences of this state of affairs is the fact that the "failure of the gaze" means sight will never encounter "what it desires to see: God. That is why men continue to make images" even though "God is thus nothing other than the name of our desire to see our similarity . . . that constantly escapes from sight." *Can Images Kill?* 16, 17, 18.

26. Jean-Luc Nancy, "The Image—The Distinct," in *The Ground of the Image* (New York, 2005), 1–3.

27. An interesting parallel text in this regard is Robert Nelson, "Living on the Byzantine Borders of Western Art," *Gesta* 35, no. 1 (1996): 3–11.

28. The book is edited by Roald Hoffmann. Most of my own entanglements with the sublime are recorded in my *Six Stories from the End of Representation*.

29. There is a third argument, which I am omitting here: that the postmodernism sublime is such an intricate concept that it is effectively useless without extensive qualification. The full essay explores Weiskel's text in some depth.

30. Jean-François Courtine, *Of the Sublime: Presence in Question*, trans. Jeffrey S. Librett (Albany, N.Y., 1993); and *Sticky Sublime*, ed. Bill Beckley (New York, 2001), which I do not recommend because it ranges much more widely than the concept of its title.

31. Mark C. Taylor, *Disfiguring: Art, Architecture, Religion* (Chicago, 1992).

32. George Steiner, *Real Presences* (Chicago, 1989).

33. Jean-Luc Nancy, "Preface to the French Edition," in *Of the Sublime: Presence in Question*, trans. and with an afterword by Jeffrey S. Librett (Albany, N.Y., 1993), 1–3. Nancy's approach is not simply ahistorical; he also observes that "beginning with Kant, the sublime will constitute the most proper, decisive moment in the thought of art"—a formulation close to Lyotard's. Nancy, "Sublime Offering," in ibid., 50. Lacoue-Labarthe comes to a similar conclusion; see "Sublime Truth," in ibid., 71–108, esp. 89.

34. Peter De Bolla, *The Discourse of the Sublime: Readings in History, Aesthetics, and the Subject* (New York, 1989), 30.

35. Jean-François Lyotard, "The Sublime and the Avant-Garde," *Art Forum* 22, pt. 8 (April 1984): 38.

36. Thomas Weiskel, *The Romantic Sublime: Studies in the Structure and Psychology of Transcendence* (Baltimore, 1976), 3.

37. Rudolf Otto, *The Idea of the Holy: An Inquiry into the Non-Rational Factor in the Idea of the Divine and Its Relation to the Rational*, trans. John W. Harvey (Oxford, 1946 [1917]), 42, 47, 65.

38. Like the sublime, the numinous is thrown around rather carelessly in art criticism. Writing on Ed Ruscha's blurred paintings of the mid-1980s, the critic Bill Berkson says you have to be "prepared inexorably for the numinous at every turn." Otto wouldn't approve of the self-assured tone here, especially when Berkson goes on to say that "we wouldn't revere it so" if the divine "logos" of the paintings "weren't an inexhaustible

blank very like the sweet nothings wafting across the page of an Ed Ruscha sunset." Berkson, "Sweet Logos," *Artforum* (January 1987): 98–101, quotation on 99.

39. See Rufolf Otto, "The 'Wholly Other' in Religious History and Theology," in Otto, *Religious Essays: A Supplement to "The Idea of the Holy,"* trans. Brian Lunn (London, 1931), 78–94.

40. *Idea of the Holy*, 26.

41. Ibid., 28.

42. Randall Van Schepen, "The Spirit of Form: From the Wax Man to Metal Cubes," in *Re-Enchantment*, ed. David Morgan and James Elkins, vol. 7 of *The Art Seminar* (New York, 2008).

43. Richard Rorty, "Habermas and Lyotard on Modernity," in *Habermas and Modernity*, ed. Richard Bernstein (Cambridge, Mass., 1985), 161–75, quotation on p. 174.

44. Lacoue-Labarthe, "Sublime Truth," in *Of the Sublime*, 84.

45. Eagleton, *The Ideology of the Aesthetic* (Oxford, 1990), 90; De Bolla, *Discourse of the Sublime*, 35.

46. This is part of Timothy Engström's trenchant critique of Lyotard's sublime, which he says "runs the risk of putting beyond narrative, beyond critical and discursive reach, the sorts of pains and excesses that narratives produce . . . a death camp here, the odd effort at genocide there." "The Postmodern Sublime? Philosophical Rehabilitations and Pragmatic Evasions," *boundary 2* 20 (Summer 1993): 194.

47. Although philosophy per se is not my subject in this essay, it is especially damaging to the coherence or usefulness of the sublime that it is so malleable that it can come to stand for poststructuralist theory itself, as Suzanne Guerlac argues, and Jean-Luc Nancy implies.

CHAPTER 9: WHAT WE SEE AND WHAT APPEARS

The following is an English translation of "Ce que nous voyons et ce qui apparaît," a lecture that Marion presented on June 24, 2003. The talk lays out the essence of his approach to the visible, an approach that sets up the parameters within which Marion himself, and many of the other contributors to this volume, consider the question of idolatry. The talk has previously appeared only in French, in *Les Cahiers du Collège Iconique* 16 (2004).

1. Translator's note: In French all four verbs in this phrase have the same grammatical structure, which can express passive (e.g., be confirmed), reflexive (e.g., confirm itself) or dual (e.g., confirm each other). Unfortunately, this ambivalence cannot be transferred to English.

2. Gustave Flaubert, *Sentimental Education* (New York, 2004). Translator's note: *Apparition* can mean arrival, appearance, coming, even development or putting in an appearance, as well as birth or first appearance, but the word can also refer to an apparition, vision or revelation of some sort. Marion plays on several of these connotations in his text. Something being a "sight" best seems to capture the flavor of what Marion wants to convey in this particular context, despite the fact that etymologically it is closer to "seeing" than to "appearing." Of course the verb *apparaître*, used in the title

and throughout the essay, is the corresponding verb to this noun and means to appear, to transpire, to emerge, to feature, to develop, to surface, to seem, etc.—it is generally here translated as "appearing" in contrast to "seeing" (*voir*).

3. Translator's note: Marion is here playing with the etymology of *objet* (object) consisting of *jeter* (to throw) and *ob* (face—in front of, before). Literally, an object would be something that is hurled in front of someone.

4. Translator's note: *Visée* (aim or project) and *viser* (aiming for, having in mind, looking at) are etymologically related to *vis-à-vis* (opposite, facing) and *visible* (visible, able to be seen, obvious). Again, Marion is playing with these connections that are difficult to render into graceful English.

5. Translator's note: Literally, "a knowledge of such a kind that when I know the 'ins' I will know also the 'outs.'"

6. Jean-Luc Marion, *Being Given: Toward a Phenomenology of Givenness*, trans. Jeffrey L. Kosky (Stanford, Calif., 2002).

7. Translator's note: *L'usuel*, actually the "common" or "everyday," but Marion is emphasizing use here.

8. "Une bonne voiture . . . c'est une voiture que l'on n'a même pas besoin d'aller voir, on n'a même pas besoin d'aller y voir, comme on dit très bien, qu'on n'a pas besoin de voir, qui n'apparaît jamais." Translator's note: The middle section of this sentence ("on n'a même pas besoin d'aller y voir") is an idiomatic phrase which means "to check whether everything works well" or "to be careful."

9. Translator's note: See note 2 above regarding *apparition*. In the following, *apparition* will be translated as "appearance," as that is what Marion emphasizes here, but the same word is used as in the quote from Flaubert where it refers more to a vision or an apparition.

10. See *Being Given*: "The Effect of the Picture" in §4, "The Reduction to the Given."

11. See Marion, "What Cannot Be Said: Apophasis and the Discourse of Love," *The Visible and the Revealed* (New York, 2008), chap. 6.

12. Hans Holbein the Younger, *The Ambassadors* (1533), tempera on wood, 207 cm.×209.5 cm. (81 in.×82.5 in.), London, National Gallery.

13. Translator's note: Marion is referring to the long anamorphic fresco along the hallway of the cloister of the Church of the Holy Trinity on Pincio Hill. Painted by Jean-François Nickron (1613–46), it portrays St. John of Patmos and San Francesco di Paola.

CHAPTER 10: ON HEIDEGGER, THE IDOL, AND THE WORK

What is worthwhile in this essay owes its origins to remarkable seminars and conversations over the years with Irad Kimhi first at the University of Chicago, then at the Avicenna Philosophy Institute of Jaffa. All errors, alas, are my own.

1. The origins of Heidegger's lecture "The Origin of the Work of Art" are not simple. Heidegger delivered a lecture on November 13, 1935, entitled "Concerning the Origin of the Work of Art" in Freiburg to the Society of Art Sciences. He gave the same lecture in January 1936 in Zurich at the invitation of the students of the university. Heidegger developed this lecture into a three-part lecture that he delivered November 17 and 24 as

well as December 4, 1936, for the Freien Deutschen Hochstift. It is these three lectures that appeared together in *Holzwege* in 1950 with the title, "The Origin of the Work of Art," followed by an afterword, written after 1936. In 1956, Heidegger wrote an addendum in which he clarified many features of the essay as a whole. In its present form, the essay "The Origin of the Work of Art" contains a brief introduction followed by three major subjections, entitled "Thing and Work," "The Work of Art," "Truth and Art," an afterword written between 1936 and 1950, and finally, the addendum of 1956. For useful discussions of the differences, see Otto Pöggeler, *Die Frage nach der Kunst: Von Hegel zu Heidegger* (Freiburg, 1984); Françoise Dastur, "Heidegger's Freiberg Version of the Origin," in *Heidegger Towards the Turn: Essays on the Philosophy of the 1930s*, ed. John Risser (Albany, N.Y., 1999); Michel Haar, *La chant de la terre* (Paris, 1988); Jacques Taminiaux, *Recoupements* (Brussels, 1982). In what follows, references to the Freiburg version will be marked parenthetically in the text as "1935," taken from: Martin Heidegger, *"De l'origine de l'oeuvre d'art," premiere version (1935)*, French trans. by Emmanuel Martineau (Paris, 1987). References to the later version will be marked parenthetically as "1956," translations taken from: Martin Heidegger, *Off the Beaten Track*, ed. Julian Young and Kenneth Haynes (Cambridge, 2002). All other translations are by the author of this essay, unless otherwise stated.

2. And so we find the first pejorative use of the Greek word *eidōlon* only with the Septuagint.

3. Michel Haar thinks that the "The Origin of the Work of Art" constitutes "the most radical transmutation of aesthetics not only since Kant but also since the Greeks" (Haar, *Chant de la terre*, 191).

4. The idea of a possible presentation of what is not material or sensible is not restricted to an aesthetics of the beautiful, but is still present in an aesthetics of the sublime, because the sublime is still negatively defined in regard to a possible presentation of what is not presentable.

5. For a rich discussion of the breakdown in meaning and the revelation of world and its structure, see Robert B. Pippin, "Necessary Conditions for the Possibility of What Isn't: Heidegger on Failed Meaning," in *The Persistence of Subjectivity: On the Kantian Aftermath* (Cambridge, 2005). See also Marion's essay in this volume.

6. Julian Young accuses Heidegger here of "lapsing into 'aesthetics,'" and hence concludes that the entire passage is "forgettable." Julian Young, *Heidegger's Philosophy of Art* (Cambridge, 2001), 49. But that we tend to look at and stare at particular works, drawn to their earthiness, hardly constitutes a relapse into the "disinterestedness" of Kantian aesthetics. Young's criticism is beside the point.

7. Maurice Blanchot, *L'espace littéraire*, (Paris, 1955), 296.

8. The artwork does not belong to the museum world, the world documented by historians, or the world of the art industry. On the contrary, the great work belongs to the world it opens up, as with the Greek temple. Now historical reflection may enable us to experience the temple at Paestrum or the cathedral at Bamburg as an "expression" of their ages; but this only means they are no longer at work. As Heidegger notes: "Our glorious German cathedrals; can be an inspiration to us. And yet—world decline and world withdrawal have broken their workbeing" (*HS 7*).

9. Martin Heidegger, *Nietzsche*, 2 vols. (Pfullingen, 1962), 1: 100–101.

10. Ibid., 108.

11. Georg Wilhelm Friedrich Hegel, *Vorlesungen über Ästhetik*, 2 vols. (Frankfurt, 1970), 1: 21.

12. Heidegger, *Nietzsche*, 106.

13. Hegel, *Vorlesungen über Ästhetik*, 25.

14. Robert B. Pippin offers a richly suggestive reading of modernism as precisely this transformation in Hegelian terms; see Pippin, "The Absence of Asthetics in Hegel's Aesthetics," in *The Cambridge Companion to Hegel and Nineteenth Century Philosophy*, ed. Fredrick C. Beiser (Cambridge, 2008), 394–418.

15. Martin Heidegger, "Die Herkunft der Kunst und die Bestimmung des Denkens," in *Denkerfahrungen* (Frankfurt, 1983).

16. Ibid.

CHAPTER 11: BEYOND INSTRUMENTALISM AND VOLUNTARISM

1. Martin Heidegger, *The Fundamental Concepts of Metaphysics: World, Finitude, Solitude*, trans. William McNeill and Nicholas Walker (Bloomington, Ind., 1995). Hereafter referred to as *FCM*.

2. Jonathan Lear, in *Radical Hope: Ethics in the Face of Cultural Devastation* (Cambridge, Mass., 2006), provides a lucid discussion of this connection.

3. As in so many other cases, Heidegger may have drawn inspiration on this score from Georg Simmel, who, in his late work wrote of a modern "crisis in culture" marked by a pervasive "formlessness" in personal interaction, religion, art, and so on. Cultural forms, Simmel observed, no longer exerted the kind of constraint that they had throughout history. Faced with this crisis, Simmel wrote: "We gaze into an abyss of unformed life beneath our feet. But perhaps this formlessness is the appropriate form for contemporary life" (Georg Simmel, *On Individuality and Social Forms: Selected Writings*, Heritage of Sociology [Chicago, 1971], 207).

4. Think of a couple discussing their relationship with terms like, "How is our relationship?"—as if it were not their relationship that was in question.

5. Interpretive questions about the difference between boredom and anxiety in Heidegger of course arise immediately, about which Ferreira provides a thorough discussion. See Boris Ferreira, *Stimmung bei Heidegger: Das Phänomen der Stimmung im Kontext von Heideggers Existenzialanalyse des Daseins* (Dordrecht, 2002). Heidegger treats both anxiety and boredom as fundamental attunements in that they both manifest the existential structure of *Dasein*—anxiety revealing our constitutive futurity, boredom revealing the constitutive fragility and contingency of our existence. See Robert B. Pippin, "Necessary Conditions for the Possibility of What Isn't: Heidegger on Failed Meaning," in *The Persistence of Subjectivity: On the Kantian Aftermath* (Cambridge, 2005). Heidegger seems to choose to discuss one rather than the other on rhetorical grounds, asking which mood will likely engage his audience more forcefully. In opting for boredom rather than anxiety, Heidegger seems to be here moving toward his later historical understanding of the "forgetting of being" as a positive

attribute of his times, and the attempt to find something "saving" where the "danger is greatest."

6. Lars Fr. H. Svendsen, *A Philosophy of Boredom* (London, 2005).

7. "Are we explicitly and intentionally to produce boredom in ourselves? Not at all. We do not need to undertake anything in this respect. On the contrary, we are always already undertaking too much" (*FCM* 82).

8. Of course, it is possible to read a boring book without getting bored, and to get bored while reading an interesting book—but when something draws us into a mood of boredom, we are saying something about what the thing in question can do. Thus, Heidegger writes, "boredom—and thus ultimately every mood—is a hybrid, partly objective, partly subjective." See also Aharon Ben-Ze'ev, *The Subtlety of Emotions* (Cambridge, Mass., 2000), 87.

9. "We do indeed say that a mood is infectious. Or another human being is with us, someone who through their manner of being makes everything depressing and puts a damper on everything; nobody steps out of their shell" (*FCM* 67).

10. "Consequently we may not make boredom into an object of contemplation as some state that arises on its own, but must consider it in the way that that we move within it, i.e. in the way that we seek to drive it away" (*FCM* 91).

11. Goodstein criticizes Heidegger for not using this description of the boredom of the train station as a wedge for condemning the historical changes implicit in the rise of rail travel—the commodification of time, the transformation of the landscape into a rational grid, the breakup of the close-knit village, and so on. But Heidegger is not engaged in historicist critique; he is not "against" trains or modern technology and science, but is instead to show that the way in which the mood of boredom can irrupt in a train station or airport reveals that there is more human depth in this situation than can be conceived with what organizes its surface, with the instrumentalist form of social organization. The goal is to make both this depth and this superficiality manifest and to bring what is buried to the fore. See Elizabeth S. Goodstein, *Experience Without Qualities: Boredom and Modernity* (Stanford, Calif., 2005).

12. "Boredom is only possible at all because each thing, as we say, has its time. If each thing did not have its time, then there would be no boredom" (*FCM* 105).

13. "Particular things, in what they offer us or do not offer us and in the way that they do so, are in each case co-determined by a particular time" (*FCM* 105).

14. "The station cannot properly be what it is supposed to be for us as long as the moment of the train's arrival is not there" (*FCM* 105).

15. "The dragging of time as it were refuses the station the possibility of offering us anything. It forces it to leave us empty. The station refuses itself, because time refuses it something" (*FCM* 105).

16. The nonteleological temporality of boredom number 1 is also registered in checking one's watch, an activity that does not have any concrete effects and is not even a way to pass the time (it is not fun, after all). But checking the time does reveal the engagement with our timeliness peculiar to boredom number 1—anticipation, from within

a situation in which everything has been "dragged" out of its own specific time, of a time when everything could be "timely" again.

17. Exactly what it means to say that this first form of boredom is superficial can be somewhat elusive. It is tempting to suggest, as several commentators have done, that this form of boredom is what is sometimes called "simple" boredom that lacks intense feelings and is easy to remedy. Deeper boredom would be more intense and harder to cure. However, Heidegger is careful to point out throughout the lectures that he is not particularly interested in the causes and remedies of boredom—not because there may not be causes or remedies, but because those are not his subject (*FCM* 103). His subject is to reveal the philosophical potential in finding ourselves in a boring situation. Being "deeper" has to do with the revelatory power rather than the intensity or curability of the various forms of boredom.

18. "Boredom springs from the temporality of Dasein. Boredom . . . arises from a quite determinate way and manner in which our own temporality temporalizes itself" (*FCM* 127).

19. This sort of language has led commentators to make comparisons to what *Being and Time* called "authenticity" and "resolution." Some have praised him for pointing out that there is more to life than cocktail party chitchat. Others have criticized him for mandarin elitism (see Goodstein, *Experience Without Qualities*, 322). But Heidegger is not "criticizing" the everyday or parties, and he is not holding up a kind any alternative for praise. The second form of boredom is for him superficial; it relies on a "petty I-ness" that Heidegger rejects as shallow (*FCM* 134).

20. The peculiar form of temporality characteristic of this sphere also shows up in the way that time feels frozen. One does not even feel the need to check the time. Gone are worries about the mortgage and the office; the present moment is everything, and we relate to our own time in a particularly segmented way: "we are cut off from our having-been and from our future" (*FCM* 124). Philosophizing begins to occur when we ask how this "cutting off" is possible.

21. "Es ist einem langeweilig." Though it is clear in the German (and, more importantly, it is clear theoretically) that with this phrase Heidegger is not referring to *das Man*, the translation of *das Man* as "the one" can encourage Anglophone readers to treat this form of boredom as a symptom of losing oneself in conformism and convention. Even a reading as careful as Mulhall is marred by treating boredom this way. See Stephen Mulhall, *Philosophical Myths of the Fall*, Princeton Monographs in Philosophy (Princeton, N.J., 2005).

22. We are now no longer speaking of ourselves being bored with . . . , but are saying: It is boring for one. It—for one—not for me as me, not for you as you, not for us as us, but for one. Name, standing, vocation, role, age and fate as mine and yours disappear. . . . This is what is decisive: that here we become an undifferentiated no one (*FCM* 135).

23. Heidegger does, however, provide a telling quasi example of a situation in which the third form of boredom can emerge, one that he cautions is "non-binding" in the sense that it includes an acknowledgment of its own openness: "'It is boring for one' to

walk through the streets of a large city on a Sunday afternoon" (*FCM* 135). In evoking the figure of the Sunday urban wanderer, Heidegger places his analysis of boredom explicitly in the tradition that links boredom with the practices of flanerie and the new forms of experience and action emerging in the modern metropolis (in a tradition that includes such figures as Baudelaire, Simmel, and Benjamin). That the (nonbinding) example is to have taken place on Sunday is especially fitting. It is a day of rest, church is out (let us say), nobody is supposed to be at work, and so nobody (need necessarily) have a destination to rush off to or be avoiding serious matters at home (at the writing desk, for example) to which they should be attending. The urban wanderer exists, explicitly and avowedly, in a state of suspension, and there is no other goal or value hovering outside of his action, structuring the contours of this space as a blocked effort to achieve a goal or as a self-evasion. The structure of this type of activity resists fixed divisions between what is serious and what is relaxed, what is activity and what is passivity.

24. Hans Joas, *The Creativity of Action, trans. Paul Keast* (Chicago, 1996).

25. Elijah Millgram, "On Being Bored Out of Your Mind," *Proceedings of the Aristotelian Society* 104, no. (2004): 183.

26. Ibid., 184.

27. Ibid.

28. David Foster Wallace, quoted in D. T. Max, "The Unfinished," *New Yorker*, March 9, 2009.

29. See Hubert Dreyfus and Sean Kelly, "Notes on Embodiment in Homer: Reading Homer on Moods and Action in the Light of Heidegger and Merleau-Ponty," in *Moving Bodies*, ed. Ejgil Jespersen, vol. 4, no. 2 (Oslo, 2006).

30. Daniel Silver, Terry Nichols Clark, and Clemente Jesus Navarro Yanez, "Scenes: Social Context in an Age of Contingency," *Social Forces* 88, no. 5 (2010): 2293–324, follow this cue to develop a conception of modern urban life as a collection of moods, ambiances, and scenes, developing empirical measures of scenes based on the number, density, type, and variety of cultural institutions (like museums, music venues, etc.), and therewith performing what Baudelaire refers to as a "botany of the street." We find that the scene and ambiance of city powerfully predict where individuals and firms reside, work, and locate, controlling for a number of economic, political, and demographic variables.

INDEX

The authorized representative in the EU for product safety and compliance is:
Mare Nostrum Group
B.V Doelen 72
4831 GR Breda
The Netherlands